"The best books about digital transformation combine a practitioner's experience together with original insight. Beulen and Dans have provided genuine insight based on strong fundamentals.

They understand and describe the need for an enhanced architecture function, the importance of data quality and how data ownership principles must be applied before significant strides can be made in analysis and enable implementation of AI capabilities.

As a Chief Data Officer this is a must-read, including interviews with top industry experts like Julia Bardmesser, the topics covered range from ethical considerations for data usage through to adoption of advanced technologies in service of a data-first organization."

Andrew Foster, *Chief Data Officer, M&T Bank and lead contributor to EDM Council's Cloud Data Management Capabilities standard (CDMC)*

"We live in an exciting era that witnesses an unprecedented adoption of digital technologies. One easily can get lost in the countless opportunities data science and AI bring. Rather than delving into technical details, Beulen and Dans explore the crossroads of Digital Transformation and Data Analytics. By doing so, they provide the reader with valuable recommendations on driving Digital Transformation in the public and private sectors.

By providing many examples, the authors put digital technologies in context. They pay attention to recent advances, such as Deep Learning and Quantum computing, but always relate these to organizational challenges including skills development and ethics. I appreciate that the book benefits from the rich experiences and own research of the authors. Also, many practical and scientific pointers are provided for further reading. Relevant current and upcoming legislation on topics such as privacy, security, and sustainability are also included in the text, making it an invaluable resource.

I can strongly relate to the emphasis the authors put on data sharing and data governance in ecosystems. I agree with the authors that we have only just begun to tap into the opportunities. By giving very practical recommendations, this book will help you in your digital transformation journey. Highly recommended!"

Prof. Dr. Jos van Hillegersberg, *Scientific Director at Jheronimus Academy of Data Science*

DATA ANALYTICS AND DIGITAL TRANSFORMATION

Understanding the significance of data analytics is paramount for digital transformation but in many organizations they are separate units without fully aligned goals. As organizations are applying digital transformations to be adaptive and agile in a competitive environment, data analytics can play a critical role in their success. This book explores the crossroads between them and how to leverage their connection for improved business outcomes. The need to collaborate and share data is becoming an integral part of digital transformation. This not only creates new opportunities but also requires well-considered and continuously assessed decision-making as competitiveness is at stake. This book details approaches, concepts, and frameworks, as well as actionable insights and good practices, including combined data management and agile concepts. Critical issues are discussed such as data quality and data governance, as well as compliance, privacy, and ethics. It also offers insights into how both private and public organizations can innovate and keep up with growing data volumes and increasing technological developments in the short, mid, and long term. This book will be of direct appeal to global researchers and students across a range of business disciplines, including technology and innovation management, organizational studies, and strategic management. It is also relevant for policy makers, regulators, and executives of private and public organizations looking to implement successful transformation policies.

Erik Beulen is a professor of Information Management at The University of Manchester/AMBS – UK. He is also a professor of Information Management & Digital Transformations at Tilburg University – NL and the academic director of the executive MSc Information Management & Digital Transformations at TIAS Business School (NL). Erik is also an external advisor at Bain & Company.

Marla A. Dans is Head of Data Management and Governance at Chicago Trading Company (CTC) – United States. Prior to CTC, Marla was Head of Data Governance at Tradeweb, consulted for data programs across multiple financial services firms, held a strategic position in JP Morgan Asset Management's chief data office, and for nearly two decades worked for Morgan Stanley in executive director roles in information technology, across application development, DevOps, infrastructure, and information security roles.

Business and Digital Transformation

Digital technologies are transforming societies across the globe, the effects of which are yet to be fully understood. In the business world, technological disruption brings an array of challenges and opportunities for organizations, management and the workplace.

This series of textbooks provides a student-centred library to analyse, explore and critique the evolutionary effects of technology on the business world. Each book in the series takes the perspective of a key business discipline and examines the transformational potential of digital technology, aided by real world cases and examples.

With contributions from expert scholars across the globe, the books in this series enable critical thinking students to excel in their studies of the new digital business environment.

Demand-Driven Business Strategy
Digital Transformation and Business Model Innovation
Cor Molenaar

Navigating Digital Transformation in Management
Richard Busulwa

Smart Business and Digital Transformation
An Industry 4.0 Perspective
Sándor Gyula Nagy and Tamás Stukovszky

Data Analytics and Digital Transformation
Erik Beulen and Marla A. Dans

For more information about this series, please visit www.routledge.com/Routledge-New-Directions-in-Public-Relations–Communication-Research/book-series/BAD

DATA ANALYTICS AND DIGITAL TRANSFORMATION

Erik Beulen and Marla A. Dans

Routledge
Taylor & Francis Group

LONDON AND NEW YORK

Cover image: © Yuichiro Chino

First published 2024
by Routledge
4 Park Square, Milton Park, Abingdon, Oxon OX14 4RN

and by Routledge
605 Third Avenue, New York, NY 10158

Routledge is an imprint of the Taylor & Francis Group, an informa business

British Library Cataloguing-in-Publication Data
A catalogue record for this book is available from the British Library

Library of Congress Cataloging-in-Publication Data
Names: Beulen, Erik, author. | Dans, Marla A., author.
Title: Data analytics and digital transformation / Erik Beulen and Marla A. Dans.
Description: New York, NY : Routledge, 2024. |
Series: Business and digital transformation | Includes bibliographical references
and index.
Identifiers: LCCN 2023029309 | ISBN 9781032160245 (hardback) | ISBN
9781032160221 (paperback) | ISBN 9781003246770 (ebook)
Subjects: LCSH: Information technology—Management. | Big data—Management. |
Management—Statistical methods. | Strategic management.
Classification: LCC HD30.2 .B4748 2024 | DDC 004.068/4—dc23/eng/20230629
LC record available at https://lccn.loc.gov/2023029309

ISBN: 978-1-032-16024-5 (hbk)
ISBN: 978-1-032-16022-1 (pbk)
ISBN: 978-1-003-24677-0 (ebk)

DOI: 10.4324/9781003246770

Typeset in Times New Roman
by codeMantra

CONTENTS

FIGURES

TABLES

ABOUT THE AUTHORS

Erik Beulen is a professor of Information Management at The University of Manchester/AMBS – UK. He is also a professor of Information Management & Digital Transformations at Tilburg University – NL and the academic director of the executive MSc Information Management & Digital Transformations at TIAS Business School (NL).

Furthermore, he is an independent member of the data committee of Royal FloraHolland and an external adviser at Bain & Company. His current research areas are digital transformation, corporate and IT governance, data analytics, and technology workforce diversity, and his work has been published, for example, in the *Journal of Information Technology*, *IT & People*, and *Communications of the Association for Information Systems*. He has also published, with his coauthor em. Prof. Pieter Ribbers, the Routledge books *Managing Digital Outsourcing* (2020) and *Managing Information Technology Outsourcing* (2021 – third edition).

Marla A. Dans is Head of Data Management and Governance at Chicago Trading Company (CTC) – United States. Prior to CTC, Marla was Head of Data Governance at Tradeweb, consulted for data programs across multiple financial services firms, held a strategic position in JP Morgan Asset Management's chief data office, and for nearly two decades worked for Morgan Stanley in executive director roles in information technology, across application development, DevOps, infrastructure, and information security roles.

Marla is an active member of the global Enterprise Data Management (EDM) Council and co-founder of the EDM Council's Women in Data Forum, a long-term member and former board member of the Women's Bond Club of New York, and an active member of 100 Women in Finance. She is a keynote speaker and panelist on data and data analytics.

PREFACE

Understanding the significance of data analytics is paramount for digital transformation success, as the exponential output of digital transformation feeds back into data analytics. In many organizations, data analytics and digital are separate organizational units without fully aligned goals which need collaboration in order to further improve business outcomes. The crossroads between data analytics and digital will be explored here.

Businesses face increasing market dynamics and hyper-competition, coupled with compliance and security burdens, along with sustainability, privacy, and ethical challenges. To disrupt and avoid being disrupted, data analytics identifies opportunities and risks. Data analytics also enables the implementation of digital transformations by delivering input for strategic decision-making, offering the ability to analyze and monitor implementation progress and business achievements.

Volumes of data are growing at an unprecedented speed, driven by the Internet of Things and unstructured data (e.g. social media content), as well as additional data generated by transforming into digital organizations. This feeds back into data analytics as well as data science, requiring even more mature data management and governance to achieve enriched insights. In addition, the need to collaborate and share data is becoming an integral part of digital transformations. This not only creates new opportunities but also requires well-considered and continuously assessed decision-making as competitiveness is at stake. This book details approaches, concepts, and frameworks, as well as actionable insights and good practices, including combined data management and agile concepts. In addition, a deep dive into privacy and ethics will be included.

This book clarifies and provides guidance on leveraging data analytics in achieving digital success and for digital transformations to advance data analytics. This book has a global focus, as competition does not acknowledge borders (and, to a lesser extent, legislation does), and digital and analytics good practices are transferable across borders and industries. Practitioners, as well as academics, MBA students, and BSc and MSc students, are the target audience. Practitioners include board of management, C-suite, and executive representatives of both private and public sector organizations.

This book reflects our observations on the crossroads of data analytics and digital transformations. Any vendors mentioned here are merely examples in a wide field of tools and solutions; the authors make no recommendations. In the case of multiple vendors, vendors are listed alphabetically. Every chief data office is responsible for conducting its own due diligence and running RFPs to determine the best suite of tools to meet their organization's data management needs.

In this book, the terms "chief data officer" and "chief digital officer" are always spelled out in full to avoid any unclarity about the acronym CDO.

We would like to thank Tata Consultancy Services (TCS) for collaborating with us on this book. We would also like to thank Dinanath Kholkar, Mandar Bhatavdekar, and Dr. Sharma Neha for their introductions and guidance. We would like to thank Joydeep Samajder for the coordination of our collaboration and the introductions to TCS case studies and TCS subject matter experts. Furthermore, we would like to thank Savita Kulkarni, Themis Michaelides, Sandeep Saxena, and Bandana Sinha for sharing their valuable insights. The insights are captured in short write-ups to highlight important points in data analytics and digital transformations.

We also would like to thank Julia Bardmesser, financial industry strategic adviser and chief data officer, for sharing her valuable insights on compliance and ethical risks.

Erik Beulen and Marla A. Dans

PART 1

Business context

Introduction: Business context

Data volumes have been growing exponentially for decades. It started with kilobytes (kBs), we are currently using yottabytes (YBs), and the next level is already defined: hellabyte or brontobyte (1,000 yottabytes). This growth in data volumes creates opportunities for any organization to improve decision-making and to enhance data-driven decision-making by making data analytics an integral part of their operations. In this book, we define data analytics as advanced analytic techniques which are applied to operating models including algorithms processing large volumes of structured and unstructured data.

In analytics, this book makes a distinction between three types of analytics: descriptive, predictive, and prescriptive analytics. Descriptive analytics is the dashboard of real-time metrics tracking. This gives an overview of the performance of the organization and how the digital transformation is progressing. Descriptive analytics highlights key trends that can trigger management interventions and even strategic pivots. The next level is predictive analytics, which is used to forecast outcomes based on changing variables in statistical modeling. Where descriptive analytics highlights trends, predictive analytics provide different paths for pivoting a strategy and producing different scenarios for management to consider. Predictive analytics is a project-based effort instead of in real time and is followed by prescriptive analytics. This will identify which predictive outcome is optimal for the strategy, including innovations to achieve the targeted and desired outcomes. Predictive analytics ensures confidence in decision-making by backing with data-driven evidence versus gut instinct. This is not limited to operational decision-making; predictive analytics can also be used in developing strategies and assessing innovative opportunities.

DOI: 10.4324/9781003246770-1

All three are instrumental in digital transformation success. Many organizations are changing and will continue to do so, and their business models innovate and improve their operations by digital transformations. In the context of this book, we define a digital transformation with a focus on data and analytics as an initiative to improve business performance by making an organization more responsive and enabling the introduction of new business models and innovation by leveraging data and data analytics.

In summary, data analytics is foundational in any digital transformation. In this first part of our book, both data analytics and digital transformations will be explained, where data analytics will be further detailed in Part 2 and applied to digital transformations in Parts 3 and 4. In Part 5, the outlook of the combination of data analytics and digital transformations will be explained.

1

DIGITAL TRANSFORMATIONS EXPLAINED

Organizations not only run the risk of being disrupted but also need to disrupt themselves. And, business strategies include more than the adoption of new technologies, as data and data analytics are at the heart of digital transformations. Archetypes of digital transformations are detailed as a foundation for this book.

For decades, data volumes have been growing exponentially (e.g. transaction data, document files, social media, and the Internet of Things), and those volumes will continue to grow. As a consequence, the insights from data analytics are becoming more valuable. These insights are not limited to operational management. Data analytics is also pivotal in strategic decision-making, including digital transformation.

Any organization should be exploring digital transformation opportunities and needs to integrate digital transformations in their business strategy. Doing so will not only enable innovation but also change business models, including Business 4.0/smart factory, smart government, smart cities, marketplace sales, and platforms, which is critical to remain competitive, as well as outpacing and leading digital natives.

Furthermore, organizations need to explore how to improve the forward and backward exchange of data in ecosystems and value chains. This will make topics such as data ownership and data quality even more important and will also further improve the operations. Of equal importance, this will also enable more enhanced data analytics and improvement of the collective competitive position of the value chain-associated organizations.

DOI: 10.4324/9781003246770-2

1.1 Introduction

Organizations are faced with changes in many shapes and forms, ranging from changing expectations and needs from customers for companies and citizens for public sector organizations, to new innovative technologies and new market entrance, as well as changing regulations. This has an impact on the lifespan of organizations. The 33-year average tenure of companies on the S&P 500 in 1964 narrowed to 24 years by 2016 and is expected to shrink to just 12 years by 2027 (Anthony et al., 2018, p. 2). To disrupt or be disrupted has become the norm (Beulen and Ribbers, 2020). But public sector organizations are also constantly changing, for example, as public sector organizations have replaced bureaucratic organizations with autonomous initiatives (Hood, 1991). This has triggered the need for coordination and has resulted in the "joined-up government" (Newman, 2020).

Digital transformation enables adoption by facilitating change. It is important to distinguish between reinforcing existing value propositions – digitization (e.g. e-commerce), on the one hand, and, on the other hand, reshaping value propositions – digital transformations (Härting et al., 2017; Gobble, 2018; Leonardi and Treem, 2020; Mugge et al., 2020; Caputo et al., 2021). This is where data and data analytics are becoming more important (Leonardi and Treem, 2020). Gartner defines digitization as "the process of changing from analog to digital form" (Gartner, n.d.-a). Digital transformations typically entail revamped business models combined with new products and services. Innovation is also more important in digital transformations than in digitization. Gartner defines digitalization as "the use of digital technologies to change a business model and provide new revenue and value-producing opportunities; it is the process of moving to a digital business" (Gartner, n.d.-b). Incumbent organizations must deal with existing operations, including underlying information technology. This hinders speed; however, these organizations have vast experience, including underpinning data, to build upon. Start-ups and scale-ups benefit from agility. Furthermore, there are new entrance organizations, also called digital natives, shaping fully digital value propositions and competing against and partnering with incumbents.

In this book, we define digital transformation as an initiative to improve business performance by making an organization more responsive and enable the introduction of new business models and innovation by leveraging data and data analytics. This definition is borrowed from many sources; some of these definitions are criticized by, among others, Gong and Ribiere (2021). Digital transformations are defined by Westerman et al. (2011) as "the use of technology to radically improve the performance or reach of enterprises" (p. 5). This definition focuses on business performance. Where Chanias, similar to Pappas et al. (2018) and Dremel et al. (2017), explains how the car manufacturer Audi leveraged data in their digital transformation, Chanias explicitly adds analytics to the definition: "The extended use of advanced IT, such as analytics, mobile computing, social media, or smart embedded devices, and the improved use of traditional technologies, such as enterprise resource planning (ERP), to enable major business improvements" (2017).

Finally, it is important to highlight that digital transformation is not a one-off project. Any organization will be in a permanent state of transformation (Matt et al., 2015; Beulen, 2020a, 2020b; Beulen and Ribbers, 2020). Continuous digital transformations are more in the DNA of digital native organizations, but should be adopted by any organization in order to survive.

1.2 Digital transformation

Prior to discussing the opportunities and threats of digital transformations, the context needs to be set. This context includes two topics: (1) top management commitment and (2) change management and ways of working.

For digital transformation success, commitment of the top management is essential (Matt et al., 2015; Adams and Bennett, 2018; AlNuaimi et al., 2022). Top management still lacks digital capabilities (Weill et al., 2019), which is a concern. Organizations address this shortcoming in different ways. By appointing chief digital officers and digital non-executives, the capabilities within the board of management will increase (Tumbas et al., 2018; Berman et al., 2020). Organizations appointing a chief digital officer need to make sure responsibilities between the chief digital officer and the chief information officer are aligned (Singh et al., 2020). Typically, the focus of the chief information officer is on technology, whereas the chief digital officer focuses on the market, the business models, and the innovation of the products and services. In some organizations, the role of the chief digital officer and the chief information officer is a combined role; however, this requires a combination of capabilities, which is very rare. Nevertheless, in the future, the responsibilities of the chief digital officer will become the responsibility of business managers, as digital will become the new norm in short time. The role of chief digital officer is considered to be a finite role, which will become obsolete when an organization has reached a level of digital maturity. Also, appointing a chief data officer is important. The chief data officer is the custodian of data governance, setting standards and policies while ensuring data quality (Earley, 2017; Brenneman, 2018). The role of the chief data officer will be discussed in Part 3 in greater detail.

To change business models and to innovate products and services, change management and adoptive ways of working are essential. Most organizations have adopted agile ways of working (Denning, 2018a, 2018b; Brosseau et al., 2019; Holbeche, 2019). By embracing agility, organizations can respond much faster, make incremental decisions, and adapt to changes in the market and/or changes customers need or new regulatory requirements (Kale, 2017). Agility is also very supportive in achieving success in digital transformations (Perkin and Abraham, 2021). Typically, agile is combined with the concept of DevOps (Hemon et al., 2020). This enables an increased release cycle, from the best monthly deployment to the daily, or even more frequent, deployment. DevOps combines the responsibility for the development and the maintenance of functionality and facilitates participation of representatives from the primary process, business representatives, or, in the case of public sector organizations, civil servants from operations, as well as strategists and policy makers (Wiedemann et al., 2019).

1.2.1 Digital transformation opportunities

Digital transformations are focusing predominantly on the introduction of new products, services, and processes, and less on improving existing products and services (Beulen, 2018a, 2018b). The new products and services can be combined with new business models and contribute mainly to the top line of organizations. In the case of public organizations, this contributes to the objectives and/or purpose of the organization. The digital transformation upside for new products and services is typically higher than for existing products and services. Digital by design simply has a bigger impact. The improved processes mainly contribute to operational efficiencies and have an internal focus, and this is no different for public organizations. Technology enables these efficiencies – a good example is robotic process automation (RPA) (Schmitz et al., 2019; Siderska, 2020).

Currently, private sector organizations face severe competition, and public sector organizations face increasing demands from their stakeholders and/or citizens, which raises the digital transformation bar. Also, increased and new legislation set high demand for digital transformations. Rethinking and revamping the products and services, and the business model, and changing the organizational structure enables organizations to disrupt competition. Many incumbent organizations are not disrupting competition, and they focus on avoiding being disrupted by digital natives. Keeping up with the pace is already a challenge for most incumbent organizations. In order to avoid being outperformed by digital natives, many incumbents simply acquire digital natives or take a stake in these companies. This not only neutralizes the competition but also strengthens the digital capabilities of the incumbent. The cost of acquiring digital natives is high, as the market cap of these organizations is off the charts. Furthermore, retaining the staff of the acquired digital native is challenging, to say the least. For example, Randstad (global leader in the HR services industry, revenue 21b euro, and 35k employees – www.randstad.com) has embraced this acquisition strategy. They continuously scan the HR technology market (+2.5k companies) and invest and acquire technology companies. (Randstad, 2017, p. 32). In 2015 Randstad acquired Smartrise,[1] an online outplacement firm in the US for 100m USD, and in 2016 Monster,[2] a global online recruiting platform for 429m USD.

In addition, some organizations also integrate their sustainability objectives into their digital transformation (Kar et al., 2019), for example by developing smart cities (Anthony Jnr, 2021). This is dominant but not limited to public sector organizations, as private sector organizations also combine digital transformations and sustainability goals (McCausland, 2021).

1.2.2   *Digital transformation threats*

In addition to the upside, embarking on digital transformations is not without risk. There are four threats organizations need to take into account. One is the risk of cannibalizing existing business, and another is the risk of underinvesting in the existing operation and insufficient management attention for the existing organization. Innovation has also increased noncompliance and increased cyber security exposure.

1 **Cannibalizing existing business:** improved services and products might impact the sales of existing services and products (Greenstein, 2010; Matzler et al., 2018). This will impact the overall performance of any organization. In embarking on digital transformations, the impact on the existing business must be taken into account. Similar to public organizations, they need to take into account the impact of a digital transformation on all their objectives.
2 **Underinvesting in existing business and not sufficient management attention:** in many organizations, digital transformation is funded by the existing business. Therefore, management for the existing business is required. In this context, attention for the staff that is running the existing business is also important. These employees might feel undervalued. This will increase attrition and potentially jeopardize business continuity. Organizations should not only focus on the implementation of the digital strategy, but also keep an eye on the existing business (Hinterhuber, 2022).
3 **Noncompliance:** Globally, any organization faces increased pressure from regulators and legislators, including organizations in the public sector (Scupola and Mergel, 2022). This is not limited to the increasing privacy regulations, such as GDPR. One example is antitrust legislation. This will be detailed in Chapter 7.
4 **Cyber exposure:** digital transformation significantly increases the digitization of the many processes, as well as the exchange of data in increasingly global ecosystems. This results in increased cyber security risks. In any digital transformation, cyber security risk assessments as well as cyber security investments need to be embedded (Möller, 2020). This will be detailed in Chapters 7 and 12.

1.3   Impact of emerging technologies

For any organization, it is essential to continuously explore, experiment, and implement emerging technologies. Any emerging technology that does not have the opportunity to scale up should not be considered. In innovation, many organizations engage with partners and partly outsource innovation (Beulen and Ribbers, 2002, 2003, 2021). Contract innovation is different from traditional outsourcing (Beulen, 2004, 2007). Innovation requires a less formal and strict contracting, in addition to longer-term commitment. This sets requirements for governance and contract management (Aubert et al., 2015).

1.3.1 The Internet of Things

The Internet of Things (IoT) connects to devices and enables data exchange. IoT can be an integral part of (automated) decision-making. It also provides opportunities to make the provisioning of services more efficient or adds services to products, such as predictive maintenance of assets. This technology can also provide data to improve the design of the next version of an asset, as manufacturers can analyze performance and maintenance data from all the manufactured assets. The ownership of the collected data and confidentiality needs to be agreed upon. The discussion of data ownership is not limited to personal data (Janeček, 2018) but also to commercially relevant data. This last aspect is often overlooked but will become more important in the near future, as this is also potentially impacting business models.

In addition, cyber security requires attention. Unfortunately, this sensor-based technology is vulnerable for cybercrime, as there is processing/edge computing in the IoT devices, as well as the communication and data transmission from the IoT devices to information systems (Lee, 2020).

1.3.2 Blockchain

Blockchain is a general ledger technology that can be used to share data and facilitate transactions. It is a technology that enables distributed non-trusting organizations to collaborate without the need to have a trusted intermediary. Blockchain also enables efficiency in sharing data and transactions enabled by smart contracts (Cong and He, 2019). There are still potential legal challenges with smart contracts, but for simple and unambiguous transactions, smart contracts are very suitable.

The negative association with cryptocurrencies has and is still not helpful in the adoption of blockchain (Kosmarski, 2020). The energy efficiency of mining is still a concern, despite the increase in applying proof-of-work consensus algorithms in blockchains (Lasla et al., 2022).

1.3.3 Artificial intelligence

Artificial intelligence (AI) is at the heart of data and data analytics. In AI, computers "imitate"/"replicate" the human brain, with the purpose of self-learning and continuous improvement. In AI humans develop features, which is different from Machine Learning (ML), where computers develop features autonomously. ML can be applied to any size data set but is typically not applied to large data sets (Murdoch et al., 2019). Also, deep learning (DL) is part of AI. In DL, complex algorithms and deep neural networks train models and patterns. DL requires significant computer power and is typically only applied to large data sets (Bengio et al., 2017). This will be detailed in Chapter 2.

1.3.4   Knowledge graph

A knowledge graph upends traditional relational data schemas with a three-dimensional semantic architecture that introduces connections (edges) between entities (nodes) (Fensel et al., 2020b). Graph visualization tools increase data analytics capabilities exponentially by adding that distinct relationship layer, enabling drill-down capabilities into nodes and edges, for never-ending fun in the search for meaningful data and insights. Knowledge graphs drive service and product improvement (Noy et al., 2019). This will be detailed in Chapter 2.

1.4   Impact of data and data analytics

Data and data analytics have become an integral part of digital transformation. Data-driven organizations are becoming the norm (Datnow and Park, 2014; Watson et al., 2021); however, they require data-driven leadership. Organizations need to increase the percentage of data-driven decisions. At the moment, many organizations still struggle with the basics, e.g. data quality, data management, data governance, tooling, and automation (Beulen, 2020b).

Data and data analytics are supportive in identifying and shaping digital transformations. Modeling and scenario planning are fueled by data and data analytics. The initiation of the analysis still starts with intuition, and final decision-making remains an executive decision. However, rigor of analysis significantly improves the likelihood of achieving digital transformation objectives and also reduces the risk profile. The confidence level of the decision-making increases by leveraging data and data analytics. Also, data and data analytics are driving operational decision-making. Pre-set rules automatically generate decisions and initiate actions. Organizations need to implement checks and balances to ensure the desired outcome and meet ethical standards. Setting thresholds and final human approvals for specific decisions is important. This requires continuous monitoring, as well as managerial and board of management oversight. Implementing proper governance is key. Chapter 3 is a deep dive into data-driven leadership.

Data-driven organizations benefit from data democratization, which in this book is defined as making data accessible for analyses and decision-making, without involving IT and data specialists, for identified employees of the organization (Espinosa et al., 2014; de la Vega et al., 2016; Maynard-Atem, 2019; Patel, 2020).

Important in data democratization is ease of use, and therefore, tooling, which is end-user friendly is essential, examples being (in alphabetical order) Google (www.looker.com), Microsoft (www.powerbi.microsoft.com), Qlik (www.qlik.com), and Tableau (www.tableau.com). Organizations need to unlock their data by ensuring data quality combined with a ruleset for data access. The quality of data remains a concern in many organizations due to poor data ownership, growing data volumes, and the increase of unstructured and external data. All of this requires proper governance and guidance of an empowered chief data officer. Access management is another challenge in many organizations, due to the significance of temporary/project roles, rotation of staff including new roles, onboarding, and attrition. In addition, there are changes in legislation that might impact the lawfulness of data access for employees, e.g. GDPR. The impact of this legislation is more substantial for international organizations and organizations dealing with end-user data, such as client data, patient data, or civilian data. But the list also includes legislation such as antitrust legislation, one example being the litigation of the European Commission against Amazon. The Commission has sent a Statement of Objections to Amazon for the use of nonpublic independent seller data and (2) has opened a second investigation into its e-commerce business practices. This case was settled in December 2022.[3]

Finally, organizations need to transform from an application-centric architecture to a data-centric architecture (Rajabi and Abade, 2012; Demchenko et al., 2014; Kwon et al., 2019). Data-centric architectures enable data democratization, as silos are inherent to an application-centric architecture. Cloud computing with advanced load balancing functionality is supporting data-centric architectures (Dasoriya et al., 2017). Data-centric architectures are also supportive of Internet of Things solutions (Liu et al., 2019) and business models such as Industry 4.0 (Martínez-Gutiérrez et al., 2021).

Aspects of data democratization will be explained in greater detail in Chapters 5–7.

1.5 Changing business models

In digital transformations, new business models are also introduced (Berman, 2012; Kotarba, 2018). The business models have many shapes and forms, but all are technology-driven and include a significant data and data analytics component (Brownlow et al., 2015). Furthermore, these new business models set requirements for partnering within existing and new value chains. Partnering is the strengthening of the competitive position of an organization combined with increasing entry barriers to a market (Adamik, 2016). Missing out on digital transformations for partnering is not an option. New business models must be explored in conjunction with partners (Visnjic et al., 2018). In this section, four of the most common new business models are discussed briefly.

1.5.1 Industry 4.0 and smart factory

In the manufacturing sector, automation and data exchange are heavily used to optimize the manufacturing process. Investments to innovate the manufacturing processes are as significant as the returns in terms of opportunities to add services to the products, make the process more efficient, and strengthen the collaboration with partners, including increasing the level of exclusivity in ecosystems and value chains. This business model also includes innovations such as the Internet of

Things and robotics. In the context of digital transformation, the focus is predominantly on the opportunities to add services to the products by enhancing the functionality and sharing client usage data of products for (preventive) maintenance of the product, and client advice including product replacement or suggestions for more efficient product usage. Most of these services are software, and not seldom apps, which is offered in combination with the physical product. Typically, the pricing of the product includes the "free" usage of additional services.

1.5.2   Smart government and smart cities

Specifically for public organizations, the new smart government and smart city business models are highly relevant. These business models include two distinct concepts: one supports the interaction with and between citizens and organizations, and a second is using data and data analytics to perform public tasks. Both concepts are highly technology-driven and data-driven. The impact of politicians on digital transformation is an additional challenge, similar to private sector organizations which face changes in board of management; however, the objectives of new politicians often contradict the objectives of their predecessors. In digital transformations, public organizations also often include less tangible goals such as sustainability goals, e.g. reduced energy consumption or support for the circular economy. On the other hand, public organizations might be able to get funding more easily approved, as long as the outcomes of digital transformations align with the objectives of the public organization and their stakeholders. Overall, the adoption of new business models such as smart government and smart cities is not straightforward and is still emerging.

1.5.3   Marketplace sales

Marketplace sales is a specific new business model of business model platforms. Marketplace sales include two different business models: business-to-consumer (B2C) and consumer-to-consumer (C2C). In this book, the focus is on B2C only, although marketplace sales combine both business models, e.g. Craigslist, eBay, and Facebook. In B2C, a platform offers the opportunity to sell goods and services for businesses, with transactions taking place over the platform. The platform is compensated by the businesses for offering the marketplace. The platform typically facilitates the payment and offers additional services, such as order fulfillment. Consumers visit the platform and can compare the products of all the providers on the platform.

There is a wide variety of marketplace sales, where platforms such as Amazon and Alibaba combine providing the platform to independent retailers with being a retailer. This potentially triggers violation of antitrust regulations. The European Union has sent a Statement of Objections to Amazon for the use of nonpublic independent seller data and opened a second investigation into its e-commerce business practices. If confirmed, this would infringe on Article 102 of the Treaty on the Functioning of the European Union (TFEU) that prohibits the abuse of a dominant market position (European Commission, 2020). In the context of the importance of and dependence on marketplace sales for many businesses, this investigation is important.

1.5.4   Platforms

Marketplace sales are an integral part of platforms. This new business model is attractive not only for the B2C market but also for the business-to-business (B2B) market. B2B platforms basically facilitate doing business between organizations, similar to how marketplace sales facilitate doing business with consumers. The facilitation between organizations is in setting up ecosystem partnering, organizations collaborate by leveraging the platform. The platform facilitates transactions. These types of platforms are very prominent in logistics, where public organizations such as Customs and Border Protection also participate in transactions over the platform.

The platform is compensated for their services in facilitating transactions, which is different from marketplace sales; this is typically on a flat-fee basis instead of a percentage of the transaction, as the transactions rarely have a significant value. Also different from the marketplace sales, the transactions on B2B platforms are not one-off transactions, as the costs associated with the initial collaboration are high.

1.6   Ecosystem partnering

In digital transformation, collaboration with partners in the value chain is becoming more important (Lewrick et al., 2018; Duan et al., 2021), and data, along with data exchange, have an important role in these developments (Curry and Sheth, 2018; Pappas et al., 2018).

The development of new business models, new services, and new products will be predominantly co-creation (Hyysalo et al., 2019). Joining forces with partners is the norm; this can be in the value chains an organization is already currently operating in or in new value chains. Market conditions are in flux, and many organizations are considering multiple options in ecosystem partnering. However, most organizations have been part of value chains for over 60 months, and only a few value chains have been established, within the last 18 months (Beulen, 2022b). However, the ability to innovate will further increase the market dynamic. This makes the potential impact of digital transformation even more significant. At the same time, this also requires partnering capabilities in the participating organizations (Davidson et al., 2018; Helfat and Raubitschek, 2018).

Structuring ecosystem partnering is not straightforward, as there are challenges related to data ownership. To avoid any doubt, we clarify here that this is data related to products and services, not large data sets which can be sold. These data increase the value of the products and services, and, consequently, there is value associated with this data. How will the individual organizations in the value chain unlock and allocate this value? Given the market dynamics, this is the biggest challenge in ecosystem partnering. Data will be shared forward in the value chain (think service and product information) but also backward in the value chain, e.g. client preferences and retail information, including pricing information. Owning the data and the ability to monetize the data strengthens the position of an organization in an ecosystem and value chain. As a consequence, organizations need to agree on sharing data in a value chain. The charging agreements are typically made for 12 months and the ecosystem partnerships are governed by both contractual and relational governance (Beulen, 2022a). Associated with the data ownership challenges are also the intellectual property challenges. Compared to data ownership, there is more legislation in place to protect intellectual property. Most of the data legislation is related to privacy and ethical considerations. However, with the upcoming Data Service Package Act in Europe, the antitrust aspects are becoming more important (European Commission, n.d.).

In Part Four, ecosystem partnering will be detailed. This will include all aspects, e.g. data sharing, data governance, and partnering in ecosystems and value chains. The focus in this book related to ecosystem partnership will be less on intellectual property and more on data.

1.7   Digital transformation archetypes

Digital Transformation archetypes need to be defined to assess the digital transformation maturity of an organization. The four identified archetypes are inclusive of the focus of digital transformation, alignment with data leadership and capabilities, and digital transformation governance. The four archetypes are in order of increasing maturity, business as usual, Digital Transformation 1.0, siloed digital transformation, and integrated digital transformations. These are detailed below, with an overview depicted in Table 1.1 (Digital Transformation Archetypes).

1 **Business as usual: steady transformation – gradually adopting new business models, gradually moving into new markets, and innovating existing services and products.** The organization has not really entered the digital era yet. Hence, there is no digital or data leadership, and data ownership is spread across the organization. Also, digital and data capabilities are both non-existent. As a consequence, digital transformation governance has not been implemented.

2 **Digital Transformation 1.0: radical transformation initiatives – top-down endorsed high-level digital strategy, launch a couple of pilot digital transformations, and put a focus on new business models.** The organization is entering the digital era. Individual digital heroes kick off radical transformations. Organizations have appointed a chief data officer to develop the enterprise data strategy; however, data ownership is not properly addressed yet. Data

TABLE 1.1 Digital maturity of four archetypes of digital transformations[4].

Archetypes of digital transformations	Digital			Data		
	Leadership	Capabilities	Governance	Leadership	Capabilities	Governance
	Digital leadership	Digital capabilities	Digital Transformation governance	Data leadership	Data capabilities (combined with digital capabilities)	Data governance
Business as usual	No digital leadership	No data leadership Data ownership across the organization	Non-existing	Data is managed by IT staff, no business involvement	Non-existing	No formal data governance strategy exists
Digital Transformation 1.0	Individual digital heroes	Chief data officer appointed – Data ownership in the digital initiative	Emerging	Enterprise data management strategy established and aligned with digital initiatives	Ad hoc program management of pilot projects	The need for data governance is acknowledged and being developed
Digital Transformation 2.0 – Siloed digital transformation	Mandated digital heroes	Strong chief data officer focusing on getting the basics right – Data ownership in the organization unit	Growing and in DNA of individuals and some organizational units	Digital data management strategy implemented in silos, data science teams are siloed, and digital transformation output data remains decentralized	De-centrally managed digital transformation	Digital data governors established in silos

Archetypes of digital transformations	Digital			Data		
	Leadership	*Capabilities*	*Governance*	*Leadership*	*Capabilities*	*Governance*
	Digital leadership	*Digital capabilities*	*Digital Transformation governance*	*Data leadership*	*Data capabilities (combined with digital capabilities)*	*Data governance*
Digital Transformation 3.0 – Integrated digital transformation	Mandated digital teams	Strong chief data officer focusing on maintaining safeguarding policies and procedures – Data ownership across the organization and optimized	In DNA of organization	Digital data management strategy across the organization aligned with enterprise data management strategy, data science teams are centralized, and digital transformation output data is looped back into enterprise data management strategy	Portfolio management for digital transformations	Digital data governors aligned with enterprise data governance strategy

ownership is with the digital transformation initiatives. Additionally, digital and data capabilities are emerging. Therefore, digital transformation governance is limited to ad hoc program management of pilot projects with a vanilla oversight from the board of management.

3 **Siloed digital transformation: radical and continuous digital transformations – top-down endorsed digital strategy with a carte blanche adoption for organization units – decentralized.** The digital strategy is also predominantly data-driven, as the importance of data analytics is growing and is implemented by mandated digital heroes. The digital heroes are supported by an emerging central data scientist team. The focus of the chief data officer is on getting the basics right by implementing the enterprise data strategy, where data ownership is still decentralized. In addition, digital and data capabilities are growing. Digital and data are no longer in the DNA of individuals but are already embedded in some organizational units. Consequently, the digital transformation governance is de-centrally organized, with a growing oversight from the board of management.

4 **Integrated digital transformation: radical and continuous digital transformations – top-down endorsed digital strategy with a coordinated adoption across the organization and agile ways of working.** The digital strategy is also fully data-driven and is implemented by mandated digital teams. Digital teams are supported by federated data scientist teams. New data output from digital transformation initiatives is looped back into enterprise data management and data governance systems and processes. As the basics are in place, the focus of the chief data officer is on safeguarding data policies and procedures, where data ownership is optimized and embedded across the organization. In addition, digital and data capabilities are now in the DNA of organizational architecture. Hence, digital transformation governance is a managed portfolio with proper involvement of the board of management.

Understanding the digital maturity of an organization is important (Gill and Van-Boskirk, 2016; Valdez-de-Leon, 2016; Ifenthaler and Egloffstein, 2020). Strategy companies, such as BCG, have digital maturity models including 36 categories, which is known as the Digital Acceleration Index.[5] The ultimate goal of any organization is the highest maturity level to integrate digital transformation. Achieving this level requires building up digital and data leadership, as well as capabilities, and adequate digital transformation governance. These archetypes will be the foundation for describing digital transformation journeys in Part 3 and enabling organizations to grow their leadership and capabilities in digital and data over time and to adjust digital transformation governance accordingly. This includes corporate governance (Beulen and Bode, 2021).

1.8   Conclusion

In digital transformation, everything is moving at pace. Competition is fiercer than ever, regulations are providing guiderails, and technology is rapidly innovating. This offers opportunities as well as creates threats. Organizations need to use data and data analytics to navigate in this day and age to avoid to be disrupted.

Notes

1 https://www2.staffingindustry.com/Editorial/Daily-News/Randstad-buys-outplacement-firm-RiseSmart-for-100-million-35489.
2 https://www.randstad.co.uk/randstad-completes-acquisition-monster-worldwide-to-accelerate-its-digital-human-resources-strategy/.
3 https://www.cnbc.com/2022/12/20/amazon-reaches-settlement-with-eu-on-antitrust-case.html (CNBC, 2022).
4 The archetypes digital transformation 1.0, 2.0, and 3.0 will be detailed in Part 3.
5 See https://www.bcg.com/capabilities/digital-technology-data/digital-maturity.

2
DATA ANALYTICS TRENDS CLARIFIED

The decades of growth of data volumes are unprecedented, and the ability to analyze data with artificial intelligence and machine learning are also on the rise. This requires mature data management and data governance. Many organizations are implementing data democratization and are exploring opportunities for data sharing with ecosystem and value chain partners beyond transaction data. This chapter not only explains the data analytics opportunities but also addresses the challenges and risks and includes a deep dive into descriptive, predictive, and prescriptive models and the technical implications wherein (e.g. cloud). In addition, the new concepts of data lineage and data provenance will be detailed. These insights into a subject matter interview will be structured by people, process, data, and technology.

Data analytics has been in the fast lane for over two decades. Data analytics speed and dynamics are increasing at an unprecedented rate. The increase of data volumes will continue to grow, especially unstructured social media data, as well as Internet of Things data. These increasing data volumes require proper data management including architectural principles. This will enable organizations to benefit from improved insights. In addition, technological innovations are enabling the increasing impact of data analytics, e.g. cloud computing and quantum computing. All are foundational for artificial intelligence. On a conceptual level, ontologies and knowledge graphs are essential in artificial intelligence. These developments are significantly expanding the analysis processing speed and affordable available storage volume. All of this fuels artificial intelligence, which includes machine learning and deep learning. The two concepts are often used intertwined, but are distinctly different. Artificial intelligence is pivotal in digital transformations.

DOI: 10.4324/9781003246770-3

2.1   Introduction

Organizations use exponentially growing volumes of data in operating and managing their organizations. Data analytics is becoming a core competency in many organizations (Ghasemaghaei et al., 2018; Amankwah-Amoah and Adomako, 2019) to ensure improved decision-making and increased insights. Extensive and increased use of data also creates challenges not limited to privacy legislation (Salas and Domingo-Ferrer, 2018).

This requires management attention for data management, which includes governance and policy making, in addition to more technology-related aspects, such as cloud computing, to ensure sufficient clean and usable data, processing power for running algorithms, storage capacity for data, and tooling to perform data analytics. To enforce governance, many organizations have appointed a chief data officer (Griffin, 2008) and have a very clear focus on data-centric architectures (Rajabi and Abade, 2012), which is becoming more important in the context of Industry 4.0 (Martínez et al., 2021). Improving governance will drive value creation and enable data-driven decision-making (Beulen, 2020b).

In addition to the basic foundation for data analytics, cloud computing also offers emerging innovations such as quantum computing (Tsai et al., 2016), which is not yet an established and widely used innovation (Eskandarpour et al., 2020).

In addition to technological innovations, conceptual developments are also happening. Organizations are defining their ontologies (Guarino et al., 2009; McDaniel et al., 2018) and are implementing knowledge graphs (Fensel et al., 2020a, 2020b; Ji et al., 2021). Ontologies can be defined as "a formal, explicit specification of a shared conceptualization" (Studer et al., 1998, p. 25), whereas knowledge graphs can be defined as follows:

> A knowledge graph (i) mainly describes real world entities and their interrelations, organized in a graph, (ii) defines possible classes and relations of entities in a schema, (iii) allows for potentially interrelating arbitrary entities with each other and (iv) covers various topical domains.
>
> *(Paulheim, 2017, p. 491)*

They are closely related, as an ontology is a data schema that provides meaning and relationships between the data – the data and relationships are visualized through a knowledge graph architecture. These ontologies and knowledge graphs significantly increase insights from data and are instrumental to artificial intelligence.

Artificial intelligence has been around for more than two decades (Russell and Norvig, 2016) and includes both machine learning and deep learning. Artificial intelligence is the umbrella term for value creation from data, whereas machine learning is algorithm-based self-learning based on algorithms. Little to no human intervention is required to improve these machine learning systems. The difference between machine learning and deep learning is the scale. Deep learning systems are self-learning systems that process significant volumes of data to improve value creation from data.

2.2 Descriptive, predictive, and prescriptive models

There can be differentiation between three models: descriptive, predictive, and prescriptive models (Greasley, 2019). Good examples of all three types of analytics in healthcare are described by El Morr and Ali-Hassan (2019). Organizations are initially focusing on the implementation of descriptive models (Lucas, 1978).

The descriptive model answers the question, "What has already happened?" The results are often visualized in dashboards tracking real-time metrics. This gives a view on the performance of the organization and how performance and digital transformation are progressing. Descriptive models focus on key trends that can trigger management interventions and even strategic pivots. Over time, the number of variables in descriptive models has increased significantly and also has expanded from univariate analyses to bivariate and multivariate analyses, significantly increasing the value of descriptive models. Typically, descriptive models are reviewed on a basis of 6–12 months, which includes testing and reviewing of any bias in the data used and making an inventory of the business requirements. The outcomes of the review process will be implemented, depending on the complexity, by the data analytics teams[1] and/or the data science teams of an organization. Usually, the implementation of these changes in descriptive models will be managed centrally.

The next level is predictive models, which answers the question, "What will happen in the future?" These are used to forecast outcomes based on changing variables in statistical modeling (Navath, 2021). Also, for these models, the number of variables used in the models is increasing (Lepenioti et al., 2020). Where descriptive analytics highlights trends, predictive analytics provides insights into alternative paths for pivoting a strategy and producing different scenarios for management to consider. Predictive models are used on a project-based effort, often focused on historical instead of real-time data, and they are followed by prescriptive analytics. This will require participation of subject matter experts combined with data scientists for designing and implementing predictive models, for example, hierarchical clustering, linear regression, and classification and regression trees (CART). These predictive models will identify which outcome is optimal for the strategy, leading to innovations that can achieve the targeted and desired outcomes. From the initial design of the prescriptive models, the involvement of senior management is required to ensure that the predictive models are aligned and supportive to the overall organization strategy. A team of subject matter experts and data scientists will design and implement predictive models using agile sprints. Model and data version control are critical to maintaining progress with iterative testing. Predictive models provide confidence in decision-making by backing forecast outcomes with data-driven evidence versus gut instinct. This is not limited to operational decision-making, predictive analytics can also be used in developing strategies and assessing innovative opportunities.

The third level is prescriptive models, which answer the question, "What should be done?" The transition requires significant effort and maturity, and among other things tackling the conditional stochastic optimization problem (Bertsimas and Kallus, 2020). These are the advanced models that provide actionable insights into support and drive automated operations and data-driven decision-making. The operational teams in organizations can focus on complex cases and on oversight and monitoring of automated decisions. Different from descriptive models, the review cycles are much shorter, as the impact of biased data is much more significant and can directly impact the performance and even jeopardize the continuity of the organization. Additionally, prescriptive models require processes to respond to alerts, indicating patterns in decision-making that require immediate investigation. The increasing threat of cyberattacks makes this requirement even more of a priority.

For any of the three models, self-service tools empower managers and subject matter experts in organizations. This trend cannot be stopped and should not be. However, this trend sets requirements for data governance and increases the frequency and rigor of reviews.

2.3   Increasing data volumes

There have been many surveys and studies exploring data growth over the last decade (Statista, 2018; Gartner, 2021b; IDC, 2021), all indicating a single direction, more than exponential growth in the past, most likely, even more so in the future. Growth is mainly coming from transaction data, human files, social media, and machine-generated data, e.g. the Internet of Things. The growth of social media and machine-generated data exceeds the growth from the other categories. All different categories are input for artificial intelligence and data-driven decision-making. There is a specific data category, which is cyber security monitoring data (Panigrahi and Borah, 2018). With the increasing number of security breaches and cyberattacks, this (monitoring) data volume is growing rapidly (Larriva-Novo et al., 2020). As Clive Humby put it in 2006, "Data is the new oil" (Humby, 2013). Like oil, data is valuable, but it cannot be used if it is not refined. Oil has to be transformed into gas, plastic, chemicals, etc., to create a valuable entity that drives profitable activity; so, data must be broken down and analyzed for it to have value. Increasing volumes of data offer significant opportunities to increase value creation in digital transformations.

Data can be distinguished between structured and unstructured data. Unstructured data requires additional data management and data governance attention as it is less searchable. Also, unstructured data is generated by humans as well as by machines, and it requires more interpretation, as it is typically stored in its native format in data lakes. Examples of formats for unstructured data are audio, images, videos, and social data e.g. Facebook, Instagram, and Twitter. Currently, an increasing number of organizations are considering adding structured data to the data lake to improve an integral view and analyses. In the mid to long term, continuous increase in processing power and "built-in" analytics might reduce the need for expensive data warehouses.

Despite the advanced analytic tools, organizations need to focus on the quality of structured and unstructured data. However, in most organizations, unstructured data requires the most attention, and usually gets the least attention – except for alternative data subscriptions for advanced analytics. There are three dimensions to assess the quality of the data: (1) interpretability, (2) relevance, and (3) accuracy (Carlo et al., 2011). In the first category are predominantly the confidence level and the percentage of noisy data that affect the quality of unstructured data.

In the second category, the level of specificity has an impact on data quality. Higher specificity, combined with efforts to interpret, for example, by tagging or classifying, increases data quality significantly, as well as potential depth of insight and confidence in the outcomes of the analytics. However, this could also impact usability and the number of relevant use cases for these niche unstructured data sets.

In the percentage of third category, accuracy is the most relevant indicator of data quality. In addition to tagging or classifying unstructured data, organizations are also investigating improvements to data generation, such as installing a higher-quality camera or increasing the frequency of data collection.

The data owner is responsible for improving the quality of both structured and unstructured data. Implementing data governance and policies supports data owners and enables the implementation of data quality measures. Ultimately, improved data quality supports value creation and digital transformations.

2.4 Basics of data management

The need to focus on compliance was triggered by the financial crises in 2008 (Hunt et al., 2012), which institutionalized the role of chief data officer. Some organizations were ahead of the pack, as Capital One appointed the first chief data officer in 2002 (Zetlin and Olavsrud, 2020). The initial compliance focus was on data governance. Data governance was defensive, thereby ensuring data quality. This focus gradually transformed into a more proactive data management strategy. Data management is a capability in support of value creation from data. Access to high-quality data is important and needed for managing operations and incremental decision-making (McAfee et al. 2012; Xiaofeng and Xiang, 2013). Important in data management are identity and access management, full analytics automation, external unmanaged data and open data, data lakes and active data warehouses, and exclusive analytics cloud solutions (Beulen, 2020a). The challenges for data management are related to all these important topics; see Table 2.1.

Regarding identity and access management, multifactor authentication combined with OAuth, which is an open standard for authorization, provides secure

TABLE 2.1 Challenges in data management

Challenges	Description
1. Identity and access management	Ensuring appropriate access to data and to information systems and platforms
2. Full analytics automation	Ensuring all analyses and data manipulation is fully automated
3. External unmanaged data and open data	Enabling the use of unmanaged data and open data in data analytics in addition to structure data
4. Data lakes and active data warehouses	Enabling the use of data lakes and active data warehouses in data analytics in addition to traditional data warehouses
5. Exclusive analytics cloud solutions	Ensuring exclusive analytics cloud solutions support for data analytics and avoid on-premises analytics solutions

delegated access (Indu et al., 2018). Analytics tools need to be fully automated, from data entry to data usage – DataOps (Ereth, 2018). This is not limited to monitoring and live updates of dashboards. For data-driven decision-making, data sets need to be extracted and loaded into the analytics platform. The analysis might trigger data updates and/or creation of new data or deletion of data, in one or more databases and/or data lakes. Interfaces between systems, platforms, and analytics platforms are essential and require fully automated analytics tooling to avoid inaccurate dashboards and impacting data-driven decision-making. This is related to the integration of data and the design, development, and deployment of functionality, and the need for exclusive analytics cloud solutions (Atwa, 2020).

In addition, data management needs to deal with unmanaged data and open data, which creates business value (Popovič et al., 2018). This sets requirements in terms of quality control of the data. Organizations need to distinguish between data feeds, which have a real-time or daily frequency, as this frequency triggers follow-up transactions and decisions in the receiving organization versus one-off data sets which are acquired to make an incremental decision, such as an external data mart with over a decade of historical data (Scriney et al., 2019). The real-time data feeds need rigorous checking as feed updates are made on a high-frequency basis, which typically requires automated profiling. This enables receiving organizations to implement adequate quality control. For the one-off data sets, it will be difficult or impossible for receiving organizations to verify the quality of the data on arrival. The procurement process of these data marts must address this risk. This requires implementing data lakes and active data warehouses (Vermeulen, 2018).

Finally, exclusive cloud analytics solutions need to be implemented. Data management needs to facilitate the required demand, which can be very unpredictable and volatile. Cloud analytics solutions are fully flexible in terms of required processing power and storage capacity.

The chief data officer is instrumental in getting the data management basics right. The chief data officer leads and drives data literacy and data governance to increase data quality (Wolff et al., 2016; D'Ignazio, 2017). Data literacy is typically a journey of 12–18 months, minimum, to onboard an organization from the board of management to the employees in the operational units. Creating awareness and explaining the potential value of data are the main objectives of data literacy programs. Training programs to increase the data capabilities of employees are also an embedded part of these data literacy programs (Frank and Walker, 2016).

In close collaboration with the chief information officer (CIO), the chief data officer needs to work on data management following the data governance focus. The role of the chief data officer is to set the requirements for information systems and tooling, the underlying infrastructure, and architecture. The requirements are based on the data strategy which has been aligned with the managers of the organization units, including concepts such as data democratization. In addition to ensuring the data management foundational platform is available, a key focus of the chief data officer is to support the organization to identify use cases: How can the organization unlock value by using data?

Essential for any successful use case is clear data ownership, as this is instrumental to data quality and availability. Data ownership has to be embedded in the business. The chief data officer often takes ownership of data used by multiple organization units, excluding reference data ("cross-business-line data" – below figure), whereas the board of management needs to embrace data and support the use of data in value creation. Therefore, the board of management should never take data ownership. Figure 2.1 provides a snapshot of a 2020 global survey with more than +100 respondents.

This data ownership will be discussed in greater detail in Part 4, particularly in Chapters 12 and 13. Data management in all of its facets will be discussed in greater detail in Parts 2 and 4.

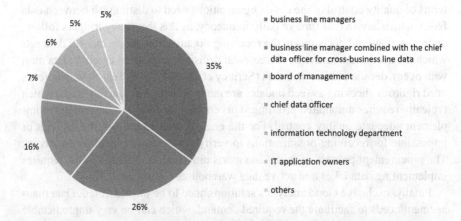

FIGURE 2.1   Ownership of data in survey organizations (N = 105) (Beulen, 2020a)

2.5   Data architecture

Data architecture puts data first in enterprise and IT architectures. The data architecture addresses two challenges: data silos, which leads to data duplication; and
master data management, which results in multiple security masters. To address the
data silo challenge, organizations need to adapt their enterprise and IT architecture
from an application-centric architecture to a data-centric architecture (Andrews
et al., 2019; McComb, 2019). This thinking is linked to Gartner's framing of data
fabric, defined as "a design concept that serves as an integrated layer (fabric) of
data and connecting processes" (Gartner, 2021a). This enables availability of not
only data within the organization, including data democratization, but also data
sharing outside the organization. It is also supportive of data ownership, which improves data quality. However, architects must prepare for answers on the increasing volumes of unstructured data. Unstructured data is of increasing importance in
the innovation of services and products. To process and embed unstructured data,
additional tools, processes, and procedures are required to refine the data and transform the unstructured data into structure data. The additional tooling needs to be
embedded in the architecture, as, for example, suggested by Kluegl et al. (2016).
The selection and maintenance of tooling and parameters in the tooling requires
the full focus of data architects, as organizations are in flux and need to respond to
many changes. These dynamics set a high bar for data architects. Furthermore, data
architecture is not all about centralizing data and data processing. In Industry 4.0,
including the Internet of Things, edge computing is a good practice. Data architects
must take into account the implications of this requirement (Li et al., 2018).

On top of that, data architecture also resolves the impact from multiple security
masters by defining more stringent data categorizations, the second challenge. This
approach results in improved security as data needs to be protected. The implementation of measure, including segmentation, can be fully tailored by data category,
where each data category has its own set of security requirements. A reduced am-
biguity results in an increased level of security (Gupta et al., 2019; Semenov and
Poltavtsev, 2020).

The above also sets demanding requirements on the capability of the data architects. Enterprise and IT architects need to have a greater understanding of business
processes, up to the point that business knowledge is even more important than
knowledge of technology and information technology (De Mauro et al., 2018).
The role of a data architect is developing into a business role. The architect needs
to be able to communicate with the data scientist as well as with representatives
from the primary and support processes, including the IT departments and external
technology partners. To be clear, the data architect is an additional role in organizations. The data architect does not replace the enterprise and/or IT architect. Data
architects take guidance from the enterprise architect and provide guidance to IT
architects as data-centric is the new mantra. In addition, data architects take guidance from the chief data officer, focusing on data classification, processes, and

procedures to ensure compliance, meet ethical standards, and safeguard security. The data architects execute the strategies of the chief data officer.

Central in data architecture is currently cloud computing and, in the future, quantum computing. These technologies will be detailed in the next two subsections.

2.5.1 Cloud computing

In cloud computing, there is a difference between infrastructure as a service (IaaS), platform as a service (PaaS), and software as a service (SaaS) (Mell et al., 2011). All are relevant for data analytics, as they facilitate cost effective storage and ensure high performance computing environments for high-speed data analytics. Data warehouse and data lake tooling such as Amazon Web Services Redshift, Google Big Query, IBM DB2, and Snowflake are pivotal in value creation with data analytics. Data warehouses and data lakes are the domain of the data scientist and data engineer. They use solutions such as Jupyter, Python, and R to build their algorithms. Industry standards and good practices for managing data in the cloud are emerging, for example, EDM Coucil's Cloud Data Management Capabilities (CDMC) framework.

In order to facilitate data democratization, SaaS platforms such as Microsoft Power BI, Qlik, and Tableau are required. Unlike data warehouse tooling, individual employees can use these SaaS platforms and perform their own analyses, and no additional solutions are needed. Individual employees are characterized as citizen data scientists.

Data warehouses, data lakes, data analytics solutions, and SaaS platforms are implemented and maintained by the IT department or a third party, if outsourced (Beulen and Ribbers, 2010). Typically, organizations opt for hybrid solutions that include both the IT department and a portfolio of third parties. The considerations for in-house versus external are typically driven by a combination of the availability of capabilities and costs, and the compliancy impact, where a high compliance impact leans toward in-house.

In the architecture, the selection of cloud platforms is a very challenging responsibility, as the functionality of any of these platforms is enriched at a high pace and the cloud service provider market is dynamic. Due to enriching functionality, the most preferred cloud platform portfolio today will be different from future preferred portfolios. Assessing the upward potential of platforms has to be included in the selection of cloud platforms. Also, there is a constant influx of start-ups which either will exit the market or grow into a scaled-up cloud service provider, followed by transforming into a mature cloud service provider. A not unusual alternative scenario is that new cloud service providers are acquired by existing cloud service providers. This results in additional complexity and increased risk profiles for any organization. The market dynamics result in uncertainty, while selecting and implementing a cloud platform has a long-term impact, and the cost and effort required to migrate to cloud platforms should not be underestimated.

Costs and vendor dependency are both important in selecting cloud platforms. The cost of cloud platforms is pay-as-you-go, whereas the pricing mechanisms are typically centered around data transfer costs. There are three data transfer cost factors in cloud computing: the same platform versus another platform, different cloud platform regions, and/or availability zones. Typically, volume will affect the unit price for data transfer. Therefore, multi-stack cloud architectures reduce vendor dependency; however, this comes at a price. Many organizations currently have a multi-stack cloud architecture, not by design but as a result of initiated successful pilots with multiple cloud platforms.

The enterprise, data, and IT architect have a combined responsibility to continuously assess the cloud architecture and balance requirements, costs, and vendor dependency.

2.5.2   Quantum computing

The increased processing of quantum computing compared to classical computing can further extend the impact of data analytics (Praveena et al., 2018; Ajagekar and You, 2020). Quantum computing was initiated in the late 1990s (Shor, 1998; Steane, 1998; Gruska, 1999; Hey, 1999); however, it is still an emerging technology (Wolf, 2017). Gartner defines it as follows:

> Quantum computing is a type of nonclassical computing that operates on the quantum state of subatomic particles. The particles represent information as elements denoted as quantum bits (qubits). A qubit can represent all possible values simultaneously (superposition) until read. Qubits can be linked with other qubits, a property known as entanglement. Quantum algorithms manipulate linked qubits in their undetermined, entangled state, a process that can address problems with vast combinatorial complexity.
>
> *(Gartner, n.d.-c)*

Examples of qubits are electronics (spins versus atomic level), photons (polarization versus position), and Bloch sphere representation (state parameterization versus vector on the unit sphere).

Currently, organizations can start to experiment with quantum computing; however, it is still not largely commercially available. McKinsey (2020a) expects that by 2030, only 2,000–5,000 quantum computers will be operational. Left alone, suitable applications will be largely available for data analytics. However, any organization should include quantum computing in their roadmap and start to investigate data analytics opportunities. In order to successfully explore these opportunities and to start pilot projects, organizations need to ramp up quantum computing capabilities and leverage quantum computing capacity that is currently available (Bova et al., 2021) – consider PaaS solutions such as Amazon bracket, Azure Quantum, Google Cirq, and IBM Qiskit.

For data architecture, organizations need to be very closely aligned with the chief information security offer (CISO), particularly in the context of quantum computing, as any encrypted traffic, files, or hardware that lands in the hands of an intelligence collector could soon be fed to their quantum decryptor (Keplinger, 2018). For example, NASA has been transitioning to quantum-resistant algorithms since 2015 (Schneier, 2015). Although this threat is not data-specific, any organization should keep this in the back of their minds and strategize on the topic (Hamilton, 2019; Cavaliere et al., 2020). This is even a threat to national security (Grobman, 2020). This threat is underpinned by the Shor algorithm: the quantum algorithm for factoring a number N in the $O((\log N)3)$ time and $O(\log N)$ space. The implication is that public-key cryptography will be broken (Shor, 1994). Furthermore, there is also Grover's algorithm: a quantum algorithm that finds with high probability the unique input to a black box function that produces a particular output value, using $O(\sqrt{N})$ just evaluations of the function, where N is the size of the function's domain. The implication of Grover's algorithm is that protection of symmetric encryption systems will be reduced (Grover, 1996). However, according to NIST, organizations still have time. NIST expects that RSA algorithms will remain secure up to 2030, as Shore's algorithm has not been applied successfully and Grover's algorithm is lacking. NIST advises cryptographers to increase the key size and consider the advanced encryption standard (AES-256) and consider secure hash algorithms (SHA-256 and SHA-3) (Chen et al., 2016).

2.6 Artificial intelligence[2]

Alan Turing famously published on the possibilities of machines with true intelligence (1950). In 1956, in the Dartmouth Summer Research Project on Artificial Intelligence, the term "artificial intelligence" was coined by John McCarthy (Dartmouth College), Marvin Minsky (Harvard University), Nathaniel Rochester (IBM), and Claude Shannon (Bell Telephone Laboratories) (Moor, 2006). Dwivedi et al. (2021) defined artificial intelligence as "the common thread among AI definitions is the increasing capability of machines to perform specific roles and tasks currently performed by humans within the workplace and society in general" (p. 2). Devices that mimic cognitive functions such as learning, speech, and problem solving are also an integral part of artificial intelligence (Russell and Norvig, 2016). Artificial intelligence also includes the ability to independently interpret and learn from external data (Haenlein and Kaplan, 2019). Furthermore, replication of both algorithms and learnings in organizations is straightforward with artificial intelligence.

This sounds very promising and relevant in the context of data analytics and digital transformations, as artificial intelligence is also relevant for any organization. Artificial intelligence enables fact-based decisions (Dignum, 2018; Dwivedi et al., 2019). Different from humans, artificial intelligence can always be "on," and AI is typically faster than humans. Gartner (2021b) differentiates in complexity of decisions as in well as time required to make a decision. Decision automation is related to quick and simple decision-making, where decision argumentation is a more time-consuming and more complex type of decision-making, and decision support is related to the most complex decisions, which require the longest time to make the decision.

Artificial intelligence also triggers fear of job losses. Some jobs will indeed be made redundant by applying artificial intelligence. McKinsey expects that 14% of the global workforce will have to find another job by 2030 (2018). However, the adoption of artificial intelligence will also create jobs. Gartner expects a net positive effect in 2025 (2017). Finding qualified professionals for performing artificial intelligence has been difficult for over a decade for most organizations, and the search will remain a challenge according to the Organization for Economic Co-operation and Development (OECD) (Squicciarini and Nachtigall, 2021).

Continuously increasing processing power and data storage capabilities will further enhance the impact of artificial intelligence on data analytics and digital transformations. Artificial intelligence is related to ontology and knowledge graphs, which support the relation between data and data categories. Also, artificial intelligence is related to machine learning and deep learning, which are distinctly different by related technology developments. The most important four technology developments will be explained in the three subsections below.

2.6.1 Ontology and knowledge graphs

To get improved insights, organizations need to develop and implement an ontology and associated knowledge graphs. Ontologies and knowledge graphs provide insights among data elements. Gruber (1993, p. 199) defines an ontology as "a specification of a representational vocabulary for a shared domain of discourse – definitions of classes, relations, functions, and other objects." Organizations are increasingly considering a multi-tier ontology to support the complexity. A knowledge graph can be defined as "a multi-relational graph composed of entities as nodes and relations as different types of edges. An instance of an edge is a triplet of facts (head entity, relation, tail entity) (denoted as (h, r, t))" (Wang et al., 2014, p. 1112). The knowledge graph was launched by Google in 2012 to increase insights from search engine data (Singhal, 2012). Knowledge graphs upend traditional relational data schemas with a three-dimensional semantic architecture that introduces connections (edges) between entities (nodes). Graph visualization tools increase data analytics capabilities exponentially by adding that distinct relationship layer, enabling drill-down capabilities into nodes and edges, for never-ending fun in the search for meaningful data and insights. An important contribution of knowledge graphs is that they create human-readable explanations. This is supportive to the design, implementation, and monitoring of both machine learning and deep learning algorithms.

2.6.2 Machine learning

Machine learning is already being applied on a large scale by many organizations (Forrester, 2019). Machine learning, also labeled as narrow artificial intelligence, is based on human pre-programmed activities to perform a task, operating by "if-then-else" statements and hard-coded knowledge suggestions.

It is important that the algorithms are trained. The data quality used to train the algorithms is more important than volume of training data; however, more training data helps improve the algorithms. Nevertheless, verification of the machine learning outcomes of the algorithms is very important.

Learning methods can be divided into two broad categories: inductive and deductive. Inductive methods create computer programs by forming rules or extracting patterns from data. Deductive methods result in a function that is as generic as the input data.

Benefits of machine learning are making employees smarter, making operations more efficient, improving strategic decision-making, hyper-personalizing customer experiences, and accelerating the launch of new products.

2.6.3 Deep learning

Deep learning allows the computer to build complex concepts from simpler concepts. Different from machine learning, deep learning is unsupervised. Organizations only monitor the data sets that are input for deep learning and deep learning outcomes.

Unlike machine learning, deep learning has not been adopted by many organizations. Currently, most organizations have initiated a pilot project and are experimenting with deep learning. In this learning curve, organizations must build up knowledge on how to interpret deep learning outcomes (Li et al., 2022).

Deep learning is also labeled as general artificial intelligence and perform tasks without explicit pre-programmed activities to perform a specific task. General artificial intelligence systems create insights based on data processing. The focus of these systems is on identifying trends (Schmidhuber, 2015).

Deep learning is used in, for example, image recognition, speech recognition, natural language processing, audio recognition, social network filtering, machine translation, bioinformatics, drug compounding, medical image recognition, and board game programs. But it is also becoming very important in detection of network intrusion and an essential component in ensuring cyber resilience (Ahmad et al., 2021).

Deep learning has also introduced the phenomenon of "deepfake" of a photo, audio, and/or video fragment due to the increased believability and accessibility of technology that creates a deepfake (Kietzmann et al., 2020). Deepfake can also be a threat to national security (Sayler and Harris, 2020).

DATA ANALYTICS TRENDS

Savita Kulkarni – Head of AI Services
TCS Analytics and Insights Unit at Tata Consultancy Services

There are quite a few important trends in data analytics. These trends can be bucketed into four areas: (1) data governance, (2) technology, (3) people, and (4) business.

1. Data governance

The most prevalent trend is all encompassing governance across data, processes, people, and technology. For decades, organizations have been doing site audits to validate data. The trend was towards data warehouses where the focus was on consolidated data and centralized analysis. Centralized governance was quite well handled.

But then came the era of Big Data around a decade ago, which ushered in the trend towards distributed data architecture. Savita Kulkarni: "Big Data is data that contains greater variety, arriving in increasing volumes and with more velocity. This is also known as the three Vs. Put simply, Big Data is larger, more complex data sets, especially from new data sources." Big Data was predominantly used for the processing side. Data warehouses continued to exist. So, there was a co-existence of data warehouses, Big Data, and mainframe systems, causing a breakdown in distributed data governance. Savita Kulkarni:

> For about the last five years, cloud and AI have been in full swing, further complicating efforts to manage and collate and corelate the data. Now with data catalogs, data fabric, data mesh and associated ontologies, as well as data sharing across organizations and ecosystems, organisations are forced to completely rethink and develop holistic, networked and federated governance frameworks.

Alternative and orthogonal datasets used and cultivated by AI need to be managed as well. The data estate itself is expanding. Savita Kulkarni: "Orthogonal data – the introduction of new, seemingly unrelated, data sets, that, combined with data already in use, produce new consumer insights."

Policies around privacy, data sharing, data quality, and even AI adoption are very important. For example, in life sciences, there are GxP (good practices) compliance or good machine learning practice frameworks. The evolving policy frameworks are driving home the fact that traditional data governance is no longer sufficient.

Governing ecosystems

One aspect of traditional data governance focuses on managing or enhancing multiple copies of the same data and ensuring the right kind of stewardship and data quality is in place. Savita Kulkarni:

> When we talk about governing an ecosystem, traditional data governance needs to be taken to the next level of scale. For example, a Finance department working with a Manufacturing department – there can be multiple departments creating similar data, like client data, that needs to be included in cross-departmental analytics, but each department is creating the data in different ways to enable their own decisions and develop their own strategies.

When external ecosystems are added into the mix, usage and governance policies must also be updated to extend to external ecosystems, business partners, and IT partners, as well as unstructured data like websites, alternative, and open data sources. Strict internal data policies and data ownership need to be reevaluated to determine if they are still applicable to external data sources. If wrong decisions are made, identifying who is responsible, how is it fixed, and what processes are applied, are policies that must span ecosystems.

Savita Kulkarni: "Using a Data Marketplace framework enables the development of governance policies that span ecosystems to be defined upfront on a holistic platform, instead of attempting to join together individual governance programs, which may have conflicting policies."

Managing bias and risk trends

Governance has become a priority and governing bodies are developing stringent compliance rules across industries. Savita Kulkarni:

> When AI is introduced, the ability to have an auditable system or ability to reconcile the results and decisions being made by AI is very important. The underlying aspects of how bias is handled needs both 'Responsible AI' and 'Accountable Human'.

Humans who are teaching AI have a responsibility to ensure that organizational ethics and risk governance are inherent in the AI. AI has to be transparent with auditability frameworks so humans can better train the AI.

2. Technology

Cloud and AI

The technology trends in data analytics of course begin with cloud technologies. At the beginning of cloud adoption, it was all about transactional applications moving onto the cloud. Cloud has now stepped formally into the data analytics space. Savita Kulkarni: "Data fabric on cloud, regional data requirements, and best of breed architectures, are driving the need for a multi-cloud strategy." Another trend in cloud adoption is enabling enterprise AI to become core to decision-making, driving the need for AI governance, including auditability and explainability for AI systems.

Multi-cloud data strategy challenges

Single cloud strategies will focus on optimizing cost, agility, and/or speed to meet a specific need and gain the full benefits of cloud. Multi-cloud strategies present challenges for data duplication, latency across cloud systems, more complex access and privacy controls, and regional regulations for data center storage. Savita Kulkarni:

> The promise of data mesh as well as data fabrics is to address these overhead challenges with a virtualization layer across data access and governance, providing a more flexible architecture allowing for pivots to replace best-of-breed cloud platforms as needed for compliance or usage optimization. On the other hand, Integration and higher costs are also a challenge that needs to be optimally handled in multi-cloud strategies.

AI challenges

While many organizations are 'testing the waters' with AI, very few organizations are productionizing it for deployment at the enterprise level. Organizations still struggle to bridge the gap for deployment of AI solutions at the enterprise level. Savita Kulkarni:

> They need to think through the data policies and define a clear AI strategy, what they wish to achieve, whether AI is adopted as an intervention in their

organization or aligned to specific organizational growth plans and agendas. AI strategies must be defined from the top down.

If each individual department builds their own AI solutions without a coordinated top-down approach, then invariably there will be challenges bringing it together and putting it into production.

Enterprise AI adoption is a big challenge because real-world data is ever changing and comes in different forms. Idealistic AI solutions may not fit unless they are very adaptable, self-learning, and there is a deep understanding of how the entire data pipeline is defined. There are multiple aspects of adopting an AI solution into the larger organization and the right strategy is required. This is a big challenge that is often not addressed. Savita Kulkarni: "Having the right strategy and governance framework is extremely critical."

3. People

Distributed workforce management

From a people perspective, the 'great resignation' and attrition has introduced a level of instability and scarcity of skills in organizations. The skills gap is affecting what organizations can accomplish versus what skills are available in the organization. The pandemic has created a distributed workforce, which is changing and driving a lot of people management trends.

Talent

To address the shortage of qualified and certified professionals and attrition, much effort is put into certifications. Savita Kulkarni: "At Tata Consultancy Services, we have developed the AI Academy. There are three aspects for developing a professional to maximize their AI project skills: (1) Service/Technology Skills, (2) Business/Management Skills, (3) Process/Soft Skills."

The first is technical skills, enhancing a professional's skills in a specific AI discipline like natural language processing (NLP) or machine learning (ML) or computer vision and Data Engineering, Data Management and Ops., etc. This is very straightforward training.

The second part is business domain and management skills involving industry/functional knowledge, business value maps, organizational change management, governance. Savita Kulkarni:

Professionals building AI models must understand the data they are working with to be able to choose the right kind of models, test and tune the data appropriately. The ability to bring domain skills to AI is very important. Developing technology skills without the domain and change management skills is only half the battle.

The third and most important part is understanding the consequences of the outcomes. This is about Process and Soft skills involving behavior, ethics, communication and agile methodology, and design thinking processes. Professionals building AI must be aware of the impact of mistakes from poor training data, for example defining voltages in the algorithms of utility organizations, what wrong decisions coming from AI can do to the outcomes of a program, a consumer, a patient, or a bank customer. Unless they are aware of the impact, they can never bring the right kind of rigor into the AI program. So, the right human oversight and ethics is very important.

Another skill and aspect often ignored or given less focus is the 'Art' part in AI systems. Savita Kulkarni:

Unless the results of AI are presented in an easy-to-understand way, the whole purpose is defeated. A normal end user should be able to understand what the AI is trying to tell them. The Art of creating User Interfaces that help end users understand what AI systems are suggesting or recommending, to enable them to infer and take right decisions is key to drive AI adoption and acceptability.

These are talent training aspects which we always ensure professionals are building into the AI.

4. Business

Business data management

As much as five years ago, the business was barely involved in data, and it was predominantly in the IT space and mostly managed by IT. Savita Kulkarni:

Fast forward five years, the trends are now showing that businesses are managing almost 50% of the data themselves. The businesses recognizing data assets, data products, and context-centric business solutions that drive data monetization and data sharing, has become a major trend.

When an organization begins to create data sets and data products intended for monetization, then it must be tied to the data strategy and roadmap defined for the organization. Savita Kulkarni: "For example, if the data strategy requires a purpose for creating a data set, how does that purpose tie to business growth?"

The business has to be involved and empowered to look at data monetization and ensure the purpose is aligned with the organizational data strategy. Centers of Excellence form policies for data sharing and monetization and Data Committees, comprised of decision makers from both Business and IT, are needed to define policies and take decisions related to the entire data lifecycle and accountability.

2.6.4 *Conclusion*

This chapter has clarified the relevant data analytics trends. Technology developments continue to develop at a pace. This sets requirements for any organization to be on top of any new developments. Organizations that are able to assess trends quickly and efficiently will be able to make decisions on exploring the adoption of any technology trend. Following a proof-of-concept, organizations need to decide which technologies are relevant to invest in, and scale up rapidly. Organizations require a dedicated team of seasoned technology experts with business experience to successfully adopt data analytics trends.

Notes

1 Previously also known as business intelligence (BI) teams.
2 An earlier version of this section has been published in Information Management and eBusiness (Beulen et al., 2022).

PART 2

Data analytics foundation

Data analytics is the foundation for any digital transformation and has two opportunities: data-driven decision-making and data monetization. This part explains these opportunities, combined with three challenges.

The use of data is no longer only a source of information for organizations to make decisions. More and more, data drives simple decision-making in many organizations. This first opportunity frees up human resources to focus on more advanced decision-making; hence, this increases the customer focus, or for public sector organizations the citizen focus. Also, this makes the work performed by employees more interesting and challenging. The additional tasks, the development and the maintenance of the data-driven decision-making workflows, and monitoring of the outcomes further increase the relevance and the profile of the involved employees.

The second opportunity in digital transformation related to data analytics is the monetization of data. Collecting and analyzing data to develop insights offers opportunities to develop new business models. The insights can be good additions and create value to the offered services and/or products. The monetization of data requires clarity on the ownership of the data and needs to take into account the ever-increasing compliance obligations. Organizations need to anticipate on upcoming compliance obligations to avoid a clash with regulators and lawmakers.

Benefiting from these two opportunities requires (1) high data quality, (2) proper data governance, and (3) data compliance, privacy, and ethics. In this part, these three challenges are addressed. Many organizations struggle with data quality, as the data ownership, processes, and tooling are not at level. Organizations need leadership in the data domain. Putting in place proper data governance is instrumental to improving data quality. Organizations have appointed chief data officers to drive improvements and ensure a data focus. This C-level role is beginning to

DOI: 10.4324/9781003246770-4

evolve into a management role of head of data and analytics. To be clear, this is not to suggest that, in the future, the role of data management will be less important. This indicates the increased overall data maturity and data capabilities of an organization. Furthermore, from having one's house in order to harvesting, it is necessary to keep an eye on data compliance and privacy – in addition to the GDPR, many data privacy legislations are in place. Finally, ethics is an important aspect in data analytics. Organizations need to develop their own moral compass and avoid biased algorithms and data sets. In data governance and data policies, ethics requires specific attention.

3
DATA-DRIVEN DECISION-MAKING

Intuition and experience need to be powered by data analytics. Organizations need to integrate data-driven decision-making into their DNA. Data-driven decision-making is not limited to incremental (investment) decisions, it also extends to decision-making in day-to-day operations and processes. Improved incremental decision-making typically supports the more strategic decision-making by senior management and higher. The decision-making in day-to-day processes is related to operational efficiency and effectiveness and typically not only replaces manual effort and reduces errors but also improves the customer experience. Data-driven decision-making is conditionally correlated with improvements in revenue-based productivity of 4%–8% (Brynjolfsson and McElheran, 2019).

Adopting data-driven decision-making requires significant change management and leadership guidance and is not achieved overnight. Additionally, data-driven decision-making is instrumental in accelerating digital transformations.

3.1   Introduction

Increasing volumes of data are available for organizations; this not only includes internal transaction, client, and supplier data, but also (un)structured and external data. This creates opportunities to improve decision-making. Despite the need to leverage data in decision-making, organizations should always complement intuition and gut instinct with data-driven decision-making. Data-driven decision-making can be defined as the practice of basing decisions on the analysis of data rather than purely on intuition (Provost and Fawcett, 2013, p. 53). To be clear, data-driven decision-making is not a new phenomenon; as early as the 1990s, financial institutions and telecommunication companies implemented large-scale information management systems to manage data-driven fraud control decisions. A decade

DOI: 10.4324/9781003246770-5

prior, less sophisticated information technology powered direct marketing to target specific segments through direct mail and telemarketing. Today, data-driven decision-making is progressing to a company-wide scope.

The literature suggests replacing data-driven decision-making by data-driven analytics (Provost and Fawcett, 2013; De Langhe and Puntoni, 2021). Descriptive analytics enables the decision maker to look back at trends that have already occurred and make future decisions. Predictive and prescriptive artificial intelligence models predict future outcomes, enabling the decision maker to choose the best future course of action.

Examples of data-driven algorithms are decision trees, support vector machines (SVM), K-means, k nearest neighbor (kNN), Adaboost, and deep learning (DL) algorithms (Tian et al., 2021). These will further drive innovation (Yablonsky, 2019). This outlook is particularly relevant for decision-making in day-to-day processes; automatic pricing adjustments based on inventory, demand, and competitor pricing in retail would be good examples for data-driven analytics. In this book, data-driven analytics is embedded in data-driven decision-making.

The business benefits of data-driven decision-making are quite obvious: improved decisions and improved outcomes, with potentially reduced costs and/or increased revenues.

The tone at the top is important in order to successfully and fully benefit from data-driven decision-making. This is not limited to providing funding for tooling, head count, and the implementation of data governance. Management must demonstrate that their decisions are also data-driven and set strict requirements for their subordinates to also focus on increasing the percentage of data-driven decision-making. Tracking the percentage of data-driven decisions and making it an integral part of performance reviews is key. This will pose challenges in the definition of a "data-driven decision," and measuring the percentage of data-driven decisions will continue to be a challenge.

The percentage of data-driven decisions as part of the total number of decisions is definitively increasing (Beulen, 2020a). In a 2020 survey, including 105 organizations ranging from revenue/budget of less than 10m euros to + 1b euros, the percentage of surveyed organizations with less than 10% data-driven decisions in 2020 was 23%, where only 23% of the organizations made 50% or more of their decisions data-driven. The envisioned percentage for 2025 was that all of the surveyed organizations will at least make 10% of their decisions data-driven and that 63% of the organizations made 50% or more of their decisions data-driven. This is detailed in Figure 3.1.

3.2   Inhibitors for data-driven decision-making

The adoption of data-driven decision-making is not straightforward. The inhibitors are predominantly in business. First, the involvement of the business is required. Due to anxieties about technology and job security, business managers are hesitant

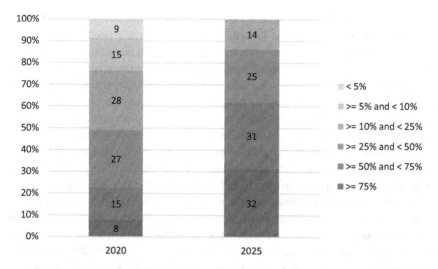

FIGURE 3.1   Percentage and number of organizations grouped by the (envisioned) percentage of data-driven decisions in 2020 and 2025 (N = 105, 102 valid responses – global survey) (Beulen, 2020a)

to fully adopt data-driven decision-making. To address technology anxiety, training and appointing champions are effective measures to increase the adoption of data-driven decision-making. Champions are not only role models but also the go-to persons for data-driven decision-making topics, including questions related to self-service data tools.

A second inhibitor is poor data quality. The data is not trusted. The implication is that the data is either not used at all, or that a significant effort is required to check the underlying data and potentially cleanse and supplement data prior to making the decision. Data quality issues remain persistent in many organizations; however, for organizations that embrace data-driven decision-making, the business case to improve data quality will significantly improve.

Third, organizations struggle with identification of the right data set. For incremental decisions, this requires a seamless collaboration between business managers who are making data-driven decisions and the data science department. For decision-making in day-to-day processes, the complexity is much lower. Business managers need to decide on which historic data need to be taken into account: e.g. last month's data or data from the last 36 months. One of the challenges for business managers in making these decisions is adjusting the data sets used and/or adjustment of the decision rules to ensure that they reflect current market conditions. In terms of process, this requires strict governance to prevent using biased data sets and/or sub-optimal decision rules.

However, lack of data science skills also hinders the adoption of data-driven decision-making. First to consider is the availability of qualified professionals; this is applicable to both business managers as well as to data scientists and technology specialists, especially data engineers who are making data accessible to the data scientists, in the IT department. The labor market is always in need of qualified resources; therefore, organizations should focus not only on recruiting and labor conditions but also on retention management. In retention management, the purpose of the organization is more important than ever. For smaller organizations, the need for data scientists has to be questioned. Alternatively, smaller organizations can embed the data scientist role into data management roles, as smaller organizations will struggle to find and successfully engage the right caliber of data scientists for the medium and long term. Typically, data scientists want to engage with business managers, as well as peers, and are looking for hyper-fast learning curves. Smaller organizations will struggle to engage their peers and offer fast learning curves.

Second, processes are hindering the adoption of data-driven decision-making. The centralization of governance provides guidance to the data scientists, as well as to the IT department on how to architect the technology infrastructure, and to business managers on how to deal with data, including the ownership of data. Centralizing governance processes facilitates data sharing, which is extremely important for data-driven decision-making. Many organizations have appointed a chief data officer and/or a head of data (analytics), which is helpful in order to improve the processes.

Finally, the absence or limitations of the tooling inhibits organizations from fully adopting data-driven decision-making. Nowadays, most organizations have data management tooling in place, where some organizations, as a consequence of mergers or acquisitions or an immature enterprise and IT architecture, have

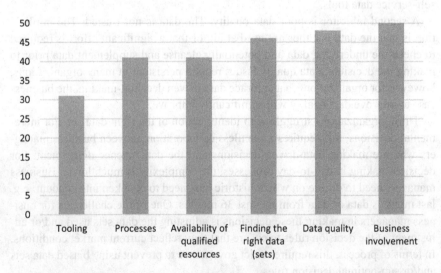

FIGURE 3.2   Inhibitors to adopt data-driven decision-making – number of organizations surveyed reporting a limitation: multiple responses (N = 105 – global survey) (Beulen, 2020a)

multiple data management tools in place. Standardization of data management tools and centralization of data management governance are typically helpful for tooling and supporting data-driven decision-making.

The results of a 2020 survey on inhibitors for the adoption of data-driven decision-making are detailed in Figure 3.2.

3.3   Aspects of data-driven decision-making

In the adoption of data-driven decision-making, there are four aspects: data quality, data governance, business collaboration, and partnership. Organizations must set their priorities to ensure data-driven decision-making is becoming part of the DNA of their organization. The four data-driven decision-making aspects are detailed in full in Figure 3.3 and are described and analyzed in the following. Both are based on a 2020 global survey with 105 responses (Beulen, 2020a).

3.3.1   Data quality

Data quality is still too low in many organizations. In a global 2020 survey, just under 50% of the 105 respondents scored a 4 or lower on a 1–7 Likert scale, where 1 = No, limited and reactive improvement in data quality and 7 = actively managing

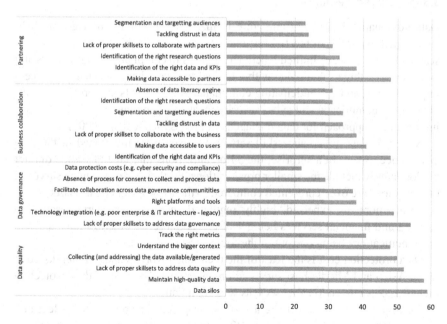

FIGURE 3.3   Overview of data-driven leadership aspects – number of surveyed organizations indicated an aspect clustered by data-driven leadership aspect (N = 105) (Beulen, 2020a)

a data literacy program and proactively and structurally improving data quality to ensure consistent and trusted data in combination with the implementation of an ontology (Beulen, 2020a).

Data silos are the biggest issue in the data quality aspect – 59 of the surveyed organizations face this challenge. As expected, large organizations with a revenue of > 1,000m euro are overrepresented by traditional sectors, such as banking and financial services and manufacturing. There is no difference in the challenges of the geographic data silo, except that all three surveyed in the Middle East face this challenge.

"Tracking the right measures" is the data quality challenge that is mentioned least – 41 of the surveyed organizations face this challenge. This is less of a challenge for the Dutch surveyed organizations, whereas this challenge is mentioned by three out of four Asian surveyed companies. There were no sectoral or size-related differences among the surveyed organizations in this regard. To address data quality challenges, it is also important to understand the larger context. This includes the data life cycle and compliance requirements.

Furthermore, assessing the data is important, and this is the starting point for improvement actions and might begin with attracting the right talent to improve and maintain high-quality data.

3.3.2 Data governance

Data governance is still too immature in many organizations. In a global 2020 survey, just over 55% of the 105 respondents scored a 5 or higher on a 1–7 Likert scale; where 1 = No, or limited reactive responses to compliance requirements and cyber security threats combined with a limited focus on data management process improvements, and 7 = anticipating compliance requirements and proactively implementing compliance and cyber security measures combined with a continuous improvement approach for data management processes (Beulen, 2020a).

A lack of data governance skill sets is the issue most mentioned in the data governance aspect. In a surprise, the 54 organizations that face this issue did not predominantly include the smaller organizations. Furthermore, the Dutch surveyed organizations are overrepresented compared to their European counterparts.

Furthermore, as expected, highly regulated sectors are underrepresented – banking and financial services being 4 of the 11 surveyed organizations, and telecommunications being one out of the four surveyed organizations.

Data protection cost is the least of the mentioned worries and not mentioned at all by Asian and Middle East surveyed organizations. The cost of data protection includes costs related to cyber security and compliance.

An organization should have a process in place for consent to collect and process data. This is not limited to B2C organizations. Furthermore, some organizations have a poor enterprise and IT architecture and legacy systems, which prevent them from exchanging data and improving the quality of data.

The enterprise and IT architecture provides guidance for implementation of the right platforms and tools.

3.3.3   Business collaboration

Business collaboration is moderate in many organizations. In a global 2020 survey, just over 65% of the 105 respondents scored a 5 or higher on a 1–7 Likert scale, where 1 = low collaboration with the business and 7 = full and proactive/strategic collaboration with the business (Beulen, 2020a).

In the business collaboration aspect, the identification of the right data and KPIs is mentioned by 48 of the surveyed organizations. Organizations with a large internal data exchange are underrepresented, only one of the five surveyed organizations in the consumer goods and distribution sector, and 4 out of the 15 surveyed organizations in manufacturing have reported this as an issue. Surprisingly, the energy resources and utilities sector is overrepresented with 8 out of the 11 surveyed organizations. This aspect was not reported by any Asian organizations.

The absence of a data literacy engine is mentioned by 31 of the surveyed organizations. This issue is mentioned the least by the surveyed organizations. There was no under- or overrepresentation of sectors, size of organization, or geographies.

It is important to tackle mistrust in data and for organizations to make data available to users. Many organizations are embracing data democratization by clear segmentation and targeting audiences. This is the basis for identifying the right research questions. Involvement of the business with self-service tooling is becoming the norm in many organizations over the next 12–24 months. However, some organizations might need a little more evangelization and increased data literacy efforts from the chief data office.

3.3.4   Partnering

Partnering is still too low in many organizations. In a global 2020 survey, just over 40% of the 105 respondents scored a 5 or higher on a 1–7 Likert scale; where 1 = No initiation of partnerships and no involvement in maintaining partnerships and 7 = high involvement, leading role in initiating new partnerships, and responsible for maintaining existing partnerships (Beulen, 2020a). Especially with the partnering aspect, there is a lot of room for improvement.

Partnering is considered the most difficult aspect of data-driven leadership. Making data accessible is mentioned as the biggest challenge by 48 of the surveyed organizations. As expected, highly regulated sectors such as banking and financial services (8 out of 11) and energy resources and utilities (9 out of 11) are overrepresented. Where sectors that are used to data exchange across ecosystems and value chains are underrepresented, only 5 of the 15 manufacturing organizations face this issue. In high-trust geographies, this challenge is low; in Asia, only one of the four surveyed organizations faced this issue. Also, small organizations (<= 10m euro) do not face this issue, where large organizations (> 1,000m) are overrepresented.

Segmentation and targeting audiences is the issue that is least mentioned. Only 23 of the surveyed organizations face this issue. There was no under- or overrepresentation of sectors, size of organization, or geographies. Also, in this dimension, data-driven leadership addressing distrust in data and the identification of the right research questions are important to ensure partnership. The difficulty is in protecting the position in ecosystems and value chains. By sharing and exchanging data, organizations can strengthen their position, but also some organizations might be pushed out. Organizations need to identify the right data to share and continuously track if and how data sharing is beneficial for their organization.

3.4 Data quality improvement actions

The data quality improvement actions include data silos, lack of proper skill set to address data quality, collecting (and assessing) the data available/generated, understanding the bigger context, and tracking the right metrics. This section dives deep into these actions. This deep dive will be presented in the order of importance to an aspect, starting with the most important action.

3.4.1 Data silos

Data quality is negatively affected if data is stored in data silos. This will potentially result in duplication of data in different silos and, consequently, in data maintenance challenges. Addressing the issue of data silos is essential to improving data quality (Accenture, 2019). Many organizations are currently focusing on centralizing their data into one or more data lakes. Centralization addresses the data silo problem (Patel, 2019) but it also introduces new challenges, including data governance and data ownership issues. Therefore, organizations are currently experimenting with structuring their data in a data mesh instead of in one or more data lakes. The characteristics of a data mesh architecture are domain-oriented and support self-service (Machado et al., 2022). Basically, a data mesh architecture is an improved version of the data silos, as there are centralized policies combined with federated governance, including core principles, on top of the decentralized distribution of data among mesh nodes. In the governance setting, clear data ownership is in many organizations the most challenging part; however, that is no different for data lake or data mesh architectures.

3.4.2 Maintain high-quality data

High-quality data comes with accountability. The role of data owners is crucial (Jin et al., 2020), as they maintain the data and guide data access and data usage.

Ownership of the data should be in the organization, not with the IT department or with the data science department.

To maintain high-quality data, data ownership is not the only important factor. Organizations should also implement an ontology (Eisenberg et al., 2019). An ontology defines a set of representational terms. To manage data, there are three architecture elements which have to be aligned: the ontology, the data sources, and finally the mapping of the ontology and the data sources (Lenzerini, 2018).

3.4.3   Lack of proper skill set to address data quality

In addition to the data owner role, which is decentralized and in the business organization, central capabilities are important to address data quality. These roles are in the chief data office and are related to policy setting and policy enforcement, in addition to awareness training. Furthermore, the cyber skill set is becoming more important, as cyber threat as well as the data volumes are growing (Akhtar et al., 2019). The chief data officer and CISO must be closely aligned. Furthermore, the continuous increase in legislation obligations leads to an increasing need to have legal skill sets also available in the chief data office. Depending on the size of the organization, these skill sets are for part-time roles or contractors.

3.4.4   Collecting (and evaluating) the data available/generated

Bringing together the data needed for data-driven decision-making is a challenge. Assuring data quality is key, for both incremental decision-making and decision-making in day-to-day processes. There can be two types of noise in the data sets: in the predictive attributes (attribute noise) and in the target attribute (class noise) (Gupta and Gupta, 2019).

Furthermore, it is important that in the collection of data that fit-for-purpose has been assessed, where missing data is the most severe shortcoming. Supplementing data sets with external data sets must be considered. However, the combination of internal and external data sets requires very strict assessments, as the data definitions of both data sets need to be fully aligned.

3.4.5   Understand the bigger context

This action has two sides, the first being that the representatives of the organization have to understand the context, as they are the data owners. However, the representatives from the data science department and IT department also have to understand the context. Understanding the context is required to assess and improve data quality in favor of improved data-driven decision-making.

The differentiation of Fadler and Legner (2022) in data ownership is helpful in clarifying the different roles, as they differentiate between data, data platform, and data product ownership. The data platform is owned by the IT department, where the data and the data product is owned by representatives of the organization.

3.4.6   Track the right metrics

For data quality, there are a large number of frameworks available (Cichy and Rass, 2019). Key for data quality are the aspects of completeness, accuracy, timeliness, consistency, and accessibility. In addition to improving the data quality, the worthiness of data also must be improved. The parameters for the data veracity are based on risk (provenance and integrity) and context (stale, biased, manipulated, or ambiguous) (Accenture, 2019).

It is important that the tracking of metrics is fully automated, and this ensures consistency and facilitates tracking of these metrics, even when the data volumes are increasing over time.

3.5   Data governance improvement actions

Data governance improvement actions to address include a lack of proper skill set to address data governance, technology integration (e.g. poor enterprise and IT architecture – legacy), right platforms and tools, facilitate collaboration across data governance communities, absence of process for consent to collect and process data, and data protection costs (e.g. cyber security and compliance). This section deep dives into these actions. This deep dive will be presented in order of importance to an aspect, starting with the most important action.

3.5.1   Lack of proper skill set to address data governance

For data governance, central and decentral skill sets are needed (Abraham et al., 2019). The central skill sets are in the chief data office and are related to policy setting and policy enforcement. Most organizations have adequate central skill sets. The lack of skill sets in most organizations is in the business organizations themselves. Business managers have many responsibilities, including data governance. Not all business managers have the skill set to fulfill the role of data owner and to be a good counterpart for data scientists and the IT department. To facilitate data-driven decision-making, skills must be developed on business processes, understanding requirements, and determining impact on the data asset and on strategic thinking. What the organization needs data to do is particularly essential (https:// dama.org).

There are good reference models for data governance available, including DCAM (EDM Council, 2020) and DAMA (DAMA International, 2017). These references provide guidance on the skill sets needed.

3.5.2   Technology integration (e.g. poor enterprise and IT architecture – legacy)

Technology integration is a concern in many organizations due to technical debt, obligations to retain data, and the continuously fast growing data volumes. The architecture, including enterprise architecture as the well as IT architecture, is not up to standards. Tracking technical debt is essential to make informed decisions about technology investments that enable data-driven decision-making.

McKinsey has identified six foundational shifts for data architecture (Castro et al., 2020), the two most relevant shifts for data-driven decision-making are the shift from an enterprise warehouse to a domain-based architecture and the shift from rigid data models to flexible, extensible data schemas. These are related to emerging migration from data lakes to data mesh.

3.5.3   Right platforms and tools

Technology is improving data-driven decision-making (Power, 2015). In the last decade, the available functionality has improved significantly, and acquisitions have consolidated the platform and tooling market. This enhances the ability to make data-driven decisions. Nevertheless, there really is no "silver bullet" at the time of this writing, i.e., no end-to-end platforms and tools available in the market. Currently, organizations are still forced into best-of-breed solutions with regard to data platforms and tools. This sets additional requirements for IT architecture, especially the uncertainty related to future mergers and acquisitions, which leads to architectural guidance that facilitates flexibility, e.g. no constraints to replace a platform and/or tool on short notice. This limitation impacts the cost efficiency of the platform and tools and results in a high cost for deploying and maintaining interfaces between the different platforms and tools.

3.5.4   Facilitate collaboration between data governance communities

For the facilitation of collaboration across data governance communities, it is important that there are clear data processes and procedures (CSF #2) and that data roles and responsibilities are established (CSF #5) (Alhassan et al., 2019). In terms of the data governance community collaboration, there is vertical communication between the chief data office and the data owners, and horizontal communication between data owners. Vertical facilitation requires the most attention, as the interests of data owners are typically more aligned than the interests of the chief data office and the data owners. Here, processes and procedures can facilitate collaboration.

3.5.5 Absence of a process for consent to collect and process data

Globally, the processing of data, including personal and sensitive data, has become more restrictive. This is not limited to the European GDPR legislation, which is in addition to the extraterritorial working of GDPR legislation, also being adopted by many other countries such as Brazil, Canada, Japan, New Zealand, South Africa, and South Korea. This sets legal compliance requirements for any organization and makes monitoring of the consents required (Robol et al., 2022).

In addition, organizations that have adopted cloud computing have to be mindful of the data processing and data storage locations of their cloud computing providers. Fortunately, large IaaS and PaaS providers have made their offering compliant, ensuring compliance over time. SaaS providers require more management attention, as compliance is not always a given. To be clear, the adoption of the cloud is almost a prerequisite for enhanced data-driven decision-making.

In terms of consent, "the right to be forgotten" sets requirements for the storage and back-end procedures. This must be addressed in the IT architecture and IT processes. Unfortunately, this is not straightforward (Politou et al., 2018).

3.5.6 Data protection costs (e.g. cyber security and compliance)

Both cyber security and compliance must be embedded in the design (Sion et al., 2019). These non-functional requirements typically cause a lot of discussion. For cyber security, a risk assessment and business case are required to make an informed decision on cyber security requirements, whereas the interpretation of legislation is typically more straightforward than the risk assessment and business case for cyber security. Not being compliant is not an option.

Cyber security risk organizations might consider insuring this risk. Insurance will also provide an organization with access to the network of first responders of the insurance company. However, insurance premiums have increased significantly in recent years and are expected to increase in the years to come. Furthermore, in recent years, insurance deductibility has increased and the exclusions have expanded. Organizations need to decide wisely on how to price the cyber risk (Romanosky et al., 2019) and decide between investing more in cyber resilience or signing up for a cyber insurance policy.

3.6 Business collaboration improvement actions

Data governance improvement actions include the following: identification of the right data and KPIs, making data accessible to users, lack of proper skill set to collaborate with the business, tackling distrust in data, segmentation and targeting audiences, identification of the right research questions, and absence of a data literacy engine. This paragraph deep dives into these actions. This deep dive will be presented in the order of importance to an aspect, starting with the most important action.

3.6.1 Identification of the right data and KPIs

For the identification of the right data and KPIs, in addition to proper data ownership to safeguard data quality, additional governance is required. In some countries, it is mandatory to appoint a data protection officer. The core responsibility of a data protection officer is to ensure data protection compliance. The data protection officer can also be instrumental in the identification of the right data and KPIs (Muscatella, 2020). In this role, the data protection officer facilitates the data owners in the identification of the right data and KPIs. For KPIs, the role of the data protection officer is more of a consulting role, where for the identification of the right data, the role is more about enforcement, as data usages might result in compliance breaches.

Furthermore, decisions on expanding data sets with external data have to be made by the data owners and the data protection officer. This expansion will improve data-driven decision-making.

3.6.2 Making data accessible to users

Data owners need to make their data accessible to their users (internal data availability). The purpose of making data available is enhanced data-driven decision-making and innovation (Ghasemaghaei and Calic, 2019).

Making data available requires proper identity and access management, which has to be facilitated by tooling. This is the responsibility of the chief data office. There are many identity and access management tools. In the context of data-driven decision-making, authorization is the most important element. Authorization entitles access control mechanisms and access control governance. Attribute-based access control, which is also known as policy-based access control, is the most fit for purpose access control mechanism. In access control governance, there are three relevant mechanisms: certification and risk score, life cycle management, and segregation of duties (Indu et al., 2018).

3.6.3 Lack of proper skill set to collaborate with business

To successfully implement data-driven decision-making, the organization needs to be able to effectively communicate with the IT department, as well as with the data scientists. As both are supporting the organization, they have to adapt to their counterparts in the organization, including the data owners.

Business and IT skill sets are required to enable collaboration. Also, internally-focused data scientists are not helpful; they should focus beyond their algorithms to support collaboration with the business. Data scientists need to be business generalists. Data scientists' ability to "speak the language" of the business avoids additional coordination costs, longer waiting times, and narrow context, e.g. no business perspective knowledge (Colson, 2019).

3.6.4   Tackling distrust in data

The tackling of distrust in data starts with a focus on data quality, as detailed in Section 3.4, and data governance, as detailed in Section 3.5. In addition to setup, regular meetings including the chief data office, data owners, and the IT department are important to increase the predictability of the data required for data-driven decision-making. A higher predictability enables timely cleaning of the data and fit-for-purpose monitoring of the quality of the data.

Also, invest in measures that monitor bias in the data used in data-driven decision-making (Dwork and Minow, 2022). This will not only increase internal trust in data but also reduce the risks and avoid associated costs for repairing the impact of the use of biased data.

3.6.5   Segmentation and targeting of audiences

Increased data volumes increase the complexity of segmentation and targeting audiences. For this process, it is important that data quality and data governance are at level. For segmentation and targeting audiences, data owners and data scientists are involved for incremental decision-making, as this is the basis for developing algorithms. For decision-making in daily processes, the data owners and the IT department are involved. Decision rules need to be implemented by the IT department. For both decision-making categories, it is recommended to also involve the chief data office and/or the legal department to ensure that the segmentation and target audiences are compliant.

3.6.6   Identification of the right research questions

For incremental decision-making, not only the right data sets need to be collected (see data governance in Section 3.5) but also the right research questions need to be identified. These research questions are the starting point for data scientists to prepare their algorithms.

The identification of the right research questions and which information to request is a joint effort of the data owners and the data scientists. Data governance should provide requirements for research questions, as well as for the composition of the meetings and the meeting frequency. In many organizations, the chief data office is also involved in a quality assurance role in the identification of the research questions.

3.6.7   Absence of data literacy engine

Important is that relevant employees can collect, manage, evaluate, and apply data in a critical manner (Ridsdale et al., 2015), whereas the emphasis on 'critical manner' is important in the context of data-driven decision-making. Data literacy is an essential skill (Leon-Urrutia et al., 2022).

The chief data office is in charge of achieving data literacy. This is more than a couple of awareness sessions. A continuous data literacy program needs to be in place, including the monitoring of the data literacy. Many organizations even have mandatory training requirements to ensure data literacy for the entire organization. Furthermore, data literacy should be an embedded part of profiles used to recruit new employees and to promote incumbent employees into their next role.

3.7   Partnering improvement actions

The partnering improvement actions include making data accessible to partners, identification of the right data and KPIs, identification of the right research questions, lack of proper skill set to collaborate with the partners, tackling distrust in data and segmentation, and targeting audiences. This paragraph dives deep into these actions. This deep dive will be presented in the order of importance to an aspect, starting with the most important action.

There is some overlap with the actions for business collaboration in Section 3.6, nevertheless, the actions in the previous paragraph are specific for business collaboration in the context of data-driven decision-making, whereas the actions in this paragraph are specific for partnering.

3.7.1   *Making data accessible to partners*

Sharing data sets requires both data quality and data governance, which are detailed in Sections 3.4 and 3.5. Data exchange is important for innovation and improving competitive position. Exchange must be automated by making use of application programming interfaces (APIs) (Borgogno and Colangelo, 2019). The automation and APIs ensure a seamless exchange but also require coordination effort to implement the APIs and connect the information systems of the partners. The exchange of data can also be implemented by smart contracts on the blockchain. For both data exchange through APIs and for blockchain, specific attention should be paid to the cyber security policies and protocols from all partnering organizations. The exchange of data also requires cross-organizational governance.

3.7.2   *Identification of the right data and KPIs*

This is in essence no different from the actions detailed in the business collaboration in Section 3.6. They are the same participants, except that there needs to be representation from all the partners. This increases the number of participants and potentially complicates and slows the speed and effectiveness of the identification.

3.7.3   *Identification of the right research questions*

This is in essence not different from the actions detailed in the business collaboration in Section 3.6. However, because of potentially conflicting interests, it is essential to spend sufficient time early in the process to explore the objectives and sensitivities of all partners. This should be an integral part of the partnership development effort of all partners.

3.7.4   Lack of proper skill set to collaborate with partners

The collaboration has a focus on the partner relation and less on the information technology, data, and data analytics, as detailed in the business collaboration actions in Section 3.6. To enable data-driven decision-making, a dedicated partner manager needs to be assigned by all partners. This partner manager is well connected and has access to the senior management of their organization. This will facilitate decision-making with respect to the exchange of data.

3.7.5   Tackling distrust in data

The distrust in partnering is limited to the exchange of data but in any other aspect similar, it is to the action described in the business collaboration improvement actions as detailed in Section 3.6. Although the risk exposure for the partners is higher than the internal risk in business collaboration, as organizations are not in control of the data, data analytics, and processing of their partners.

3.7.6   Segmentation and targeting of audiences

For segmentation and targeting audiences, partner managers also have an important role in aligning segmentation and target audiences to improve data-driven decision-making between partners. Partner proposals are prepared by the stakeholders of the respective partners, e.g. data owners and data scientists and the IT department, and discussed by the partner managers. As relevant stakeholders, they can join meetings as subject matter experts.

DATA ANALYTICS ADOPTION FOR GOVERNMENTAL ORGANIZATIONS

Bandana Sinha – Program Director
Tata Consultancy Services

Governmental organizations are huge entities and can be compared to a conglomerate of enterprises. Their purpose is the creation of public value. This is not limited to outcome achievement and service delivery, quality, and efficiency, but also trust and legitimacy are important. Bandana Sinha: "Governmental organizations have to use data analytics to safeguard the citizen's rights, to enforce the citizen's obligations to society, the state and one another and to support government's policies as well as policy making."

Governmental challenges

Using data analytics requires data sharing. Especially for governmental organizations, data sharing is a very responsible and intricate exercise. The long-term obligations to retain data add to this complexity, typically data have to be retained for 15–20 years. Bandana Sinha: "As a consequence, most governmental organizations have legacy processes and information systems which keep data hostage and hinder leveraging data analytics opportunities."

Furthermore, in general, governmental organizations and civil servants are conservative in risk taking. This slows down governmental organizations from a full data analytics adoption. The size and volume of data being exchanged between most governmental organizations is also hindering adoption. Bandana Sinha:

> A good example are tax departments. They receive data from a large number of governmental, public and private organizations. These data are difficult to analyze and aggregate as in most countries there is a lack of uniformity, each department and each organization has their own standard.

Governmental organizations are also more vulnerable for court cases and parliament questions. Public opinion is also a potential (and unpredictable) factor which further increases the data analytics risks for governmental organizations. All of the above results in an even greater need for governmental organizations to ensure data security and privacy and implement proper backup and restore processes in the context of data analytics.

Governmental data analytics types – examples

As is the case in the private sector, for governments a distinction can be made between small data analytics and large data analytics. Bandana Sinha: "Both offer opportunities to fulfill the ambitions of governments to maximize the creation of public value with the help of data analytics."

Small data analytics has a short-term focus, is relatively low cost, and requires little interpretation. The emphasis is on status reporting and small data analytics typically has a single purpose. Bandana Sinha:

Therefore, small analytics are perfect for achieving quick wins. The government can provide dashboard information on the weather conditions to enable farming and fishing, but also more fundamental insights related to, for example, in India, hygienic sanitary conditions in schools impact young girls dropping out of the school system. A combination of sensors, edge computing and data analytics can make the difference.

On the other hand, large data analytics, which includes social media and geospatial data, is important for governmental organizations. This is more true of data analysis including complex algorithms; however, small data analytics should not be marginalized.

Governmental data analytics basics

For any organization, including governments, trust and transparency are important for the adoption of data analytics. Bandana Sinha: "This includes avoiding misinterpretation, where measures are publishing business glossaries, establishing check lists/maintaining data catalogues, offering certified training programs and appointing Chief Data Officers are critical."

An emphasis on data management tooling will increase the automation level and improve data quality. The introduction of 'worthiness score' (e.g. external, regulatory and not checked) and data catalogs will further enhance data analytics which support improving social fabric and other public value governmental goals.

Cloud computing adoption?

With regard to cloud adoption, many governmental organizations have not made up their minds. Cloud is a data analytics enabler; however, currently many governmental organizations have not embraced cloud computing due to the significant volumes of sensitive data (e.g. military, financial, and scientific data). Bandana Sinha: "Most governmental organizations currently select private cloud solutions over public cloud solutions. However, the trend toward public cloud, even for sensitive data, cannot be denied."

The cloud computing debate urges need for a proper qualification of sensitive data. Governmental organizations have a track record in document classification, access to confidential and restricted government documents have always had tight authorization processes, controls, and tracking, long before digitization. Bandana Sinha: "For governments, data classification is just the next level. Nevertheless, the increasing use of 'unstructured data' makes data classification more difficult."

Governmental approach

To successfully leverage data analytics in creating public value, governmental organizations have to focus on competency management. Specific for Indian governmental organizations, it is particularly beneficial to provide sabbatical leaves to senior civil servants. During senior sabbaticals, junior civil servants are encouraged to expedite data analytics adoption as they are less constrained by historical ways of doing things and bring more digital native ideas to the approach. Bandana Sinha: "Sabbatical leaves avoid that data analytics is put on hold until the retirement of senior civil servants."

In attracting and retaining data analytics talent, governmental organizations must emphasize the purposefulness of their mission. This is essential as the compensation and benefits of governmental organizations are typically less attractive than in the private sector.

In order to leverage data analytics opportunities, some countries, such as India, have created specialized vehicles to support the development of analytics. Bandana Sinha: "In order to be successful, these initiatives are identified as 'mission mode', to designate appropriate priority and resources for achieving the mission." Clearly defined objectives, scopes, and implementation timelines and milestones, as well as measurable outcomes and service levels are needed more than ever. Also, setting data rules and regulations is important, in this respect Botswana is a lighthouse country with their data protection act. Furthermore, recent governmental organizations are migrating their data analytics operating model from data lake centric to data mesh centric.

Bandana Sinha: "In summary – governmental organizations need to continue to propose data analytics opportunities to create public value. This will not be easy and straightforward but a worthwhile mission to pursue!"

3.8 Conclusion

Most organizations have high ambitions with regard to data-driven decision-making, but there are significant prerequisites to meet these ambitions. Poor data quality and data governance are the focus areas. This stresses the need for data leadership, appointing a chief data officer and/or a head of data (analytics) is obvious. The initial focus should be on creating data awareness and including data in the enterprise and IT architecture. Organizations need a solid foundation for data-driven decision-making to successfully embark on digital transformations.

After laying the groundwork for data quality and data governance, the focus of data leadership must be on business collaboration in order to enhance data-driven decision-making. Managers must be further educated on data and the integral usage of data in performing their jobs. This will further mature data-driven decision-making and will trigger product and/or service innovations, which will pivot and propel the digital transformation.

The partnership aspect of data-driven decision-making is even more challenging. Organizations need to exchange data beyond transaction data with partners in their ecosystem to further enhance data-driven decision-making and to innovate. Innovation in partnerships is beyond product and/or service innovations, and the focus is on co-creating new products and/or services and to improve the competitive position. This will enable ecosystems to successfully embark on the next level of their digital transformation.

The adoption of data-driven decision-making will change job profiles but will not result in unemployment. Existing jobs will be automated, while new jobs will be created (United Nations, n.d.b). Adoption will have an impact on the required profiles and the organizational culture. This will require management attention, and more specifically attention from the human resources department in evaluating and promoting existing employees, and in the development of training programs, including certification and recruiting new employees.

4

MONETIZATION OF DATA AND DATA ANALYTICS

The ultimate goal of many organizations is to monetize their data by increasing insights and advancing data analytics. This is a matter of not only optimizing processes but also adding additional services to products to increase the value and/or the margin. Monetization requires changing organizations, processes, and capabilities.

4.1   Introduction

Many organizations are exploring how to monetize their data. By advancing data analytics, the value of data can be further increased. The insights from data are used not only for optimizing processes but also for adding additional services to products and/or product services to increase value creation. Furthermore, organizations are exploring selling information. The selling of information can be to existing ecosystem partners or to new partners in existing or new markets (Wixom and Ross, 2017). Setting the price for data is complex (Mehta et al., 2021).

There are two obstacles in monetizing data: the accessibility of data and the quality of data. Both are intertwined; providing access to high-quality data is less problematic, as high-quality data and data governance go hand in hand. Data governance is also a key to providing access. Data ownership and approving access rights are more difficult for most organizations than the implementation and maintenance of the technical architecture, including application programming interfaces in order to exchange and transact data.

In monetizing data by adding additional services or selling information, data quality is even more important than when only used to optimize processes, as optimizing processes have an internal focus. Adding additional services or selling information creates potential liability toward users and/or ecosystem partners. If

DOI: 10.4324/9781003246770-6

the data is of low quality, commercial opportunities will naturally recede and potentially impact customer trust. This sets additional requirements for data governance to safeguard data quality. Additionally, organizations need to consider at what level data analytics will be applied, as this requires an additional layer of data governance. Typically, advanced data analytics is related to optimizing processes and adding additional services, whereas the selling of data is typically raw data, e.g. transaction data or location/status information. However, the trend is to use artificial intelligence models to develop newly derived data sets with insights.

To overcome the obstacles of accessibility and data quality, organizations need to have a monetization strategy in place. What type of data monetization enhances the general strategy? Typically, organizations start monetization with using data to optimize processes, followed by adding additional services and finally by selling information. Organizations can take the lessons of these distinct different types of monetization to the next type. The approach enables organizations to improve the accessibility and quality of data over time.

In order to execute the strategy, organizations need to free up budget to invest in making the data available and ensuring top data quality, which is mostly related to information technology and data tooling investment in combination with freeing up resources for improving the data awareness and the data governance, including the improvement of processes.

4.2   Organizational data versus personal data

In order to ensure compliance, it is important to distinguish between organizational data and personal data (Malgieri and Custers, 2018), as both capture business value. Increasingly, individuals start to realize that personal data represents a monetary value. The European Union has acknowledged that personal data can be used in exchange for digital content (EU Directive 2019/770), which improves the entitlement of individuals from passive defense to active empowerment. However, not many individuals are fully exercising this right, as they are having difficulty in understanding the value of their personal data (Malgieri and Custers, 2018; Birch et al., 2021). The rights related to personal data of individuals are protected in the EU Regulation 2016/679 (the "GDPR"). The GDPR prevails over the EU Directive 2019/770.

For data monetization, it is important to focus on organizational data. The most common basis is that the data is necessary for the fulfillment of the contract, legitimate interest, compliance with legal obligations, and individual consent. The latter is related to the monetary value of personal data as explained above. In addition to transaction data, also data related to the execution of the services and/or related to products are organizational data which can be monetized by organizations – e.g. Internet of Things (IoT) data. Blockchain could be a trusted, cost-efficient, automatic monetization technology concept for IoT data (Suliman et al., 2019).

4.3   Monetization of data and data analytics maturity

The focus of monetization is to support the business model. Once data and analytics investments have been made, the data insights gained will be the guide toward monetization. The maturity level of monetization is currently still low. In a 2020 survey (N = 58), there were only eight organizations that reported the implementation of data monetization as an improvement area, whereas we would expect a much higher response given the low monetization maturity of the surveyed organizations (Beulen, 2020a). These are all smaller organizations, none with a revenue of more than 1,000m euro. The eight organizations included two in the banking and financial services and two in the energy resources and utilities sectors.

Survey data on monetization maturity contradict the abovementioned low response on monetization as an improvement area. The surveyed organizations did not rate their ability to monetize very high, over 50% had a score of 2 or lower, of which over one-third ranked 0 on a 0–7 Likert scale. In general, more mature organizations are better able to monetize data insights. Interestingly, a cluster of eight organizations had a high data and analytics maturity and a low score on monetization of data insights (0 or 1 on a 0–7 Likert scale). This cluster consists of five organizations with a revenue over 250m euro, including one organization with +1,000m euro, and covers a large variety of sectors, including hi-tech and professional services, retail, banking and financial services, consumer goods and distribution, information technology, life sciences and healthcare, and energy resources

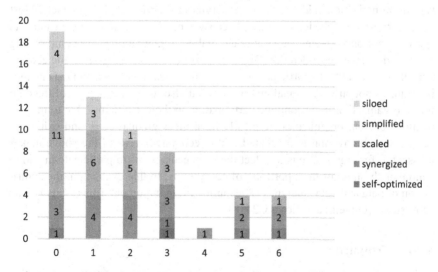

FIGURE 4.1   Monetization of Dutch organizations on a Likert scale (0–7: 0 = no monetization and 7 = full monetization) grouped by data and analytics maturity – siloed, simplified, scaled, synergized, and self-optimized (N = 58) (Beulen, 2020a)

and utilities. On the other hand, there are five organizations that have a relatively low data and analytics maturity but a high score on monetization of data insights (5 or 6 on a 0–7 Likert scale). This cluster consists of three manufacturing organizations, three large organizations with a revenue of +1,000m euro, and two small organizations with a revenue between 25m and 100m euro. This outcome of the survey challenges the assumption that data and analytics maturity is positively related to monetization (N = 5 + 3). It is also important to realize that monetization requires change and change potentially increases the risk profile. Therefore, the participants in this study concluded that change takes courage. However, the importance of monetization is undisputed.

4.4 Monetization of data and data analytics inhibitors

In Section 4.1, the obstacles to data monetization are discussed, including the accessibility of data and the quality of data, as well as actions to address these obstacles. There are four areas that require specific attention in getting monetization on track: leveraging ecosystems, levering universal data, implementing data monetization, and adopting free exchange in the data marketplace (Beulen, 2020a). What should be done to address these inhibitors?

The insights from data and data analytics are obviously relevant to the internal organization. More significant are insights that are made relevant for the ecosystems that organizations are operating in this is predominantly related to the second type of monetization: adding additional services to services and/or products. Most organizations are embedded in multiple ecosystems. Monetization of data and data analytics not only creates value but also makes collaboration more complex and creates additional dependencies. Organizations need to be decisive on the ecosystems they would like to participate in, as the monetization of data and data analytics requires not only additional investments but also limits the degrees of freedom for an organization to discontinue participation in the ecosystems. Due to the rise of monetization, organizations typically have more gradual entry and exiting in ecosystems. Innovation is facilitated within ecosystems. All of the above makes it essential for organizations to select the right ecosystems to participate in and to continuously monitor their portfolio of ecosystems. In that evaluation, the contribution of data and data analytics is becoming more important. This results in data ecosystems (Oliveira and Lóscio, 2018).

4.4.1 Ecosystems

In leveraging ecosystem organizations, the contractual agreements participating organizations make are becoming more and more important – think treatment data from medical devices. Manufacturers of medical devices can improve their devices which will result in improved health care (Karpen et al., 2021). Despite the worth of discussing privacy aspects, patient data (a.k.a. the commercial transaction between a manufacturer of medical devices and a hospital) requires even further discussion. Can the hospital monetize the data? And if so, how? Does the manufacturer grant access to data coming from other hospitals? This creates interesting debates and requires an ecosystem-oriented lens from both the manufacturer and the hospital. These debates will be centered not only around monetization but also around public value, which makes these debates even more complex.

There are similar debates in the retail sector. In this sector, point of sales information is highly relevant for the upstream ecosystem partners, particularly if their products are sold at full price, discounted price, or not sold at all. This information will help the upstream ecosystems partners to improve and adjust their products, and of course, it is ultimately also relevant for the retailer, as retailers would like to sell products at full price. The setup for data sharing in retail is complex due to the number of ecosystem partners. There will predominantly be business cases in high-value and high-volume products.

4.4.2   *Universal data*

The second inhibitor was universal data. Universal data models can replace bespoke data models and provide an extendable ontology with standardized reference data definitions for customization and harmonization of applications (Cover and Ordentlich, 1996; Silverston, 2011; Bramson, 2020). Most standards are sector-specific, which facilities monetization. This inhibitor is closely related to data quality, since mapping relations between data elements increases data quality. Implementing an ontology is at best emerging in most organizations (Leal et al., 2019). This inhibitor, different from the first inhibitor, requires a data and technology approach instead of a strategic approach. Leveraging universal data by implementing universal data model(s) as well as an ontology (across universal data models) needs heavy lifting from data owners, the chief data officer, the CIO, and the information technology department, including their tech partners.

The data owner needs to provide input related to their processes and current and future value creation. What data points are important, and how do the data elements relate to each other? This is the basis for the data model(s) and the ontology. In the context of monetization, it is important to extend the input to data sharing in the organization's current ecosystems and future ecosystems. External alignment is crucial. Data owners need to align, as part of the agreement with external stakeholders, with all ecosystem partners, on the data elements in the universal data model(s) and ontology. This is where chief data officers can support data owners, first with the internal data owner stakeholder alignment, then followed by external alignment. For both the internal and external alignment, strong central governance is required; the focus of the governance is on processes, tooling, and (architectural) requirements, not on data elements, which is at the sole discretion of the data owners. Critical in universal data models is establishing data classification at the start. This is foundational for universal data model success. Finally, the CIO and the information technology department, including their tech partners, play an important role in the implementation of tooling and application program interfaces (APIs).

In the case of monetization in ecosystems, organizations face increased complexity, especially when organizations leverage external tech partners. The contractual arrangements of the tech partners have to facilitate and make, if required, changes to the environment. Unfortunately, this flexibility is not embedded in all outsourcing contracts (Beulen and Ribbers, 2021) and in the case of offshore outsourcing contracts, it is even harder to achieve flexibility (Beulen et al., 2005; Carmel and Beulen, 2005; Beulen, 2008; Beulen and Tiwari, 2010; Beulen et al., 2011).

4.4.3 Implementation of data monetization

The third inhibitor, the implementation of data monetization, is closely related to the second inhibitor. The most fundamental challenge for implementation is in the information technology architecture. Most organizations face too many deviations from and exceptions to the information technology architecture, as well as noncompliance to the non-functional requirements, including but not limited to technology choices, which are also known as standards, compliance, and security guidelines. This is also indicated as technical debt (Rios et al., 2018). The CIO is responsible for the information technology architecture. When setting up and maintaining the information technology architecture, it is important that the CIO takes into account the collaboration of the organization with ecosystem partners. Aligning the information technology architecture of the owner's organization with the information technology architecture of the ecosystem partners is essential. This transforms the role of the CIO from a predominantly internally oriented role to a more externally oriented role – in the context of digital transformations, issue selling is essential (Chen et al., 2021a).

The information technology architecture is the foundation for the implementation of data management tools. The CIO should enforce data management tooling standardization, where unfortunately there is no best-of-breed data management tooling, at least not as of this writing. This further complicates data monetization across ecosystems. This also complicates the implementation of application programming interfaces. Finally, organizational dynamics and ecosystem dynamics complicate the implementation of data monetization. This drives information technology architectural standards toward proven technology suppliers over innovative niche suppliers. The stability of the data management tooling is in a better position to absorb the organizational dynamics as well as requiring less customization. The building blocks of proven technology suppliers are more robust, along with the implications of innovation niche suppliers, bankruptcy, or the impact of being acquired. Both will have a detrimental impact on data and data analytics monetization opportunities.

4.4.4 Free exchange in the data marketplace

The fourth inhibitor is the adoption of free exchange in the data market. No different from transactional data and data analytics monetization, free exchange in the data marketplace can also be classified as monetization (Spiekermann, 2019). Data marketplaces stimulate innovation within the organization as well as within the ecosystem and are mostly related to the third type of data monetization: selling data. The exchange of data in the data marketplace is not related to the ecosystems in which an organization operates. Therefore, the conditions under which data can be sold to any third party have to be clearly documented. The creation of an organization should never be jeopardized by transacting data in the data market. Understandably, many organizations are still reluctant to adopt the free exchange of data in data marketplaces. In transacting data, blockchain and smart contracts can be instrumental not only for efficiency but also to strengthen trust (Serrano, 2022). Nevertheless, for most organizations, there will not be a beneficial business case for the adoption of free exchange in the data marketplace. From the perspective of the platform owner, the data marketplace might also be a challenge to solve the chicken-and-egg problem. A data marketplace is only relevant if there are sufficient data producers and data consumers. The responsibility for the quality offered on the data marketplace should also be clear and can never be with the platform, although this should not stop the platform from performing curation activities, which is different from being liable for poor data quality.

Needless to say, organizations can use procured data for further monetization of all three types of monetization in their own organization as well as in ecosystems. However, the processing and enriching of purchased data with the purpose of selling the data is currently unlikely, but might be more feasible in the future due to the increasing data volumes and the increasing availability of processing power.

DATA SHARING AND MONETIZATION

Sandeep Saxena – Data Mesh, Monetization and Marketplace
Center of Excellence Lead
Tata Consultancy Services – Global BFSI data and analytics

There are two aspects of data monetization: internal data monetization and external data monetization.

Internal monetization pertains to using and extracting value from an organization's own data and then determining how best to apply the value of that data to improve the top and bottom-line, so there is an indirect impact on profit/loss. Sandeep Saxena: "This is where most large organizations are using analytics for monetization. The challenge is getting access to the right data at the right time for the right stakeholders." Using analytics for monetization across many domains, the heterogeneity in terms of the approach to analyzing the data and tooling can vary greatly across organizational domains, divisions, and lines of business. The result is the total cost to the organization is much higher. So, although there are centralized data architecture teams to support analytics, data science, and analyst teams, different lines of business are still using different tools, which is costing the organization more.

External monetization, also called commercialization of data, is not yet mainstream in most large organizations. Sandeep Saxena:

> There are industry branches that are exploring the commercialization of data, even politically conservative sectors like the governmental sector are slowly willing to sell their data, of course with all the proper privacy and consent built into the whole transaction.

Retail companies have been commercializing data for quite some time. A few South African Telecoms have also started commercializing data and are looking to institutionalize and scale up this initiative. For now, data commercialization is fairly ad hoc and has not yet become mainstream.

To understand monetization better, the business-to-business perspective and the combination of data democratization and data mesh concepts, as well as data sharing, needs to be understood.

Business to business

From a business-to-business (B2B) perspective, the retail industry is primarily commercializing point of sale data, which is relevant to a lot of other domains, most notably consumer product goods (CPG). So, for example, large retailers like Walmart or Target have two models for selling goods. One model is where retailers charge a fee for dedicated retail space to a specific CPG company and let them manage the space on their own. The CPG company then collects and manages their inventory and replenishment data. The other model is where the retailer manages the commodity stock and retail space directly. Sandeep Saxena:

> The retailer can either buy the commodity directly from the CPG company, or let the CPG company own the inventory and shelf management and can also have their own brand which they manufacture or outsource manufacturing of . In the case of a CPG company's commodity getting sold, the retailer may seek a discount or financial benefit from the CPG company in lieu of the point-of-sale data, which gives visibility of how the CPG company's products are faring in the retailer's store.

For Telecom companies, the B2B model is more a data transaction. Telecom companies are more horizontal in the sense they are providing services and data and connectivity pipelines to multiple domains. Sandeep Saxena:

> They may tie up with companies that actually own the data to make an arrangement for commercialization. Telecom data is primarily in terms of location data that they sell for advertising purposes, where privacy and consent are critical. A US telecom major came under fire back in 2014 when they started sharing individuals' contacts with companies looking to market products. They had to eventually stop the initiative.

The Financial Services industry is already in the data-selling business – data pertaining to financial securities, niche data about companies' financial performance, etc. Sandeep Saxena:

> Companies running or participating in financial marketplaces, for example, are partnered with niche providers and academia for creating models to gain insights on raw data. They tie up with such companies and jointly go to market with that particular type of product OR they build that capability in-house so that insights can be derived from the raw / aggregated data and commercialize that for a much higher price point.

Data democratization and data mesh

Data democratization is happening across many domains. Most of the time, the focus is on large organizations, including banks, insurance companies, automotive companies, or utility companies. Internal monetization is seen much more in the Financial Services industry (FSI) and even in the government space, like Smart City. Automotive Original Equipment Manufacturers (OEMs) are also looking to democratize data. Sandeep Saxena:

> However, data democratization has been handled in different ways, like replicating data which leaves many copies of data floating around. So now the trend is to look for non-data replication solutions, like through data virtualization or concept of data as a product, defined by meta data and can be searched and discovered, and using the data mesh concept to source the domain specific data without replication. So, these are the trends and there

are many enterprise data management companies, like Alation, Denodo, Zaloni, etc. that are operating in this space.

Sandeep Saxena: "Data mesh can be construed as either a new recipe or an old recipe in a different label." There are certain aspects which require interim storage for specific domains. For example, payments or credit risk-related data may not be in just one line of business, it is coming from multiple lines of business. So, the data would not be ingested into a data lake, but rather into a smaller interim storage, which is for a very specific topic, like risk management or payments, where the analysis is performed. Sandeep Saxena: "There are technologies now which do not require storage, but in some cases it is not optimal to hit operational systems for data analytics, another reason for interim storage as part of the data mesh." Operational data may not be a candidate to do advanced analytics prediction models or prescription models. These would require interim storage, where the raw data is not replicated and the consumption entity needs to identify how it is going to be consumed, and what is the purpose of that consumption. The raw data undergoes some transformation and then stored for analytical consumption purposes only, instead of storing another copy of the raw data itself. There is no replication of the original source and the sanctity of the single source of truth is maintained.

Data sharing

Commercializing data in the supply chain can be difficult because the different parties up and down the supply chain have different interests. Sharing supply chain data may jeopardize an organization's position in that value chain. Sandeep Saxena:

> One example of successful commercialization of supply chain data was for manufacturing COVID diagnostic tests. Two years ago, the Indian government was looking for a million COVID diagnostic test kits manufactured per day. The Prime Minister's office was looking at ways to encourage indigenous manufacturing of these test kits so that the scale could be there because there was no central mechanism or digitized way to connect SMEs, micro, small and medium manufacturing organizations, who were producing these raw materials, with the accredited or certified test kit manufacturers. The million-per-day goal was being hampered by lack of a digital marketplace. The Tata Consultancy Services (TCS) chairman was part of the scientific advisory committee to the Prime Minister. TCS's Data Marketplace Solution was used as an information exchange enabler across the test-kit manufacturing supply chain. Raw material providers were the start of the

supply chain, supplying the mid-tier organizations who create polymers and biochemicals, provide peripheral equipment and services, to the test kit manufacturers for final manufacture of the various types of COVID19 test-kits. All of these organizations were enabled through the information exchange platform, and though initially the visibility of each others' products was restricted due to apprehensions, with continuous education through round-tables with the stakeholders we could convey the intent and value that the platform would bring for everyone's benefit. With the apprehensions put to rest, the flexibility of the platform enabled us to eventually open it up for more competition and bring prices down. Bids and terms were published and competitive offers could be tested, accepted or rejected before deciding to buy. Competitive bidding brought prices down for certain components by as much as 70 times.

Sandeep Saxena: "Another example is in the supply chain." A large US logistics provider has customers with big consignments that are coming in from one place or another. Delays can be communicated to the customer in a timely manner using the marketplace. For example, a customer can use the marketplace to schedule with the provider an important pickup at one warehouse in Dallas for shipment to another warehouse in Cincinnati. This is what was missing. Sandeep Saxena:

> They are looking to democratize data internally at the logistics company, but also externally with key customers for real time tracking. Customer satisfaction increased as well as efficiencies in the routes. There is value not just for the logistics company, but also their clients can be offered better prices and more efficient services.

4.5 Conclusion

The future of monetization of data and data analytics is full of opportunities. Organizations are only at the beginning of monetization of data and data analytics. To expedite data monetization, organizations might consider exploring reuse and recombination of data, as data can be reused and recombined freely with degradation (Wixom et al., 2021).

The increasing data volumes and data analytics tooling and algorithms that are becoming increasingly more powerful will drive large-scale monetization. Additionally, data awareness and data technology capabilities will increase significantly in the years to come. Also, ecosystems will progressively compete on data. The chief data officer has to educate, orchestrate, and direct organizations.

In the future, the monetization of data and data analytics will also face more restrictive legislation, not limited to data privacy legislation. Antitrust legislation will become more important; a good example is the Digital Service Act package, upcoming European Union legislation. Anticipation of more restrictive legislation is recommended as the implementation of monetization requires a significant investment and typically takes over 12 months to implement. In addition, from the perspective of more restrictive legislation, the involvement of the chief data officer is required. For legislation, the involvement of the legal department in a supporting role is essential. Both will provide good information for the risk management process.

Finally, the continued increasing threat of cybercrime and espionage, also called cyber spying, will have an even bigger impact on the future of monetization of data and data analytics than today. Organizations will face cost impacts as well as risk impacts, which will be reported more frequently in organizational risk registers (Cunliffe, 2021). With regard to espionage, it is important to understand that there is a third party involved who is willing to pay for the data. In the process of espionage, this is labeled as the "information sale" phase (Rivera et al., 2022). In cyber espionage, typically botnets are used as a tool (Bederna and Szadeckky, 2020). To be clear, the cybercrime requesting ransom and the selling of stolen data in espionage are not data and data analytics monetization. Cybercrime and espionage only slow down the monetization due to the increased costs of protecting data.

5

DATA QUALITY – DATA MANAGEMENT IN ACTION

In enabling data-driven decision-making and monetization, data quality is a prerequisite for data and analytics, which includes five domains: data management, analytics automation, type of data used, type of analytics platforms, and cloud adoption. The data and data analytics maturity can be detailed in four attributes: data, processes, people, and technology, including addressing architectural and security challenges. Both the five domains and the four attributes will be detailed in this chapter. This chapter also describes roadmaps for improving data quality.

5.1 Introduction

The definition of data quality is associated with the fitness-for-use principle (Tayi and Ballou, 1998). Data quality is a prerequisite for data-driven decision-making and monetization and requires focus in any organization. It is business critical (McGilvray, 2021); according to Gartner, "Every year, poor data quality costs organizations an average \$12.9 million" (Sakpal, 2021).

Data quality includes the intrinsic data quality dimensions of completeness, accuracy, format, and currency (Wixom and Todd, 2005). Completeness is based on the elements of a data set, where the accuracy is on both the field and record levels. The format is related to adherence to the rules, which requires domain knowledge and is typically applied at the table or database level. Currency, also called "timeliness," is about suitability of the data for the organization. This includes both the update frequency and relevance.

In addition to intrinsic data quality, there are three other dimensions: contextual, representational, and accessibility (Wand and Wang, 1996; Wang and Strong, 1996; Batini et al., 2009; Ofner et al., 2012; Cappiello et al., 2013; Ehrlinger and Wöß, 2022). The contextual dimension includes accessibility, believability, and

DOI: 10.4324/9781003246770-7

relevancy, also known as added value, reputation, and quantity. The representational dimension is conciseness, consistency, ease of understanding, interpretability, and difficulty to manipulate. The third dimension, accessibility, includes access, identification, and security.

Based on the work of Goodhue et al. (1992), Trieu et al. (2022) researched the contribution of data integration to data quality in the context of business intelligence. Trieu et al. (2022) refuted the hypothesis that there is a positive relationship between data integration and business intelligence representational fidelity. Nevertheless, data integration supports the exchange of data in different systems, databases, and data lakes and contributes to data quality. The need for data integration is increasing due to the emerging data mesh trend. The data mesh will be addressed in the next chapter on data governance.

To improve data quality, organizations must cleanse their data. This process identifies and corrects erroneous data and/or data glitches (Dasu and Johnson, 2003). Many organizations use tooling to identify and fix data quality issues for data cleansing, such as IBM Infosphere Quality Stage, OpenRefine, previously known as Google Refine, and TIBCO Clarity. However, this process potentially introduces the risk of inserting new errors; organizations therefore continuously need to verify and revalidate cleansed data (Ridzuan and Zainon, 2019). Furthermore, legal aspects need to be addressed (Stöger et al., 2021), and this is not limited to medical artificial intelligence, as the potential introduction of new errors can be a breach in any sector. Monitoring and improving data quality is a continuous process and requires dedicated focus in any organization. Senior management should take a close look at data quality management projects to understand the impacts of data quality on the organization and provide guiderails to their organization (McGilvray, 2021).

5.2 Basics of data and analytics

To ensure that organizations have their data and analytics in place, there are five domains they should focus on: data management, analytics automation, type of data used, type of analytics platforms, and cloud adoption. The domains are interdependent; for example, the automation of analytics requires the adoption of cloud computing and the use of unstructured data set requirements for data management.

5.2.1 Data management

There are many definitions of data management, which ensures effective and efficient use of data by collecting and sharing data. To facilitate the use of data, data management includes enabling data processing and storage, as well as continuous data quality improvement.

Typically, data management is centralized in an organization and combined with centralized as well as decentralized data ownership. Data management is an integral part of the chief data office and includes data, technology, and process subject matter experts, not data scientists. Data scientists work closely with the data owners, as well as with the IT department and its technology partners and suppliers.

The focus in data management is on both the monitoring of the use of data and data quality improvement projects. Data management also contributes to improving and updating the data strategy and policies.

5.2.2   Analytics automation

In data analytics, the process of data collection should be automated, including quality assurance, allowing access, and making data available. Unfortunately, the maturity of the tooling is still emerging, and currently, there are no end-to-end best-of-breed solutions available.

Analytics automation is essential for dashboarding. Business intelligence tools need to be configured in such a way that report generation is fully automated. Any human involvement jeopardizes the quality of the report, in addition to the inefficiency of human involvement. Currently, very efficient tooling, such as Looker, Microsoft Power BI, and SAP Business Objects in addition to QlikSense and Tableau, are widely used by organizations.

In the context of data democratization, the automation of analytics has become even more important, as not only data scientists but also citizen data scientists embedded in the business are starting to request data for the purpose of analyzing data beyond dashboarding.

5.2.3   Type of data used

Most organizations focus on internal transactional data, which typically have reasonable data quality, as well as on employee and client data. Examples of internal transactional data are purchase or sales data.

Furthermore, external data, including open data, are becoming significantly more important, and the growth of external data is also exponential. The data quality of external data is typically more of a challenge.

However, external data and data sharing are very important in the context of digital transformations, as these types of data enable the introduction of new business models and/or enriching existing products and services. Examples are Internet of Things (IoT) data that improve the effectiveness and efficiency of equipment maintenance, as IoT data can trigger preventive maintenance and consequently avoid downtime and enables efficient planning of service engineers to perform maintenance.

5.2.4   Type of analytics platforms

The variety of analytics platforms is increasing and ranges from traditional platforms, like enterprise data warehouses or department data marts to perform ad hoc analyses, to makeshift management information systems and active data warehouses and/or data lakes and data meshes. As volumes of data grow, improving and maintaining data quality has become even more important. By introducing more advanced analytics platforms, organizations can not only improve their data quality but also increase the effective and efficient use of data. Data management tooling is closely related to the types of analytics platforms but is distinctly different. Organizations first select their analytics platform(s) of choice, following decisions with regard to data management tooling, whereas the latter has to be aligned with the enterprise architecture and the IT architecture.

5.2.5   Cloud adoption

Regarding cloud adoption, assessing cloud maturity is very important. The cloud maturity level is related to the data quality level; see Table 5.1 for an example of a cloud maturity model. Typically, organizations with a cloud maturity level of 4 or 5 are well positioned to achieve and maintain high data quality levels. A high cloud maturity is instrumental in fully automating all processes, from data validation, to providing access to data, to data processing and data analytics, as well as in removing volume constraints for data processing, data analytics, and data storage.

With cloud adoption, organizations must focus on the access compliance components of cloud solutions for infrastructure as a service (IaaS) solutions. In the context of data and data analytics, this is centered around the location of data storage (compliance obligations) and protection of the cloud solution (cyber security requirements). The public cloud trend is irreversible; nevertheless, there will always be organizations which require a private cloud solution or even their own physical data center.

With regard to platform as a service (PaaS) solutions and software as a service (SaaS) solutions, the ability to interface with other applications is an additional challenge to the IaaS challenges. All this has to be addressed in the enterprise and IT architecture of an organization.

5.3   Data and analytics attributes

The data and data analytics maturity is detailed in four attributes: data, processes, people, and technology. These attributes will be detailed in the following four paragraphs. Unfortunately, many organizations still have a limited focus on processes and people (Gartner, 2021c). Furthermore, many organizations still struggle with the data attributes, as most organizations predominantly focus on technology and the data quality challenge will not be resolved by implementing tooling.

TABLE 5.1 Cloud maturity model including ten maturity areas and five cloud maturity levels (Beulen, 2022b)

#	Maturity areas	Level 1 – Initial	Level 2 – Managed	Level 3 – Defined	Level 4 – Qualitatively managed	Level 5 – Optimizing
1	Business value	High-level business case for cloud solutions	Detailed business cases for all cloud solutions and focus on managing cloud consumption	Tracking business cases for cloud solutions and demand planning mechanisms are in place including reporting to budget holders	Continuous tracking the business case for cloud solutions including automated cost control reporting to budget holders	Continuous proactively managing the business value for cloud solutions including automated cost prediction reporting to budget holders
2	Strategy	Some non-core applications in the cloud (predominantly rehosted and replatformed)	All non-core applications and some core applications in the cloud (predominantly rehosted and replatformed)	All non-core applications (PaaS and SaaS) and some core applications in the cloud (predominantly replatformed and re-architected)	All non-core applications (PaaS and SaaS) and most core applications in the cloud (predominantly repurchased, rearchitected and renewed)	Both none-core and core applications are in the cloud
3	Culture	IT culture	Engineering culture	Aligned engineering and business culture	Business engineering-driven culture	Continuous improvement culture

(Continued)

TABLE 5.1 (Continued)

#	Maturity areas	Level 1 – Initial	Level 2 – Managed	Level 3 – Defined	Level 4 – Qualitatively managed	Level 5 – Optimizing
4	Organization	Ad hoc – multiple agile and waterfall projects	IT driven – all new project are in agile mode	Cloud Center of Excellence and being fully agile	Federated Cloud Centers of Excellence	Business driven
5	People and skills	Limited trained/ skilled cloud group in IT department	Fully certified/ skilled cloud group in IT department	Fully certified/ skilled cloud group in IT department and limited trained/ skilled business organization	Fully certified/skilled cloud group in IT department and partly trained/skilled business organization	Fully certified/skilled cloud organization
6	Governance	Operations and Project management for all cloud solutions	Steering committee covering all cloud solutions in place	Cloud solutions are aligned with IT strategy – governed by portfolio management board	Cloud solutions are aligned with business strategy – governed by business-steering committee	Cloud strategy is fully integrated in business strategy – governed by business-steering committee and active oversight by the executive board
7	Risk and compliance	Isolated cloud risk management and catching up compliance approach	Integral cloud risk management and re-active compliance approach	Integrated technology risk management and practical compliance approach	Aligned business and technology risk management and proactive compliance approach	Integral risk management and compliance by design

#	Maturity areas	Level 1 – Initial	Level 2 – Managed	Level 3 – Defined	Level 4 – Qualitatively managed	Level 5 – Optimizing
8	Architecture	Functional cloud architecture requirements are detailed	Functional and non-functional, including security, cloud architecture requirements are detailed	Defense-in-depth by applying authentication between components, and by minimizing the trust between components	Components are stateless at all times	Continuous architecting including security by design
9	Operations and cyber resilience	Qualified subject matter experts deliver secure cloud services focusing on application telemetry	Certified subject matter experts deliver secure cloud services focusing on workload telemetry	Certified organizational unit delivers secure cloud services (e.g. ISO) focusing on activity telemetry	Educated business counterparts for the delivery organization focusing on dependency telemetry and transaction traceability in order to achieve business value and cyber-resilient cloud services	SecDevOps cloud delivery is integrated in the business operations
10	Automation	Combination of manual and stand-alone tooling provisioning tooling	Combination of manual and integrated provisioning tooling suite	Integrated provisioning tooling suites	Fully automated provisioning tooling	Fully automated and self-healing provisioning

5.4 Open and unstructured data

In the Introduction, the basics of data quality are described in detail. The focus in this section will be on open data (e.g. social media data from platforms such as Facebook, Instagram, and Twitter,[1] the U.S. Census Bureau[2] for demographical data on U.S. inhabitants, and also European Union Open Data Portal[3] for insights on energy, education, commerce, agriculture, and international issues) and unstructured data (e.g. images, audio and video media content, as well as business documents and communications including live chat, messaging, and web meetings).

In addition, some organizations buy external data, such as market information. Obviously, the quality of this type of external data is less of an issue, as organizations are willing to pay for these data and the quality is typically higher. But even for purchased external data cleansing and normalization might be necessary. Also, data provisioning is typically not an issue, as data is the primary business model of the data provider. The data is offered in different formats, and the data provider has multiple interfaces to transfer the data to their customers.

5.4.1 Open data

Open data is typically a continuous stream of data and has large volumes. This provides opportunities for data-driven decision-making, as well as improved decision-making based on real-time dashboards. The main problem with open data is that organizations cannot control the data or the provisioning of the data. This presents challenges in obtaining the data. To address these challenges, most organizations have a source-agnostic interface to obtain the data, such as screen scraping. Nevertheless, most social media platforms offer a paid service to obtain data.

The large volumes of open data create additional challenges for organizations in evaluating/selecting data and in retaining data. Assessing open data can trigger significant costs. For selecting data, organizations must decide on the duration of the data storage. Typically, open data is only assessed and used in direct decision-making, data-driven decision-making, or indirectly by dashboarding. If the dashboards are archived, the underlying open data is typically not stored.

5.4.2 Unstructured data

Due to a lack of schema and structure accessing unstructured data requires more advanced techniques than accessing structured data. Indexing unstructured data is more complex, as the structure is less clear and there are no pre-defined attributes. This also affects error frequency and accuracy levels, which need to be taken into account in the data set certification. However, there can be much value in combining structured and unstructured data. Related to the cost and effort required, organizations need to make informed decisions on which unstructured data is worth the effort of accessing, producing, and onboarding.

5.5   Processes

Data collection should also include data classification. In the production and on-boarding process, data classification is important for the use of the data. In data analytics, classification can be taken into account by the data scientist. Furthermore, data classification is helpful for the data owner to set priorities for data security, data cleansing, and/or adjusting the data collection process to improve data quality.

Allocating and maintaining access rights to data is another important aspect. The data catalog plays an important role in this. Organizations need to constantly monitor access rights and, if required, differentiate between internal and external staff and/or permanent and temporary staff, but also ensure that, when personnel leave the organization, their rights are revoked. Also, for personnel who are changing roles, access rights need to be reassessed and potentially adjusted. Processes require alignment with HR processes and a proper authorization approval mechanism. Identity and access tools provide functionality to automate the allocation and maintenance of access rights. The challenge for organizations is the setup and implementation of these tools.

Monitoring the use of data is also important. Logging each data request and transaction is becoming the norm in many organizations, starting with highly regulated organizations, such as hospitals and financial institutions. Any organization should have a data policy that clearly details how data can be used in addition to the allocated rights. In the use of data, the purpose is also important. For example, client service employees of a bank should have the right to access balance details of a client when, in a conversation with a client, this becomes relevant. Access rights should then be revoked as soon as the conversation is complete and the client case is closed. Client service employees should not access balance details of family members or neighbors out of curiosity or at random times not associated with a client conversation. This makes AI-driven provisioning even more important to ensure that automated real-time access rights approval and revocation is built into the process.

Furthermore, ethics and transparency with regard to data analytics rightfully increases attention in many organizations. Ethical committees are typically not well equipped to assess algorithms. This requires a separate committee to assess the processes of collecting and selecting data and algorithms to avoid biases. The level of technical experience for the members of this committee needs to be quite advanced, and audit firms, including the big four, offer support services in the assessment of algorithms. These audits focus on data processes and audit only a subset of the algorithms.

5.6   People

The chief data office drives data quality and is headed by the chief data officer,[4] which collaborates with data owners and data stewards in the organization, as well as the IT department and its suppliers. Collaboration should be seamless, where the strategy and policies are set by the chief data office, thereby enabling the chief data office to provide guiderails for the organization.

The profile of employees in the chief data office is T-shaped, where data owners and data stewards have a business profile. Embedding data ownership in the organization is still a struggle for many, which is why organizations are exploring the breakdown of their data lake into a data mesh and creating federated governance structures. This will bring the data closer to the data owners, which will result in increased dedicated data ownership and, consequently, in increased data quality. The data mesh will be explained in the next chapter on data governance.

Whether organizations embrace the data mesh or not is not changing the involvement of the IT department and its suppliers. They provide the technology and tooling, whereas the data management tooling is architected by the chief data office within the parameters set by the enterprise architecture and IT architecture. The operating model and different roles will be explained in greater detail in the next chapter on data governance.

Collaboration requires the full participation of highly qualified professionals in all roles. In the current labor market, this is for many organizations still quite a challenge. Only a combination of providing (awareness) training and actively recruiting data-savvy professionals throughout the organization in conjunction with retention management will do the trick. To be clear, the challenge is beyond data scientists, and the people challenge is across all data management-related roles in organizations.

5.7   Technology

In technology, the focus is on data and analytics architecture and cyber security challenges. The maturity of the tooling landscape is emerging but is not limited to tooling only to cleanse data. Therefore, data and analytics architecture is becoming more and more complex. Due to the increased data volumes, the enhanced compliance obligations, and more restrictive legislation, cyber security has become an even bigger burden for most organizations. All of this negatively impacts data quality.

5.7.1   Data and analytics architecture

Data producers have the tools to generate data, including systems in the primary and secondary processes, as well as business intelligence systems. This data needs to be approved for analytics. For this approval, organizations can use workflow tooling such as JIRA. Furthermore, there needs to be tooling for the data catalog and to improve data quality and classifications – think Collibra or Informatica. In order to improve data transparency, scanning, and lineage, additional tooling such as BigID and Informatica are required. Many of these tools converge in functionality and integration points.

In data analytics architecture, cloud computing strategies are essential, whereas multi-cloud computing strategies are unavoidable. This requires thinking through data flows and architecture data storage accordingly, to avoid excessive cost related to the downloading of data, which is the typical cost trigger in infrastructure as a service.

There are additional architectural challenges; as we can conclude from the above, there is no best-of-suite tooling available at this point. Tooling is still emerging and in the future, more convergence is expected to ensure that organizations can enable as many data science tools as possible as well as support multiple data analytics languages such as Java, Python, R, and Scala. Also, in terms of underlying technology, there are no notebook restrictions. In other words, organizations offer both Jupyter *and* Zeppelin rather than Jupyter *or* Zeppelin. Also, consider Graphical Processing Units (GPUs) instead of Central Processing Units (CPUs), as GPUs accelerate processing artificial workloads by leveraging parallelism. In terms of computer operations, mandate a zero-copy architecture to avoid unnecessary data copies, saving processing power and memory bandwidth, thus improving data analytics performance.

5.7.2   Cyber security

The cyber security challenges are in data storage (data at rest), as well as in data access and processing (data in motion and data in use). The volumes of data that organizations store are exponentially increasing in conjunction with data democratization, which requires access to data by an increasing number of citizen data scientists embedded in the business, in addition to the highly specialized and often centralized data scientist organizations. This significantly increases the cyber security risk profile.

As for any cyber security threat, and also for data analytics cyber security, the risk comes from outside as well as inside. Unauthorized export of data out of the organization and data manipulation are serious cyber security threats. As for any system, organizations have to implement security operations center (SOC) monitoring for data analytics. Improving data transparency, including scanning and data lineage, is essential, and tools like BigID, Informatica, and Manta can be instrumental in this area. Additionally, biometric scanners play an important role in the authentication of users. Biometric scanners like Mantra and Thales are linked to the identity and access management systems of many organizations.

Also, data classification and data collection are extremely important in assessing the risk and impact of a cyberattack and ensure that organizations can make the right decisions with regard to cyber threat, and in case of a cyberattack, can inform authorities and relevant stakeholders accurately and swiftly.

5.8 Roadmaps for improving data and analytics maturity

In order to improve data and analytics maturity, organizations need a clear roadmap, and setting priorities is of the utmost importance. Gartner (2021c) suggests the implementation of enterprise-wide data quality standards as an important means of improving data quality. Gartner also suggests engaging with the organization, including board of management attention on data, as well as increasing data awareness across the organization. Gartner presents a descriptive framework to develop a roadmap.

Organizations should first understand their current and required data quality, which is typically done by scoring data quality. Implementing processes for accessing and processing the data should be the next focus. Boosting processes with the implementation of tools will elevate organizations to the next level. Many organizations iteratively alter the focus from implementing processes to the implementation of tools. Organizations should engage from day one with their data owners in order to increase data awareness and better understand their requirements. Obviously, the roadmaps of individual organizations are different and very specific to the organization.

Nevertheless, many organizations struggle with managing ongoing data processing combined with managing data improvement projects. The struggle is not limited to resource and/or budget constraints but is driven by the lack of a clear strategy and priorities and the limited involvement of the rest of the organization. Successful data-mature organizations have a strong data project management office,[5] as part of the chief data office, and committed data owners. Empowering the data project management office is key to the successful implementation of the data improvement roadmap, whereas the commitment of data owners is a prerequisite for initiating and endorsing the data quality improvement projects. This will be detailed in the next chapter on data governance.

TATA CONSULTANCY SERVICES CASE STUDY: UNIFIED DEVICE DATA PLATFORM FOR MICROSOFT

Microsoft develops unified business intelligence analytics platform

Challenge

Disparate business intelligence solutions on devices prevented effective data analysis.

The Business Intelligence (BI) units handling data from various Microsoft devices such as Xbox, Surface, Phone, HoloLens, Band, and Windows operated in silos. The Windows and Devices Group (WDG) wanted to consolidate these units into a single analytics organization. They sought to deliver performance-based insights into various Microsoft devices like user adoption and user awareness. If Microsoft could transition from point solutions to a platform approach, they could gain stakeholders' confidence by delivering rich insights, optimize repeatable tasks, and promote self-service.

Enabling real-time analysis of diverse device data on unified platform

- Developed a unified, extensible, and scalable data platform, and in the process migrating disparate systems onto COSMOS, Microsoft's Big Data solution. Our solution helps identify data quality issues, provides self-serve capabilities, and enhances user experience. Data marts created empower their data science team with faster and more accurate analysis, insights, and reports. We also help build complex survey workflows and statistical models to enable a deeper understanding of customers' attitudes and behavior.
- Leveraging our solution, WDG delivered key initiatives and projects on time, exceeding quality expectations. With our focus on continuous improvement, we enabled automated monitoring, minimized data latency, and improved processes across all their products.
- Using our Global Network Delivery Model (GNDM™) and Integrated Services delivery framework, we support Microsoft across Europe, the Middle East, Asia Pacific, and North America. Our delivery framework leverages best practices, tools, and processes across engagements to enhance Microsoft's data and analytics efforts.

5.9   Conclusion

Data quality is a prerequisite for enabling data-driven decision-making and monetization. However, many organizations still struggle to improve data quality. The decades-long war on talent (Beulen, 2011), the continuous growth of data volumes, and increased regulations, combined with an increasingly severe cyber security threat and public pressure to use data ethically, does not reduce the effort required to improve data quality. In fact, there is increasing need to improve data quality. Organizations must focus on improving and strengthening their data governance and data compliance. These topics will be addressed in the next two chapters of this book.

Improved data quality will also fuel digital transformations by enabling the enrichment of the current services and products with data, developing new data-centric services and products, and creating new data-centric business models. This will be addressed in Parts 4 and 5.

DATA AND ANALYTICS MATURITY SURVEY

In a survey which included 62 organizations across many sectors and revenue/budget ranging from under 10 m to more than 1 b euros, the maturity of data and analytics was investigated (Beulen, 2018b). Understanding adoption levels in data management, analytics automation, types of data, types of analytics platforms used, and cloud adoption, helps us better understand the data quality challenges that organizations are facing. This is the basis for analyzing the data and analytics of the surveyed organizations. No organization surveyed can be qualified as best in class in all five aspects. There are eight organizations that qualify as laggards on all five aspects, which are in the following sectors: government and public services (2 laggards), life sciences and healthcare (2 laggards), consumer goods and distribution, insurance, and manufacturing and other (agriculture). The remaining organizations are highly diverse in data and analytics basics. Let us take a closer look at these organizations for data and analytics basics, as this foundation contributes to data and analytics maturity.

By analyzing the adoption levels of the five aspects of the surveyed organizations, we continue to distinguish between laggard, average, and best-in-class per aspect; see Figure 5.1.

Data management. From the organizations surveyed, we conclude that the adoption of data management is low – a score of 2 or below on a 0–7 Likert scale (N = 24): laggard. This affects the ability to derive insights from data gathered from processes and transactions across these organizations. Most of these organizations are smaller, with revenue below 1 b euro (N = 19). There are no surveyed organizations using entirely digitized data management – a score of 7 on a 0–7 Likert scale, only two organizations in manufacturing and energy resources and utilities reported a 6 score. Organizations need to focus on data governance, including master data management, to be able to improve data and analytics maturity.

Analytics automation. Reducing the need for human intervention is the objective. Unfortunately, the adoption of analytics automation is also low, as more than 50% of the organizations surveyed report analytics automation under 25% (N = 34): laggard, with a limited difference in the size of the companies. As expected, the Dutch surveyed organizations in banking and financial services reported higher degrees of analytics automation adoption.

Type of data used. For the type of data used in the analysis, we concluded that adoption was medium, half of the Dutch organizations surveyed derive insights from open data and/or unmanaged external data (N = 31): average and best in class. This includes eight of the ten energy resources and utilities organizations. The most widely-used type of data by surveyed organizations is, as expected, internal managed data. Adding open data will expand the ability of organizations to derive insights.

Type of analytics platforms used. Most of the organizations surveyed use transitional platforms, such as enterprise data warehouses (N = 42) or department data stores (N = 15). Only a few organizations use traditional management information systems to perform ad hoc analyses, makeshift management information systems (N = 11), energy resources and utilities organizations are well represented, four out of the ten. Advanced organizations (70% of the large organizations) use active data warehouses and/or data lakes (N = 31): average and best in class. Therefore, the ability to derive insights from advanced analytics platforms across all surveyed organizations is classified as medium. Investing in the implementation of more advanced analytics platforms, such as active data warehouses and data lakes, will enable improvements in data and analytics maturity. To optimize platform usage, some participants have set up a data and analytics center of excellence.

Cloud adoption. In this day and age, cloud computing is largely used in analytics by many organizations. In this research, one-third of the surveyed organizations have a low analytics cloud computing score (0, 1, or 2 on a 0–7 Likert scale – N = 26). Surprisingly, the maturity of data and analytics of these organizations is no different from the maturity of the remaining two-thirds of the 62 surveyed organizations.

In conclusion, most of the organizations surveyed have to take immediate action to keep their house in order. They have to improve the effectiveness of their business by leveraging data and data analytics – and disrupt and avoid being disrupted. Organizations must focus on ensuring alignment of their data and analytics capabilities within their value chains. A greater focus on data literacy, analytics automation, and modern data governance techniques can help achieve the required data-driven result.

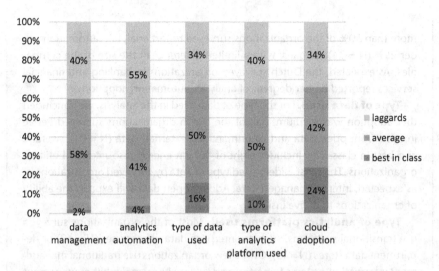

FIGURE 5.1 Data and analytics adoption aspects: data management, analytics automation, types of data used, type of analytics platforms used, and cloud adoption; by level: laggards, average, and best in class (N = 62) (Beulen, 2018b)

Notes

1 https://www.facebook.com/, https://www.instagram.com/ and www.twitter.com.
2 https://www.census.gov/data.html.
3 https://data.europa.eu/en.
4 For smaller organizations, the chief data office is also called the data office, which is run by the head of data; as for smaller organizations, this is a manager/director role instead of an executive role. The reporting lines of both the chief data officer and the head of data are discussed in the next chapter on data governance.
5 The project management office for data is in some organizations part of the chief data office.

6

DATA GOVERNANCE – BUSINESS AND IT COLLABORATION

Assuring data governance is essential for data analytics and enabling data provisioning to power digital transformations. This chapter details the organizational embedding, processes, and tooling, as well as the required business involvement. In the (RACI) tables, the responsibilities in data governance are explained, and the governance meeting structure is detailed.

There are two questions that any organization should ask themselves. First, what are the opportunity costs of not getting data governance right? Poor data governance can impact digital transformation success and the ability to make data-driven decisions, and it can also jeopardize compliance. Second, what are the data governance in-house capabilities? Building data governance requires experience, focus, and effort. Assigning experienced and qualified professionals to drive data governance is important when implementing data governance, as well as when executing and improving data governance over time. Most organizations appoint a senior person, such as a chief data officer or head of data, to pivot data governance and start with a small team of data management professionals to ensure a proper implementation of data governance.

6.1 Introduction

In addition to the opportunities to use data, data governance also reduces risks and increases return on investment. This is why data management requires C-level attention (Ladley, 2019) and a data-steering committee to drive data governance. Unfortunately, in many organizations, there is a limited sense of urgency. It is important to understand that proper data governance enables responsible use and reuse of data (McKinsey, 2020b). The largest benefit is with the reuse of data. Data governance provides guidance by the data strategy and data policies and orchestrates

DOI: 10.4324/9781003246770-8

data processes and data management tooling. This enables data owners to make their data available (Benfeldt et al., 2020).

In the context of growing data volumes and data usage, the importance of data governance is obvious (Khatri and Brown, 2010; Micheli et al., 2020). As a consequence, the mantra for data management in any organization should be fully automated.[1] This is why processes and tooling are very important in data governance (Almeida and Calistru, 2013). Full automation is also supportive of ensuring compliance and ethical use of the data. Full automation is an assurance that an organization is in control and that the focus in data governance is on enabling the use and reuse of data instead of on resolving data management and data quality issues (Plotkin, 2020). Data governance must enable data to flow faster, cleaner, and more efficiently to add value destinations. Data governance removes friction points and bottlenecks in data flow.

The data management framework from Abraham et al. focuses on data governance (2019, Figure 4, p. 429). Governance mechanisms include structural mechanisms, procedural mechanisms, and relational mechanisms. In addition, there is the organizational scope, which entails intra and interorganizational governance. Due to ecosystems and the rise of the platform economy, data sharing with partners is becoming more important and requires interorganizational governance (Mukhopadhyay and Bouwman, 2019). This requires alignment on policies, procedures, data formats, and, to a lesser degree data management tooling. Both internal data usage and external data exchange impact the domain scope. This addresses: data quality, data security, data architecture, data life cycle, metadata, and data storage and infrastructure. Ensuring data governance for this domain requires a close cooperation between data owners, data management, and supporting teams, such as information security and information technology. In this domain the data scope is detailed, and traditional data and big data are distinguished.

TATA CONSULTANCY SERVICES CASE STUDY: VOLTAS PREDICTIVELY MAINTAINS ITS CHILLERS

Voltas develops a Remote Chiller Monitoring System to prevent chiller breakdowns across India.

Voltas initiates steps for preventive maintenance to avoid chiller equipment breakdowns.

India's premier air conditioning and engineering services company, Voltas, needed to train and deploy field engineers to regularly maintain its chillers at 1000+ locations across the country.

Often, it took multiple visits to problematic sites to identify the operational issues and eventually fix the problem.

This resulted in additional maintenance costs. Voltas needed to leverage their vast experience in chiller management to track breakdowns in advance and avoid unexpected failures and unavailability of spare parts.

TCS enables centralized HVAC equipment monitoring with an IoT-based solution.

TCS utilized their IoT framework, Intel deployed their IoT gateway, and Voltas leveraged their chiller expertise – to jointly develop a centralized system that could remotely monitor chillers across different geographies.

The end-to-end solution helped Voltas:

- Diagnose real-time health of their chillers through a live dashboard
- Identify anomalies in the equipment parameters to facilitate alerts and notifications to their field engineers
- Predict failures in equipment for proactive maintenance

We leveraged our in-house Sensor Data Analytics IoT Framework (SDAF) to acquire data from the IoT gateways and send it to a Big Data based cloud platform for:

- Real-time data processing
- Complex event processing
- Storage for batch processing

This enabled real-time reports and dashboards.

Voltas is envisioning a predictive maintenance system leveraging Big Data & Analytics to increase their equipment availability and improve customer satisfaction.

6.2 Effective data governance[2,3]

In effective data governance, there are three responsibility areas. First is the foundational area. This addresses the data strategy, the data policies, and standards. Second is the management area, focusing on the use of data. Third is the processing area, which facilitates the use of the data.

In data management, a large number of roles are involved. These roles can be clustered into three domains: business, data, and support. The distinction between business and data is the most ambiguous clustering. In some organizations, data stewards are in the business, and in other organizations, this role is embedded in the data management office or both the business and the data management offices.

Similarly for data scientists, in most organizations, the data scientists are part of a central team and linked to the data management office. However, in some (typically larger) organizations, there are also business employees who are career data scientists as well as citizen data scientists.

Effective data governance requires clear roles and responsibilities. In this section, the data governance will be detailed by the three areas. These areas include five responsibilities by area. A RACI is applied to provide guidance on the responsibilities for the identified roles. This is summarized in Table 6.1. The numbering in the below subsection refers to the responsibilities in this table. In Section 6.3, the responsibilities will be linked to the data governance meeting structure. Also, this section includes the link with roles clustered by domain.

6.2.1   Data governance – foundational area responsibilities

In the foundational area, there are five responsibilities. The accountability for this area is with the data management office. The chief data officer develops and maintains the data strategy (# 1.1) and is supported by the data management office team and consults the legal team, compliance and risk managers, the IT architect and the information security manager. A typical update cycle for the data strategy is three years.

The data governor maintains and develops the data policies and standards (# 1.2) and consults with the data quality manager and the legal team, compliance and risk managers, as well as the IT architect and the information security manager. The data policies and standards are typically updated every year or in the event of unanticipated changes to the applicable regulations. To ensure proper data governance monitoring, adherence to standards is important (# 1.3). The data governor is driving adherence in close collaboration with the data quality manager and the legal team, compliance, and risk managers.

Data classification is important in data governance (# 1.4). The data quality manager is in charge of defining the data classification, with support from the legal team, compliance and risk managers, and the information security manager. The actual data classification is an integrated part of the data production and onboarding process. Any new data must be classified to ensure responsible use of data.

In order to make data governance effective, it is important to increase the data quality awareness in the organization (# 1.5). The data quality manager drives awareness. To increase awareness, training is provided as well as a point of contact to address questions. The data quality awareness program might also implement an (internal) data certification and/or gamification to ensure and improve data quality awareness.

6.2.2   Data governance – management area responsibilities

The business drives the management area and also includes five responsibilities, typically governed by the data-steering committee. The first responsibility is to own, manage, and share data (# 2.1). The ownership must be in the business and performed by a designated data owner, working in close cooperation with data stewards and data governors. A good starting point is that the producer of data is by default the owner of the data, because the producer is generally closest to the data: this person understands the purpose and is responsible for setting the business rules and performing updates. For this responsibility, the business manager, the data quality manager, the legal team, compliance and risk managers, the IT architect, and the information security manager support the data owner.

To create value, the data owner must explore data monetization opportunities (# 2.2). Similar to the first responsibility, this responsibility works closely with data stewards. As this responsibility is closely related to the data strategy also, the chief data officer is involved in this responsibility. For this responsibility, the business manager, data governor, legal team, compliance and risk managers, IT architect, and information security manager support the data owner. Typically, these sessions are twice-yearly and facilitated by the data management office.

To ensure data needs are met, the business manager must drive exploration of the data consumers' needs (# 2.3). Data consumers are both citizen data scientists and career data scientists. Data consumers have access to data and might also be data producers if they make any changes to data. Driving the exploration of the data needs of consumers is also the responsibility of the data owners, data stewards, chief data officer, and data governor. Typically, these are (twice) yearly sessions facilitated by the data management office. Input for these sessions is also the overviews of historic data requests.

In this area, data management investment decisions are also made (# 2.4). In most organizations, the business manager and chief data officer have a data management budget. Together with the data owners, investment decisions are made. The data management investments are supported by the legal team, compliance and risk managers, IT architect, information security officer, and IT manager. Understanding the technical implications of any investment is essential. Many organizations have difficulties in innovating data management strategies. Legacy tooling and technical debt slow innovation. This is where enterprise architecture is important. The IT architect is the linking pin for the enterprise architect.

Finally, data management issues (#2.5) also have to be resolved. Data management issues range from data access to tooling downtime, and a service ticket tool registers the data management issues. The chief data officer drives resolving the issues supported by both the data owner for more data user-related issues and the data governor for more technical-related issues. To resolve issues, the information security manager and the IT managers are closely involved, and if needed, the business manager, legal team, compliance and risk managers, and the IT architect are involved.

6.2.3 Data governance – processing area responsibilities

Data processing is the primary subject for data governance, and this is predominantly driven by technical support roles. Nevertheless, the first responsibility, approving and verifying data access, is driven by the data governor on behalf of the data owner (# 3.1). The data quality manager supports the data governor. Related to this responsibility is the second responsibility, which is the implementation and maintenance of the data access processes (# 3.2). Also, this is the responsibility of the data governor supported by the data quality manager and the IT manager. The IT architect and the information security manager are closely involved in this responsibility.

The third responsibility is to improve the data quality (# 3.3), which is obviously the responsibility of the data quality manager, who orchestrates the activities related to this responsibility. Most of the data governance roles are involved in supporting this activity. This includes the data owner and the data stewards, as well as the data consumers and the data governor. Also, more technical roles are involved, as many of the improvements are related to data management tooling.

Related to data management investments (# 2.4) is the fourth responsibility to monitor adherence to IT architectural standards (# 3.4). This is driven by the IT architect supported by the information security manager and the IT manager. The challenge in this responsibility is the balancing act between business requirements and the long-term impact of not meeting all defined non-functional requirements. Technical debt is not a problem as long as it is measured and endorsed by the business manager, chief data officer, legal team, and compliance and risk managers. The IT architect needs to ensure that the noncompliance with IT architectural standards will be resolved in the future.

The fifth and final responsibility is the implementation and the maintenance of data management tooling (# 3.5). In combination with the data management processes responsibility (# 3.2), this will facilitate the use and reuse of data by data consumers. The IT manager drives this responsibility and is supported by the IT architect and the information security managers, as well as the data governor and the data quality manager. The data management tooling landscape of most organizations consists of best-of-breed solutions, as there is not really a best-of-suite solution. This sets additional requirements for adhering to the IT architectural standards (# 3.4).

6.2.4 Overview of data governance roles and responsibilities

Table 6.1 provides a starting point for designing and implementing data governance and must be adjusted to specific needs of the organization. Also, over time, the roles and responsibilities must be reviewed. Typically, an annual review is sufficient.

TABLE 6.1 Data governance responsibilities clustered by nature and mapped to data governance roles clustered by domain

Data governance responsibilities clustered by nature			Data governance roles clustered by domain											
			Business			Business/Data		Data				Support		
			Business manager	Data owner	Data citizen analyst	Data steward	Data scientist	Chief data officer	Data governor	DQ manager	Legal advisor & compliance and risk manager	IT architect	Info sec manager	IT manager
1 Foundational	1.1	Develop and maintain data strategy	I					A/R	R	C	C	C	C	I
	1.2	Develop and maintain data policies and standards	I		I	I	I	A	R	C	C	C	C	I
	1.3	Monitor adherence to data policies and standards							A/R	R	R			
	1.4	Implementing and maintaining data classification	C		I	I				A/R	C		C	
	1.5	Improve data quality awareness								A/R				

(Continued)

TABLE 6.1 (Continued)

Data governance responsibilities clustered by nature			Data governance roles clustered by domain											
			Business			Business/Data			Data				Support		
			Business manager	Data owner	Data citizen analyst	Data steward	Data scientist	Chief data officer	Data governor	DQ manager	Legal advisor & compliance and risk manager	IT architect	Info sec manager	IT manager
2 Management	2.1	Own, manage, and share data	C	A/R		R			R	C	C	C	C	I
	2.2	Explore data monetization opportunities	C	A/R		R		R	C	I	C	C	C	I
	2.3	Explore data needs of data consumers	A	R	C	C	C	C	C					
	2.4	Approve data management investments	A/R	R				R			C	C	C	C
	2.5	Resolve data management issues	C	R				A/R	R		C	C	C	C

Data governance responsibilities clustered by nature

		Data governance roles clustered by domain											
		Business			Business/Data		Data			Support			
		Business manager	Data owner	Data citizen analyst	Data steward	Data scientist	Chief data officer	Data governor manager	DQ manager	Legal advisor & compliance and risk manager	IT architect	Info sec manager	IT manager
3 Processing	3.1 Approve and verify data access	A						R	C				
	3.2 Implement and maintain data access processes	I	I	C	C	C		A/R	R	C	C	C	R
	3.3 Improve data quality	I	C	C	C	C	I	C	A/R	C	C	C	C
	3.4 Monitor adherence to IT architectural standards	R					R			C	A/R	R	R
	3.5 Implement and maintain data management tooling	I	I				I	C	C	C	C	C	A/R

Legend: R = Responsible // A = Accountable // C = Consulted // I = Informed

6.3 Business involvement[4]

Business involvement is essential in data governance. The role of the data owner is instrumental; nevertheless, in many organizations the IT department is still too involved, and the maturity and capabilities of the data management office are emerging. In order to make data accessible, the data owner needs to step up with support by data stewards, which enables use and reuse of data.

The data owner needs to organize data cleansing; this requires business involvement supported by the data stewards. The data owner is closest to the data and understands best the business rules that can create data and maintain data quality. Before onboarding, data checks are required. Not all data owners are very eager to perform these tasks, but business involvement is an imperative. It is not for the data management office or the IT department to judge the quality of the data. However, both can support data cleansing by implementing process and tooling.

In addition to data cleansing, data classification is important. Data classification standards are set by the data management offices, and the process is automated by the IT department. Nevertheless, data classification in the onboarding process remains a responsibility of the business.

Furthermore, data lineage is becoming more important, not only because of compliance but also in relation to data quality. Also, automation is essential to be able to explain where data is produced, how it is transformed, where it is consumed/accessed, and for what reason. In the future, with anticipated continually increasing legislation, data lineage will be even more important. The business needs to ensure, in close collaboration with the chief data officer that data lineage is at level and that there is sufficient budget available to meet future requirements.

To facilitate the business involvement, there needs to be in place structural mechanisms including a data-steering committee on a strategic level, a data management committee on a tactical level, and an ethical rule board to ensure ethical use of data and algorithms. The size of an organization, the importance of data, and regulatory scrutiny drives the required structural mechanisms. Organizations might consider holding additional meetings on regional and/or service/product domains. However, typically, there is only one ethical rule board due to the highly specialized profile required for this board.

In the next subsections, data governance meetings will be detailed, which will be summarized in Table 6.2.

6.3.1 Data-steering committee

The data-steering committee is the strategic governance meeting, led by the chief data officer. In close collaboration with the data owners, the data strategy is discussed and approved. Furthermore, the budget for the data management project is approved. For specific topics for this meeting, business managers, data governors, the legal team, compliance and risk managers, and the information security manager also can be invited.

Also, the data-steering committee is the escalation level for the data management committee and the ethical rule board. Typically, the data-steering committee meets every quarter to ensure that the required decision-making is not hindered.

6.3.2   Data management committee

The data management committee is at a tactical level, led by either the chief data officer or the data governor, and supplemented by the legal team, compliance and risk managers, and information security manager. Also, the data owners, data quality manager, IT architect, and IT manager can be invited to this meeting. In this meeting, data policies are nevertheless approved for major adjustments, it might be advisable to endorse the data policies by the data-steering committee. In the meeting, anticipated upcoming legislation and compliancy requirements, including budget implications, are discussed to minimize risks. Furthermore, data consumer needs are prioritized, including the budget allocation for meeting the data consumer needs. Also, the status of the data management project is discussed to ensure that there are no blocking factors to implementations.

Non-business critical issues from the ethical rule board can be escalated to the data management committee. Typically, the data management committee meets every month to ensure that the required decision-making is not hindered.

6.3.3   Ethical rule board

The focus of the ethical rule board is on monitoring the algorithms and data used. Algorithms are currently predominantly used by data scientists; in the future, citizen data scientists use of algorithms will also grow. Based on the values and moral principles of the organizations the algorithms and data used are assessed. The chief data office, data governor, and data quality manager, supplemented by legal representatives, compliance, and risk managers, assess whether the algorithms and data are used ethically. This requires advanced technical skills, ethics, and risk management expertise to perform this assessment. This can also be combined with a model risk management review to ensure that the models are both ethically sound and risk managed according to the organization's policies. Furthermore, it is important that the review process including detailed risk assessments has been implemented. The data scientist needs to provide a lot of information. These data scientists need to be transparent. To be clear, all in-use algorithms have to be assessed prior to each ethical rule board meeting, and only a subset will be discussed in the meeting. Therefore, the effort for both the members of the ethical rule board and the data scientist is significant but ensures ethical use of data.

Based on the outcome of assessments, the ethical rule board also provides advice to the chief data officer by proposing updates of the data policies and standards.

Depending on the number of algorithms of an organization, the frequency is either every quartile for the organizations with high number of algorithms or twice a year for organizations with a low number of algorithms.

6.3.4   Overview of data governance meetings and responsibilities

Table 6.2 provides a starting point for data governance meetings and must be adjusted to the specific needs of the organization. Also, over time, the roles and responsibilities must be reviewed. Typically, an annual review is sufficient.

TABLE 6.2 Data governance meetings mapped to data governance roles clustered by domain

Data governance meetings	Participants clustered by domain											
	Business			Business/data		Data			Support			
	Business manager	Data owner	Data citizen analyst	Data steward	Data scientist	Chief data officer	Data manager	DQ manager	Legal advisor	IT architect	Info sec manager	IT manager
Data-steering committee	(X)	X				L	(X)	(X)	(X)		(X)	
Data management committee	(X)	(X)				L	(L)	(X)	X		X	(X)
Ethical rule board					(X)		L	X	X			X

Legend: L = Lead // X = Present // (X) = Optional

6.4   Data governance processes[5]

In data governance processes, there are two types of processes: data consumption process and data production and onboarding process. To enable data analytics, these processes are very important and must be supported by tooling, which is detailed in Section 6.5. The combination of processes and tooling support the full automation of both data consumption and data onboarding. Full automation also increases data quality and transparency and it also enables fulfilling compliance requirements. All these elements are part of the business case for investing in data governance processes.

In order to be in control, data governance processes need to be centrally implemented, as data resides in decentralized organizational units (siloed data), and organizations might have an international footprint, and therefore need to comply with regulations applicable in the countries where they are operating. A central implementation facilitates data-driven decision-making.

6.4.1   Data consumption process

The data consumption process is related to data access of data consumers – career data scientists and data citizen scientists. In getting access, not only authorizations need to be set by the data owner, but identity management also has to be at level. The combination of identity and access management ensures proper data consumption and is essential from a risk management and a compliance perspective.

In the data consumption process, there are five steps. Data consumers search for and discover data in a data catalog market (#1). If data consumers have identified the data they want to access, they put in a data access request (#2). Dependent on their authorization, the data consumers obtain approval to access the data (#3), and they are provided access to the data set (#4). These first four steps are needed to ensure that data is only made available to authorized persons. Then the data consumers use the data, potentially also generating additional data from the received data (#5). This generated data will be input for the data onboarding process, which is detailed in 6.4.2. Steps 1–5 of the data consumption process are detailed in Figure 6.1 – Data governance processes.

6.4.2   Data production and onboarding process

Data onboarding involves the collection and evaluation of data from various sources and is often used to understand trends and patterns in the data. It requires a progression of steps that organizations can use as a framework to understand their data. If the data does not meet the required data quality requirements, a root cause analysis is required to identify how the data quality can be improved. Root cause analyses are often performed by a data operations team. Typically, the root cause has to be fixed upstream, not in the onboarding process. Only a structured approach will improve the data quality. This also enables data lineage, which is important not only for the data quality but also for compliance requirements. Data is generated by data producers using transactions or external data, including open data. To ensure data quality, the onboarded data set needs to be approved (A) prior to being stored by an organization. This data storage includes a classification of the data and access rights (authorization). Both are set by the data owner. In this context, the business and data quality rules are applied on the data sets in the data management domain (B). The data management domain also drives continuous improvement in data quality (C). This is not limited to the stored data but is also applicable to the external vendor data, which is either stored or accessed with an API. This is also applicable to the data quality scores in the data catalog marketplace (D). The data onboarding process increases the volume of data available to data consumers in a structured way. Steps A–D of the data onboarding process are detailed in Figure 6.1 – data governance processes.

6.4.3   Overview data governance processes

Figure 6.1 provides a starting point for the data governance processes and must be adjusted to specific needs of the organization. Also, over time, the processes must be reviewed. Typically, an annual review is sufficient. In Section 6.5, the tooling for the data governance processes is detailed.

6.5   Data governance tooling[6]

Data governance tooling is important, and full automation is the single objective. The defined business and data quality rules, policies, and data strategy dictate the starting point for data governance tooling, that point being automated

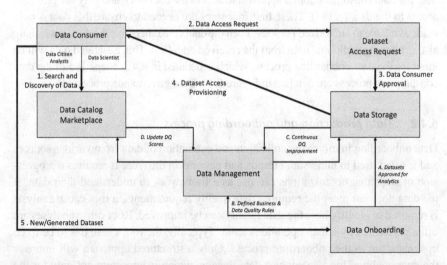

FIGURE 6.1   Data governance processes – Data consumption processes (1–5) and Data onboarding processes (A–D)

classification of data inventory across the organization in order to enable search and discovery. This requires business ownership of data and accountability from data owners. This will result in reducing time to access data and increases transparency and compliance. In improving transparency, it is important to enrich the data catalog with personal identifiable information (PII) and sensitive information classification. Data quality can also be improved by adding data set certification to the data catalog.

In data governance tooling, there are two tooling landscapes: end-user and data management data governance tooling. The end-user tooling for citizen data scientists, includes user tools such as Microsoft Power BI, Qlick, or Tableau, and for data scientists, Python, R and Jupyter notebooks are used in order to obtain insights from the data. Organizations typically accept multi-tool landscapes. Interfaces to data sources and data exchanges are mostly not a concern, as these are standard tools that have good APIs to seamlessly operate in the data domain.

Data management tooling consists of a data catalog (e.g. Alation, Collibra), data access request (e.g. BMC, ServiceNow), data storage (e.g. Amazon Web Services, Microsoft Azure, Oracle, Snowflake, SQL), data quality (e.g. Collibra, Informatica), data discovery and classification (e.g. BigID, Forcepoint), and data scanning and linage (e.g. Manta, Solidatus). Many of these vendors have offerings that span multiple categories. Technology companies such as IBM, Microsoft, Oracle, and SAP have a presence in most of these categories as well, and there are many other niche solutions. Also, data engineering tooling (e.g. ETL, streaming, publishing, data warehouse, etc.) is its own category and not covered in this book, although there are many crossover solutions.

The tooling also needs to contain a dashboard indicating data quality (Ehrlinger and Wöß, 2022); any BI tool is suitable for preparing this reporting. The data management tooling is based on best-of-breed tooling, as a best-of-suite tooling has not yet emerged.

6.6   Conclusion

Data governance is essential and instrumental for data analytics. Organizations must go beyond improving data awareness and create excitement about data. The focus should be on implementing seamless data consumption and data onboarding processes and fully automated and integrated tooling, and the governance mechanisms to drive data usage and analytics in an organization. As most organizations have a data legacy, the implementation of data governance requires a phased and agile approach. It is simply too significant and complex to consider a big bang implementation; multi-year implementation programs are not uncommon. Therefore, securing top management commitment and aligning with digital transformation themes are needed. Strong data ownership is an important cornerstone of data governance. This ownership will improve data quality and the right allocation of data usage authorization. The chief data officer and data owners need to work hand in hand in the data governance domain.

Notes

1 https://www.cio.com/article/189464/how-automation-helps-to-solve-the-data-management-challenge.html (accessed 5 February 2023).
2 The section is based on both authors' experiences in data governance and consulting roles.
3 For further reference, see frameworks such as the DCAM framework from EDM Council (EDM Council, 2020) and the DAMA DMBOK from DAMA (DAMA, n.d.).
4 The section is based on both authors' experiences in data governance and consulting roles.
5 The section is based on both authors' experiences in data governance and consulting roles.
6 The section is based on both authors' experiences in data governance and consulting roles.

7

DATA COMPLIANCE, PRIVACY, AND ETHICS[1]

Legislation is constantly evolving, and there are distinct differences for each country. Both the financial and healthcare sectors are highly regulated, e.g. the Anti-Money Laundering and Counter-Terrorism Finance Act, Know Your Customer, the Dodd-Frank Act, the Foreign Account Tax Compliance Act, and the Health Insurance Portability and Accountability Act. Also technology companies face regulations, e.g. the Digital Services Act package which includes the Digital Services Act and the Digital Markets Act.

In addition, a significant aspect of compliance is related to privacy (e.g. GDPR, CCPA, and the upcoming PIPL). The effort and expertise required to be in control is increasing. As a consequence, a growing number of regulatory technology companies (RegTechs) offer software to address these compliance obligations. Also, ethics is an emerging topic. The application of company values and moral principles put additional demands on organizations. Furthermore, the increasing data volumes and analytics processing power are setting an ever-rising bar for organizations. Processes and tooling need to be more robust and in-house capabilities need to be more advanced.

7.1 Compliance

Legislation and regulatory requirements are on the rise, and more and more sector-specific requirements are entering into force. The legislation and regulatory requirements are no longer only enforced in the financial and healthcare sector, every sector faces these requirements. This has a significant impact on digital transformations and data analytics. Not being compliant is not an option. The focus of organizations should be on processes and tooling. Important in achieving compliance is the ability to report. This also includes ad hoc reporting, which is more difficult

DOI: 10.4324/9781003246770-9

to produce than reporting which has to be done at a set pace, e.g. daily, monthly, or annually (Axelsen et al., 2022). Ad hoc reporting capabilities require a solid foundation to set the parameters that will deliver the reporting requested by the legislator or regulator. The measurement of compliance-oriented key performance indicators (KPI) is important (Panitz et al., 2010). A good KPI is the average effort and lead time required to deliver an ad hoc report, as well as the percentages of ad hoc reports that were delivered within the requested timeline set by the legislator or regulator. These KPIs will provide qualitative insights to improve compliance.

Due to the continuous flow of new legislation and regulations, agility is important (Kirchmer, 2018), as compliance unfortunately is not static. This creates additional requirement for both the processes and the tooling as well as for the required capabilities, which is typically a combination of internal (i.e. in-house) and external capabilities. In Section 7.3, regulatory technology will be explained. In addition, many organizations involve external legal advisers, compliance and risk managers, and technology experts to ensure compliance.

TATA CONSULTANCY SERVICES – COMPLIANCE

Bandana Sinha – Program Director
Tata Consultancy Services

For data compliance, the challenges are first knowing the policies, rules, and regulations, and then implementing systems and creating reports to address and prove compliance to the policies, rules, and regulations. But this is only one part of it. Bandana Sinha: "With large scale deployments across any organization there is an extra challenge – defending yourself."

Policies, rules, and regulations are intended to prevent misuse of data. But if that misuse happens anyway, if the policies do not hold, they can be openly challenged with public court cases or sensational news from opposition parties in politics or rivalries in business trying to find weak spots. Bandana Sinha: "To defend against these attacks, there are agencies who can test robustness of policies end to end across large ecosystems, not just one enterprise, but across countries and nations."

Bandana Sinha:

For example, India's National ID card is similar to US Social Security Number for identifying citizens. The India ID card is proving to be much more efficient for managing citizen welfare schemes and programs, than previous governments without the ID card. However, there is still much opposition to using the ID card, that it can be tampered with, and someone even created an ID number for a dog. That news was sensationalized to prove ID cards are bad and cannot be trusted. These are the types of situations that need to be prevented, but there is always someone testing or trying to break it. If preventative measures are breached, these also need to be defended.

Preventative measures and independent testing needs to be considered at scale, across ecosystems of multiple enterprises, government bodies, and nations. 'Defending compliance' should become a buzzword because large ecosystems and governments are holding data versus just enterprises alone.

Another challenge of compliance is managing personal devices – bring your own device schemes in corporations are growing exponentially due to perceived cost savings with deploying corporate solutions to personal devices. However, even in smaller scale enterprises, not entire ecosystems, but enterprises spread across hundreds of countries with varying regulatory requirements, personal devices are making it very challenging to manage data compliance. The cost of preventative measures to secure personal devices is quickly outpacing the original cost savings driver. Bandana Sinha:

> For example, in some countries, taxation staff will look at tax data as part of their day job, but use that information outside of the office for other purposes. They are not hacking databases, they are doing legitimate work with the data and 'screen tapping', taking screen shots or photos to use elsewhere. Personal devices which have taken images need to be detected and trapped. This is a lot of security and stealth mechanisms for simple operations, and it's bogging down the compliance industry and disproportionate to the value of the data. This extra layer of compliance has to be designed and built, but the costs to cover it can be quite large. We are building compliance by design, leveraging common frameworks, instead of point solutions for one situation or another.

Right To Information Act

In India, the Right To Information Act (RTI)[2] grants a basic right to any Indian citizen to ask the Parliament under oath or any government organization for information. RTI gives people the right to hold the government and organizations substantially funded by the government accountable. The Right To Information Act gives citizens the right to ask for information and decide, based on the information received, whether their constitutional rights have been met. This generates a lot of inquiries which must be answered, increasing the burden of compliance. In addition to processing data to achieve stated compliance goals, now you are dealing with many clarifications of information, permutations, and combinations of questions from individuals and a variety of agencies. Bandana Sinha:

> Thousands of people may join in to ask different aspects of these questions, making scale extremely important to defensive compliance. Compliance is no longer just trying to do the right thing, it must also be proven and defended if something goes wrong. Another health care example is choosing the best recipient for organ transplant. Using an algorithm to make this decision, the algorithm logic will be questioned. Algorithms cannot be black box and will need transparency to prove ethics in AI decision making.

GDPR

For privacy, Europe is leading the way with GDPR being the most comprehensive privacy rules that exist to date. Users must consent to what data is being used and for what purpose. Where there are challenges are in non-technical citizens, senior citizens, or illiterate citizens. Bandana Sinha:

> For example, ensuring health care data privacy for non-technical citizens who consent to sharing their medical information with doctors, as well as employers. Non-technical citizens may be told by employers their medical information is being collected for one purpose, but employers use it for another purpose. If they have a certain illness, employers may not send them on front facing or choice assignments. Non-technical citizens need to understand the potential ramifications of sharing health data and ensure employers are using this health data ethically.

Bandana Sinha: "Another example is high pressure jobs, like policing, military defense, or locomotive operators, 24×7 jobs under extreme situations which has impact on large number of people and the larger public good." Medical and behavioral data should be shared with the organization to ensure timely rotations, spot outliers who may be over stressed, and avoid mishaps. So privacy and ethical usage must be ensured to provide confidence for consent. However, the privacy rules can be either too loosely defined to address consent confidence or too tightly defined for usefulness and full benefits of data analytics. Privacy rules may also not address the broader ecosystems across organizations and governments. If the privacy rules work for one organization, data sharing across ecosystems is impacted if those privacy rules change across the ecosystem. It is important that ecosystems agree to principles-based privacy rules, so that privacy rules from all organizations in an ecosystem are working off the same principles-based playbook in how to treat private information.

The challenge is how to ensure principles-based privacy rules are implemented uniformly across ecosystems and achieve scale. Principles-based privacy rules must be broad for the ecosystem, but also leave some autonomy for individual organizations to make decisions for their needs as long as it doesn't break the agreed principles. Bandana Sinha: "This mix is most optimal." Privacy by design ensures enterprise training at every level, to make privacy a conscious part of the everyday work environment. Data requirement documents become extremely useful for ensuring data is treated the same across the organization.

Regional data usage

From a regional perspective, economic priorities are becoming more and more relevant. Countries are accelerating their efforts to control their digital information from their citizens, government agencies, corporations, etc., not just driven by security and privacy but also economic interest. Data needs to be kept balanced throughout the ecosystems. Technology offers a lot of solutions as well as developing privacy by design intelligent frameworks that can work across ecosystems. Bandana Sinha: "The risks have to be evaluated and prioritized, which can vary by industry, because there will always be challenges that have to be defended. Currently these are being applied broadly versus areas that can be segmented by sensitivity." The Right To Information and GDPR are regional privacy policies that are dealt with in the country or region but also have to be applied within the global ecosystem. Similarly, medical health care decisions will be challenged. Insurance for enterprises will also increase to cover the challenges to data leakages, etc.

For ethics, transactional transparency in the algorithms is the most recent development to support ethical mandates, in addition to data ownership and purpose. There must be transparency where algorithms are being used, the data inputs, how data is being aggregated, and validated outputs. Bandana Sinha: "Ethics by design is becoming one of the key parameters to algorithms and model design." Ethics is also important in public health, social fabric, and how citizens are classified when determining welfare schemes. These algorithms are becoming more transparent as ethics is questioned by larger audiences. Bandana Sinha: "Also remote medical equipment, where do we draw the line on managing patient welfare with embedded equipment from afar?" Sharing medical information and ensuring, it is not used for other purposes. Should medical equipment be tested for 100% success before deployment versus not delaying deployment?

Both ethical and privacy data must together support the organizational needs. Most organizations are forming governance boards to define ethical principles and privacy rules. What kind of data and algorithms will be acceptable to use and which will not, based on ethical principles. Often individual disputes come up, so a federated model providing some autonomy for ethical decisions at the region or sector levels can help resolve these local disputes. Also, institutionalized training at all levels is needed. Everyone needs to understand and interpret the ethical principles of the organization, because not every situation is documented or solution written down. Bandana Sinha:

> Every developer and tester needs to understand corporate ethics and incorporate ethical principles into the testing cycles. Testing for data protection is fairly standard, but testing for privacy and ethics is more difficult, more abstract, however also more important to reducing the outlier issues.

7.1.1 Data classification

In being compliant with data, classification is important (Mahanti and Mahanti, 2021). To be able to determine the classification of compliance data is a first step, as any compliance obligations require data. The granularity of the data classification has to be in sync with the business requirements and with the compliancy requirements. This will enable compliance reporting. Data management needs to review the alignment of the data classification on a regular basis to ensure that the granularity of the data classification is at level, typically annually or twice a year, as the lead time for entering into force of legislation is predominantly +12 months.

7.1.2 Identity and access management[3]

In addition to data classification, identity and access management are also important. There are three components to identity and access management: authentication, authorization, and access control.

Organizations need authentication to ensure that persons and/or systems are indeed the persons and/or systems which they claim to be. Cyber security plays an important role in this, e.g. physical access, credentials, and multifactor authentication.

Many organizations have also implemented single sign-on by applying OAuth, an open standard for authorization that provides secure delegated access with tokens rather than credentials (Indu et al., 2018). The increasing number of machine-to-machine interfaces, and growing fully automated data exchanges, raise the need for advanced identity management and identity management tooling.

Access to data is next. The most advanced mechanism for access control is Attribute-Based-Access Control (ABAC) based on the subject, object, policy, and environmental attributes. ABAC enables regulatory compliance (Indu et al., 2018). Access control is more advanced and requires additional involvement of management such as the allocation of authorizations. As a consequence of the increased granularity in access management, organizations are more in control.

7.1.3 Logging

In addition to data classification and identity and access management, logging is also important in ensuring compliance. This is predominantly related to the purpose of the data access and processing; consider that medical staff only should access patient files if they are involved in the treatment of that patient. Analyzing the logging of data access and data processing ensures compliance. In most organizations, the analysis of the logging is highly automated and powered with artificial intelligence. Nevertheless, as an integral part of data governance, the data owner needs to review the analysis and, when required, take the appropriate action if there are breaches. If there is reason to do so, external forensic auditors can also be involved to investigate the data access and processing (Achar, 2022).

7.1.4 Partner selection

Organizations need to ensure compliance first; nevertheless, in collaborating with partners and exchanging data, the compliance obligation will be extended. Therefore, organizations need to set and agree on compliance requirements with their partners. This must be an integral part of the partner selection process and governance during the collaboration.

There is additional compliance that organizations need to take into account while partnering, that being antitrust compliance (Pasquale, 2012). In digital transformations, and especially in the platform economy, antitrust legislation has become more and more important (Parker et al., 2020). Due to the large volumes of data available and the increasing strength of algorithms, this requires attention. Recently, the EU settled with Amazon on (1) using data from independent sellers to its advantage and (2) using nonpublic data on independent sellers for its retail business. This settlement precluded a fine which could have been as high as $47b, which is 10% of the global annual revenues of Amazon. In particular, independent sellers were impacted; nevertheless, protection of consumers is important (Jin and Wagman, 2021).

COMPLIANCE RISKS – SUBJECT MATTER EXPERT INTERVIEW

Julia Bardmesser, financial industry strategic adviser and chief data officer

What do you see as the most significant compliance risks related to data (processing) in financial services?

Taking a broad view of compliance that includes compliance with financial (Basel, CCAR), AML, and privacy regulations, I see three types of data risks. First is the risk of getting it wrong: incomplete, inaccurate, or incoherent data can lead to making the wrong decisions. Let me give a few examples. Systemic risk evaluations depend on the ability to connect multiple sources of data relating to the same companies – for example, the ability to identify and fully understand the entire activity spectrum of Lehman Brothers under all of its names and legal entities before deciding to allow it to go bankrupt. Also, the accuracy of RWA calculations depends on having complete, accurate data about a borrower, either an individual or a company; inaccurate RWA can lead to insufficient capital put aside or, conversely, to too much capital put aside and taken out of revenue-generating activity. In addition, KYC due diligence and AML monitoring can easily produce the wrong results if different sources of customer data cannot be connected in real time or do not have sufficient data.

Second is the risk of regulatory action based on the regulators' lack of confidence in the company's reporting. Here I would like to share some additional examples. Large fines are often levied on financial institutions when regulators examine the quality of data pipelines, the available metadata such as lineage and descriptions, and the sufficiency of the controls. Also, business divisions can lose their license to operate in certain countries if regulators find significant gaps in the control environment, especially as it relates to AML and credit risk monitoring.

Third is the reputational risk. Consumer loss of confidence due to, for example, mishandling of the Personal Identifiable Information (PII) data or misidentifying customers in Know Your Customer (KYC) process.

How can these risks be mitigated?

Generally speaking, there are two ways financial institutions mitigate these risks: first, by implementing exhaustive manual controls across the entire data supply chain with associated people and process costs; and second, by investing in data management capabilities including data governance, master data management, metadata management, data quality management, and data integration automation.

Usually, large financial institutions have a mixture of both manual operational controls and some data management capabilities, with more mature organizations relying more on automation and data management vs. manual and, often, human error-prone operational checks.

7.2   Privacy

Privacy legislation, in the context of data analytics and digital transformations, is a key element in compliance. Many countries have implemented privacy legislation[4] – currently, the General Data Protection Regulation (GDPR) of the European Union and the California Consumer Protection Act in the United States are seen as leading privacy legislation (Peukert et al., 2022). Each legislation is different and sets detailed requirements, such as in country data storage. The cost of breaching privacy legislation is very different by country. Nevertheless, organizations must also take into consideration reputational damage in case of noncompliance with privacy legislation. The reputational damage is not limited to their customers or citizens, but also includes the partners of the organization. As technology, including data analysis, has created opportunities which are not all compliant, data governance is more important than ever to ensure privacy (Quach et al., 2022).

Sharing data with other organizations not only creates opportunities. In addition to managing the commercial risks of data sharing, organizations also need to manage the privacy risks. This is not limited to consent but also to data protection; the implementation of sufficient cyber security measures, and data encryption and masking are also important (Binjubeir et al., 2019). Organizations should consider the impact of algorithms on their encryption. With artificial intelligence, encrypted and masked data can be traced back. Furthermore, it is a misconception that privacy legislation is only relevant in business-to-consumer, government-to-government, and government-to-citizen relations.

Data privacy is also affected by mass surveillance by nation states.[5] Nation states can use mass surveillance to monitor their citizens and/or target specific individuals such as activists and journalists (Lyon and ZUreik, 1996; Parsons, 2015), which is a concern of human rights watchers (Watt, 2017). Nevertheless, also individuals with bad intentions might be subject of nation state mass surveillance by law enforcement (Dryer and Stroud, 2015). The nation state can also use social media (Mateescu et al., 2015).

7.3   Regulatory technology

There is a growing market, predominantly in the highly regulated financial sector (Anagnostopoulos, 2018; Butler and O'Brien, 2019), of companies that offer software to manage regulatory compliance. The regulatory change triggered by the 2008 global financial crisis ignited the rise of the RegTech sector. For compliancy changes, RegTechs provide updates to the software. This ensures compliance in a more efficient and faster way than internally updating the information systems. RegTechs are better positioned to anticipate upcoming compliance changes as this is their core business.

The core technology that RegTechs use is ETL (Extract, Transfer, Load) technologies to consolidate and report data (Arner et al., 2016; Deloitte, n.d.-a, n.d.-b). In the context of compliance and regulatory requirements, data needs to be decoupled, analyzed, and structured to be presented in reporting. Reporting is the outcome of the service performed by the RegTech. The main challenges are the decoupling and analysis, despite the fact that the analysis is predominantly focusing on the categories detailed in the applicable legislation and regulations. The analysis performed by RegTechs is also valuable input for organizations to minimize their risk profile as well as to enhance their services and products. The midsize and larger RegTechs are also offering consulting services in addition to the technology solutions to support their clients in enhancing their service and products.

RegTechs can be categorized by domain ranging from regulatory reporting, compliance, transaction monitoring, risk management, and identity management and control (Deloitte, n.d.-a). This is a maturing market that can be described as best-of-breed. Due to the large diversity in requirements on regional (region or city), national (country), and supranational (confederation of nations) level, it will remain best-of-breed for the foreseeable future. As a consequence, organizations need to continue to maintain deep expertise on applicable regulations and regulatory requirements to ensure an organization can select and manage RegTechs, while ensuring that all obligations of their organization are integrally met. This also has implications for the enterprise and IT architecture. Involvement of architects is essential, as the RegTech applications need to interface with the systems of the organization. RegTechs offer standard application programming interfaces (APIs) to simplify data acquisition. This reduces both the effort required from organizations and the risks related to the data consolidation performed by the RegTech.

In the long term, the RegTech market might attract the attention of big tech, such as AWS, Google, Microsoft, SAP, Salesforce, or ServiceNow. Big tech might consider acquiring start-ups and scale-ups and integrate this functionality into their product portfolio. When the diversity in legislation requirements converges, big tech acquisition can be expected.

7.4 Ethics

Organizations are bound by legislation and regulations. Noncompliance will have consequences and will be enforced. Organizations can deliberately decide to be not compliant and accept the consequences, which is not limited to the verdict, e.g. fine or revoking of license to operate, but includes also reputational damage, which will potentially impact the relationship with current and future stakeholders.

In addition to being compliant, an organization can decide to embrace values and moral principles that govern the organization's behavior. Ethical behavior starts here. The United Nations Sustainable Development Goals (UN SDG) are generally accepted as the starting point for driving ethical behavior in organizations (United Nations, n.d.a). In the context of data analytics, the UN SDG #5 (gender equality), #10 (reduce inequalities), and #16 (peace, justice, and strong institutions) are relevant. Organizations and individuals must be mindful that cultural differences drive different ethical behaviors. Values and moral principles change over time and, unlike legislation, are difficult to anticipate. A single event combined with activism can require an immediate re-evaluation of the values and moral principles of an organization.

Ethics is not a new topic; for decades, organizations are integrating ethics in their ways of working and engaging (Jones and Gautschi, 1988). Activism and intrinsic motivation drive ethical behaviors of organizations and push both law makers and regulators to sharpen their pencil, as organizations define and continuously update their value and moral principles.

In the context of data, the increasing volumes of data and the artificial intelligence (AI) and machine learning (ML) technology organizations require proper governance and are predominantly related to data analytics. In 6.3.3, the ethical rule board is introduced as a governance mechanism to ensure that only ethical algorithms are used.

In addition to governance, creating awareness is essential. This should not be limited to data scientists but rather should be expanded to citizen data scientists, data owners, and data stewards. Ethics must be an integral part of the DNA. When working with data, key questions must be asked: Does the solution deliver fair and equitable outcomes? Does the solution introduce or exacerbate bias? Will this solution result in humans feeling a sense of loss of control or agency? And, what is the impact on existing roles and employees? (SAS, n.d.)

Ethics has also an impact on the partnerships and ecosystems in which organizations are participating (Oliveira and Lóscio, 2018). Alignment on values and moral principles is important with regards to data processing and data analytics and needs to be addressed in the selection of partners and in the evaluation of partnerships and ecosystems. Addressing ethics in an organization is already challenging; addressing the topic in partnerships and ecosystems is even more difficult. It requires involvement at a senior level of all involved organizations, candid discussions, and being transparent. For private sector organizations, the latter requirement is sometimes in conflict with commercial interests. Building trust can solve this potential challenge. For public sector organizations, proper internal stakeholder management is important, including involving politicians. Due to constantly changing politicians and from the impact of elections, managing stakeholders is even more difficult for public sector organizations. This is specifically for the ethics topic very impactful, as the values and moral principles of politicians can be very diverse and typically are more diverse than the variations of replacements of executives and management.

ETHICAL RISKS – SUBJECT MATTER EXPERT INTERVIEW

Julia Bardmesser, financial industry strategic adviser and chief data officer

What do you see as the most significant ethical risks related to data (processing) in financial services?

Ethical risks are not yet as well understood as compliance risks. The major risks I see come from using customers' data in a way that is not approved or intended by a customer, for example, monetizing customer data without their knowledge or, even worse, without depersonalization.

The other set of ethical issues can arise from using historically biased data sets to train ML/AI models and perpetuating existing biases in the future decision-making, such as mortgage lending decisions.

How can these risks be mitigated?

For the first set of risks, robust end-to-end preference management capability fully integrated into all of the ways customer data is consumed would be an approach to mitigate these risks.

The industry is still very immature on the ways to mitigate the second set of risks. While the new approaches and tools to create unbiased data sets continue to be developed, as we can see with ChatGPT experiments, there is still a long way to go.

7.5 Conclusion

Organizations are taking advantage of having their house in order in terms of data quality and data governance as detailed in Chapters 5 and 6. This is instrumental for data compliance, privacy, and ethics. Organizations need to anticipate adjustments in legislation and values and moral principles. Agility and continuous monitoring are essential and avoid exposure. The only way to work for organizations is via fully automated processes. Human intervention increases noncompliance risks. Tooling to onboard, process, and store data and to manage identity and access management need to be fully integrated.

This sets requirements for the internal capabilities, and typically the in-house data quality manager is in charge. Organizations need to have sufficient knowledge in-house, despite the fact that many organizations are engaging with RegTechs to address the complexity and dynamics in the compliance area. In addition to in-house tooling and processes, the RegTechs also needs to be managed.

Notes

1 Also, proper cyber security is of utmost importance to ensure that organizations adhere to the law and are meeting the requirements of their regulators; nevertheless, this is a topic on its own and not the core topic of this book.
2 https://rti.gov.in/.
3 This will be detailed in Chapter 11.
4 In addition to European Union countries and the United States, examples are Brazil Lei Geral de Proteção de Dados (LGPD), China – Personal Information Protection law, India – Personal Data Protection Bill, Japan – Act on Protection of Personal Information and Taiwan Personal Data Protection Act.
5 Also, COVID apps during the pandemic raised privacy concerns. See – Ribeiro-Navarrete, S., Saura, J. R., & Palacios-Marqués, D. (2021). Towards a new era of mass data collection: Assessing pandemic surveillance technologies to preserve user privacy. *Technological Forecasting and Social Change, 167*, 120681.

PART 3

Digital transformation phase powered by data analytics[1]

In this part, three digital transformation phases are detailed. The emphasis is on the evolving role of data analytics over the three phases toward data-driven organizations. Innovation and the introduction and management of technology enable the change of business models and the addition of services to the portfolio of an organization.

To provide some context for this part, innovations such as the Internet of Things (IoT) and the metaverse can be a meaningful addition to the portfolio of an organization. Introducing these new technologies generates large volumes of data which can be used to improve performance, whereas blockchain technology and in the future quantum computing can power a digital transformation and enable the processing of data, among other things. Organizations that want to be successful in digital transformation must have the capability to adopt and integrate new technologies. Innovations need to be managed as a portfolio, and innovations that are piloted and cannot be scaled up must be disregarded.

Technology innovations go hand in hand with the maturing of data analytics. An organization must update its data processes and tooling, as well as improve their capabilities, not limited to data scientists. The chief digital officer and chief data officer are instrumental in orchestrating and aligning technology innovations, and maturing data analytics is key in successfully entering the next phase of the digital transformation. The focus of the chief digital officer is on implementing the change, whereas the focus of the chief data officer is on implementing structure to support the change. The structure includes a data strategy, as well as data processes and tooling.

The three digital transformation phases are detailed in Chapters 8–10: Digital 1.0, 2.0, and 3.0. Each phase will include a section on digital leadership, operating model, digital transformation model, digital governance, capabilities, data

DOI: 10.4324/9781003246770-10

leadership, and data analytics. The third phase, Digital 3.0, is the phase where digital has been embedded in the DNA of the organization and fully leverage data analytics. Any organization must quickly enter this phase to avoid being disrupted. These phases are summarized in the table below.

TABLE P3.1 Characteristics of the three phases of digital transformation

Characteristics	Digital transformation phase		
	Digital 1.0	Digital 2.0	Digital 3.0
	CIO-driven	Chief digital officer and chief data officer-driven	Board of management-driven
Digital leadership	Internal digital pioneer reporting to management	An external digital expert is aboard, which reports to management	Digital leadership embedded in DNA of the board of management and the senior leadership team
Operating model[2]	Tweaking operating models for pilot digital transformation projects	Redesigning operating models for core services/products and managing individual digital transformations initiatives	Redesigning operating models for all services/products and managing portfolio of digital transformation initiatives
Digital transformation model	Centrally-managed handful of digital transformation projects and experiment with agile ways of working	Increasing the number of digital transformation projects and setting up portfolio management for digital transformation projects and to implement agile ways of working (framework and processes)	Scaling up the number of digital transformation projects and managing the digital transformation projects as a portfolio and converting fully to agile ways of working

(Continued)

TABLE P3.1 (Continued)

Characteristics	Digital transformation phase		
	Digital 1.0	Digital 2.0	Digital 3.0
Digital governance	Directly managed by the board of management	Managed by steering committee that includes board of management members, senior business management, and innovation and technology leaders	Governed by the board of management and managed by senior business management and innovation and technology leaders
Capabilities	Intrinsically motivated professionals for both digital and data	Dedicated human resource management focus on attracting, retaining, and training digital and data professionals – including the setup of certification programs and career tracks	Full management focus on digital and data talent management
Data leadership	Chief data officer appointed and focus on data literacy	Chief data office in place including data governors and data quality managers and focus on improving the data quality, basic reporting, and develop a data management tooling strategy	Data ownership in place and data stewards appointed, and focus on advanced reporting and the implementation of data management tooling
Data analytics	Focusing on transaction data	Focusing on transaction data and internal data	Focusing on all data – including external data

Notes

1 Most organizations are embarking on Digital 3.0. For this reason, Chapters 8 (Digital 1.0) and 9 (Digital 2.0) are written in the past tense.
2 To ensure this characteristic is applicable to both private and public sector organizations we use "operating model" as a label. This can also be read as "business model."

8

DIGITAL 1.0 – SUPPLEMENTING THE GOING CONCERN WITH DIGITAL INITIATIVES[1]

In Digital 1.0, organizations are starting digital initiatives. The predominant focus is on the initiation of digital initiatives. A small team of digital enthusiasts ignites the digital transformation, and not much changes in operating models. The governance is simple, direct oversight from senior management. Digital initiatives are powered by data analytics but hindered by the lack of data and the low data quality. Not only is this a necessary first step in the implementation of digital transformations, but also there is a lot of room for improvement.

8.1   Digital 1.0 – Digital leadership

Digital leadership did not exist before this phase. Organizations needed to explore and find their way in the digital era. The difficulty many organizations faced was that the orientation of digital was too much toward technology. As a consequence, the information technology department was appointed to lead digital transformations in many organizations. Digital is about innovation powered by information technology.

Digital leadership in many organizations was born by way of an internal digital pioneer who initiated digital transformation projects. The background of the digital pioneer varied, sometimes sales and marketing and delivery management, but also general management. The digital pioneer has a passion for innovation. Typically, the digital pioneer had a long tenure in the organization and was well connected. This is instrumental in the initiation of digital transformation projects. Although pilot digital projects are typically small and stand alone, they can only be rarely executed in isolation.

In this phase, the digital leadership of management is limited to facilitating the digital pioneer. Whereas the digital experience of management is very limited, the

DOI: 10.4324/9781003246770-11

fear of missing out is a dominant factor to facilitate the digital pioneer. To enhance the digital leadership of the management team, the digital pioneer sometimes also puts forward efforts in driving a digital awareness program for the management. This can include a study trip abroad, experiencing digital transformations in other organizations, combined with company visits from technology partners and business schools (Beulen, 2018b). The costs and effort for the awareness program is significant; nevertheless, an intensive study trip can boost the digital leadership skills of the management.

8.2   Digital 1.0 – Operating model

Organizations started to tweak their operating models from the traditional transaction-based models to service subscription model (Caputo et al., 2021). Typically, the operating model was a combined operating model in which the traditional transaction is supplemented by a service fee. To keep the operating model simple, there were two contracts, one contract for the traditional transaction and the second contract for delivering the services. The services are delivered in addition to the traditional transaction.

Pricing and cost of services increases the risk exponentially. Therefore, the service contracts were typically short-term subscriptions. Organizations targeted trusted clients to build experience in service subscriptions. The pricing of these subscriptions was typically cost-plus pricing. To avoid additional complexity, organizations also provided the additional services internally and typically did not collaborate with partners in the delivery of services.

To be able to deliver the services in combination with the products, organizations embarked on aligning infrastructure in their organization. This enabled not only the provisioning of the services but also ensured that the data collection required for the pricing and costing of the services was available. Also, for many organizations interfacing their infrastructure with the infrastructure of their clients was technically a challenge. Also, organizations had to deal with compliance obligations and cyber security threats. As the maturity of the infrastructure was low and a significant part of the activities was not automated, the risks related to the infrastructure were substantial.

8.3   Digital 1.0 – Digital transformation model

Organizations centrally managed a handful of digital transformation projects. The digital projects were managed directly by senior management. The absence of defined key performance indicators for digital transformation success leads to a low success rate. Many digital transformation projects should have ended earlier. Also, it was not always possible to scale up. However, the direct and often personal involvement of senior management in decision-making on digital transformation projects was not always based on commercial grounds, but rather on pet projects (Fernandez et al., 2022).

To be able to innovate at pace, agile ways of working were introduced. Agile was limited to the information technology domain and was based on the Manifesto for Agile Software Development (Beck et al., 2001). Technical enthusiasts collaborated to innovate. The agility in digital transformations was to support omnichannel and had an emphasis on data and analytics.

Many organizations separated the digital transformation projects, even to the extent that they were housed on separate floors or even in separate buildings, and/or set up separate legal entities. The implication was that, in many organizations the best and most valued employees were involved in the digital transformation projects. This obviously had implications for the morale and motivation of the rest of the workforce, including attrition and even sabotage of digital transformation projects. In career development programs, organizations should have paid more attention to the HR implications for all employees. In addition, organizations experienced the impact of the pandemic, where employees were forced to work from home. Working from home negatively impacted the ability of organizations to innovate in the new agile context (Denning, 2018a, 2018b) and more specifically in a technology context with concepts such as DevOps (Beulen, 2019).

8.4   Digital 1.0 – Digital governance

Traditional governance was structured top-down and focused on the alignment of organization and information technology. The traditional governance was also very descriptive, including process, roles, and responsibilities. This was a good starting point for digital governance, which was not fundamentally different despite the nature of the digital transformation projects. Risks and dependencies were much more complex, and external conditions were much more dynamic, while technology was innovative (Chen, 2017; Green and Daniels, 2019). These differences resulted in direct involvement of the board of management in digital governance. They felt that digital transformation projects were of strategic importance and therefore required their full attention.

Due to the nature of digital transformation projects, digital governance required an effort and dedication which proved to be difficult to commit and live up to for members of the board of management. At a minimum, the members had to compromise on other responsibilities. As a consequence, there was much room for improvement. Also, the digital profile of most members was not at level (Beulen and Bode, 2021). Many organizations improvised by involving strategic advisory firms in initiating digital transformations, as well as in implementing and managing the governance. However, their one-size-fits-all "project management offices" offerings also lacked true experience in digital transformations.

8.5   Digital 1.0 – Capabilities

The capabilities were emerging with a small group of intrinsically motivated professionals for both digital and data. Digital capabilities were and are necessary to drive value (Khin and Ho, 2018). No organization had any experience and were figuring out on what capabilities were needed and how to grow these capabilities best. Organizations hand-picked their team members. The teams involved in digital transformations grew over time in terms of number of team members, as well as in capabilities. Basically, it was on-the-job learnings, sometimes combined with external consultants transferring their skill and building up the digital transformation skills of an organization.

The focus in this phase was predominantly on digital transformation projects and was less focused on data and data analytics. Data availability and data quality issues were resolved by the digital transformation project teams.

To develop the digital as well as the data and data analytics capabilities, well-developed information management and flexible infrastructures were and are essential (Levallet and Chan, 2018). The rise of agile ways of working, including short cycle sprints, made alignment between the organization and the agile teams, which consisted of organization representatives and technology specialists, more needed than ever. The agile frameworks were and are not fully addressing these challenges; proper information management was needed. Agile also increased the need for flexible infrastructures even further. Nevertheless, standard cloud deployment platforms, e.g. Amazon Web Services, Google, IBM, Microsoft, and Oracle, were and are a solid foundation for developing any functionality.

8.6   Digital 1.0 – Data leadership

In the early days, the management of organizations did not understand the importance of data. The main argument to appoint the chief data officer was that this "seemed to be the right thing to do." Mimicking was not necessary to provide the best starting position for a chief data officer. To put this into context, the chief data officer was a new role: 84% of the chief data officers were holding this role for first time in their organization (Egon Zehnder, 2019).

In shaping their role, chief data officers had a lot to discover and many chief data officers faced a dominant involvement of the IT department and experienced resistance from the InfoSec team, as well as from other parts of the organization. Unfortunately, the participation of the organization was also limited. Data was considered a problem that should be sorted out by the IT department.

The main objective of the chief data officer was to save money by improving the creation, management, and usages of data (Treder, 2020). Typical cost savings came from the reduction of headcount due to improved data quality. This was why the focus of most chief data officer's was on improving data literacy. Improving data literacy increases data quality (Inghirami, 2021).

By initiating data literacy programs, awareness in the organization increased. This included also awareness of the management, which was important for securing budget for future data-related projects. But it was also helpful in establishing relationships with the organization.

8.7   Digital 1.0 – Data analytics

The focus of data analytics was on getting insights from transaction data, as the data quality of transaction data in most organizations was reasonably good for descriptive analytics. This is basic dashboarding with a low-frequency refreshment of the report, at best weekly but typically monthly. This provided good insight into the historic performance. These insights could be used for making decisions and for the optimization of processes. The interpretation of the insights remains a management responsibility and this could not be considered as data-driven decision-making. Data analytics basically automated the process of information provisioning to the organization but still required a lot of manual activities. IT specialists performed most of these data analytics activities. Nevertheless, these are the first steps away from basing decisions on intuition only (McAfee et al., 2012).

The main driver for leveraging data analytics was the contribution to the performance of the organization (Ferraris et al., 2019). A lot of organizations struggled with unlocking the resources with the capabilities to perform data analytics activities (Amalina et al., 2020). Not many universities were offering programs in this area; typically, professionals with education in mathematics, statistics, or computer science were involved in data analytics activities.

TATA CONSULTANCY SERVICES CASE STUDY: GREENHOUSE PERFORMANCE SYSTEM (GPS) FOR A SWISS MULTINATIONAL FOOD AND DRINK PROCESSING CONGLOMERATE CORPORATION

Client business imperative

* The organization emitted around 92 million tons of Green House Gas (GHG) in 2018. The organization wanted to understand the detailed aspects behind the emission, so that this huge emission operation can be tackled. The major issues are –
* New and continuously evolving data platform – Existing Snowflake implementation – Lack in scalability of the systems
* No reference architecture readily available – The complexity was high with multiple business functions spread across value chain
* Lack of integration scenarios with tens of source systems – No data harmonization across existing source systems
* Data quality issues and varied data granularity – Huge data quality issues across systems
* Lack of streamlined business processes – Scattered processes and data owners are working in silos

Engagement scope

- The organization has selected TCS as the trusted partner to create a Greenhouse Performance System (GPS) – a global system for better tracking and management of its carbon emission at the corporate level. This multi-year global program aims to
- Measure and Analyze Greenhouse Gas (GHG) Emissions
- Track progress in emission reductions compared against corporate targets
- Provide greater transparency of the greenhouse gas (GHG) emissions across multiple business unit

The program is initiated with the completion of an Emissions management platform for Mexico Market.

Solution and differentiators

A data maturity framework was developed for storing and selecting the right emission factors based on emission factor provider, spend category, country of origin, confidence level
  Key solution features:

- Emission Factors Database – Snowflake based data warehouse with extensible and unified data model
- Calculation Methodology – Alignment with GHG protocol with customization of methodologies
- Scalability – All markets, all BUs, all applicable functions of the supply chain with consumer use and end-of-life, almost all emissions categories (in CSV scope)
- Security, Reliability, and High Availability – The solution is built on Azure cloud platform and Snowflake ensuring very high availability with all the security features
- Auditability – To enable external audits and reporting (e.g. CDP reporting)
- Cost Effective – A cloud-based low operational-cost solution

Business benefits/outcomes

The solution implemented by TCS enables the Swiss corporation to

- Adhere to their Climate Commitments by having a control on the Supply chain emissions
- Strengthen their brand positioning by laying out a Decarbonization capability through the control of Supply Chain emissions
- Penetrate into Green consumer markets by being a sustainable brand

Value delivered C&O benefits

By integrating primary data and creating a robust greenhouse performance management system, the organization is expected to reduce carbon footprint to a huge level and offset costs by 10%–20%, estimated CHF 100+ M over 5 years.

8.8 Conclusion

Digital 1.0 was just the beginning of the digital transformation journey. Organizations started to innovate and leverage data. In Table 8.1, the characteristics are summarized.

TABLE 8.1 Characteristics of the first digital transformation phase – Digital 1.0

Characteristics	Digital transformation phase, Digital 1.0 – CIO-driven
Digital leadership	Internal digital pioneer reporting to management
Operating model[2]	Tweaking operating models for pilot digital transformation projects
Digital transformation model	Centrally-managed hand full of digital transformation projects and experiment with agile ways of working
Digital governance	Directly managed by the board of management
Capabilities	Intrinsically motivated professionals for both digital and data
Data leadership	Chief data officer appointed and focus on data literacy
Data analytics	Focusing on transaction data

Notes

1 Most organizations are embarking on Digital 3.0. Therefore, this chapter is written in the past tense.
2 To ensure this characteristic is applicable to both private and public sector organizations, we use "operating model" as a label. This can also be read as "business model."

9

DIGITAL 2.0 – SILOED DIGITAL TO INTEGRATED DIGITAL[1]

In Digital 2.0, organizations rapidly mature their digital and data capabilities and are expanding their portfolio of digital initiatives; accordingly, the business models and operating models take shape. As a consequence, advanced governance is required, which involves business, innovation, and technology leaders. Data analytics is a key enabler in this phase. The chief data office is in place and large volumes of transaction and internal data are available to power digital initiatives. In addition to data analytics, basic reporting is available to support managers in performing their tasks, and this is a good second step in maturing the organization and enhancing value creation.

9.1   Digital 2.0 – Digital leadership

Many organizations had mixed experiences in the first phase of digital transformation. In order to enter into the second phase, organizations realized they needed an experienced digital leader. Many organizations decided to appoint a chief digital officer to lead the digital transformation, typically an external candidate. This definitely strengthened the digital leadership of many organizations. The profile of the chief digital officer is a change maker who is adaptable and who understands technology (Kane et al., 2019). The focus is on improving the customer/citizen experience, which drove the implementation of new business models. This phase required a more active involvement of the management (Eberl and Drews, 2021).

It is important that organizations invest in technology to power digital transformations. In order to facilitate digital transformations, challenges related to agile ways of working need to be managed (Bresciani et al., 2021). This was new territory for many organizations and required a culture that cultivates experimentation.

DOI: 10.4324/9781003246770-12

The management had to facilitate the experimenting on one hand, and on the other hand manage the portfolio of digital transformation projects on key performance indicators – this is not counterintuitive, as it is aligned with agile ways of working. It also required the need to hire curious employees.

Before entering into the next phase, Digital 3.0, the positioning of digital leadership at C-level, chief digital officer, was discussed. Having a board member accountable for digital transformations   hinders achieving the ultimate objective, in which all board members feel accountable for digital transformations. Therefore, many organizations debated whether to reset the positioning of the role and changed it to a director or head of digital transformation role. Digital transformations still have the full-time dedication of an experienced person and their team, but the role is no longer positioned at the C-level. This also changes the reporting line, typically from reporting to the chief executive officer to other members of the management team, such as the chief operating officer (Beulen, 2018b). For technology-centric organizations, reporting to the chief technology officer is also a viable option, reporting to the chief information officer is still not advisable, as digital transformations go beyond information technology.

9.2   Digital 2.0 – Operating model

After experimenting, the organizations focused on adjusting the operating models of core products and/or services. Additionally, contracts were transformed from a traditional contract supplemented by a service contract to service contracts only. The structure of these contracts was modular and included additional services such as guarantees and a service desk.

It was essential for organizations to start experimenting with these more advanced operating models and contracts, as competition was innovating at a rapid rate (Kraus et al., 2019). This experience was also helpful in the next phase in order to involve partners in the delivery of the services. Service contracts also resulted in closer relationships between the organization and its clients. Due to the relatively short contract duration of the service contracts, typically 12–24 months, unless the economic life of the product was longer, the threat of a vendor lock was relatively low.

In terms of pricing, organizations shifted from cost-plus pricing to value-based pricing (Cheng and Wang, 2022), as the comparability of the services was much harder than comparing the pricing for the transitional transaction and the service subscription in the previous phase. Value-based pricing in combination with scale opened opportunities to increase margin while at the same time decreasing the risk profile.

The internal and external infrastructure fully supported the delivery of the service and the exchange of information between the organization and its client. The involvement of humans in this highly automated technology reduces the risk profile. In addition, a lot of effort was put into the implementation of processes, which is essential since organizations were sharing data on a large scale. By agreed procedures, compliance and commercial interest were safeguarded.

9.3 Digital 2.0 – Digital transformation model

Many organizations have set up portfolio management to manage the growing number of digital transformation projects. The implementation of agile frameworks such as Scaled Agile Frameworks (SAFe) and Large-Scale Scrum (LeSS) helped organizations set priorities and facilitated adaptivity to change, but was not mature in most organizations. In addition, these frameworks provided guiderails and bridged the distance between team members. In most organizations, predominantly the information technology specialists worked in different organizations/locations (Busse and Weidner, 2020). While the number of organization representatives in the agile team was growing, which was positive and needed, the remote participation of the information technology specialist required a lot of management attention in many organizations. The availability of information technology specialists and the growth of the number of self-employed information technology specialists was a global challenge.

From managing digital transformation projects top-down, these frameworks enabled organizations to also manage their projects bottom-up (Denning, 2019). This increased the agile digital transformation projects' success rate and ensured improved budget control. Nevertheless, agile software development is based on story points, and output-based contracting is difficult, as a story point is not an objective unit that represents a certain effort. Building up experience over time eventually might result in the opportunity to contract based on a fixed price per story point (Beulen and Ribbers, 2021).

9.4 Digital 2.0 – Digital governance

In addition to agile frameworks, such as SAFe and LeSS, that were embedded in the digital operating model, there are a lot of frameworks that drove digital governance. The frameworks are as diverse as human rights frameworks from the EU, the council of Europe, or the OECD and 5G technology frameworks from ITU and IEEE, as described by Gasser and Almeida (2022, p. 30). This complicated digital governance, as it was difficult to ensure coherence in governing the digital transformation projects. Furthermore, the complexity of ethical, societal, and compliance issues increased (Gasser and Almeida, 2022). All of this in the context of the experimentation with new technologies in a growing number of digital transformation projects required a step up in digital governance. The traditional top-down approach and direct involvement of the board of management was no longer effective or efficient. Digital governance must grow with agile growth (Vaia et al., 2022). As a consequence of the conversion from waterfall projects to agile projects, dictating functional specifications was off the table and replaced by sprints. As it was still the early days for digital transformations, most organizations still felt that the involvement of members of the board of management was necessary, but they realized that digital governance required additional dedication and in-depth knowledge and experience with digital transformations. Therefore, organizations installed a steering committee to manage the portfolio of digital transformation projects, which consisted of members of the board of management and senior business managers, as well as innovation and technology leaders. This enabled the steering committee to assess proposed digital transformation projects, make informed decisions on projects in progress, and respond to changing internal and external circumstances, as detailed by Vaia et al. with their phrase "sense, decide, and respond" (2022).

9.5   Digital 2.0 – Capabilities

After ramping up, many organizations concluded that a more structural approach toward capability building was needed, but many organizations also experienced that building the capabilities was a challenge (Svahn et al., 2017). Therefore, many organizations instructed their human resource management to focus on attracting, retaining, and training digital and data professionals. This dedication resulted in a significantly increased attrition of digital and data subject matter experts, as well as in increased salaries and improved packages. Basically, organizations were searching for the same small group of experienced and talented professionals. As a result, retention management was added to the human resources department.[2] Many organizations offered specific digital and data career tracks, as well as knowledge certification programs.

Regarding the training of their employees, many organizations experienced that building dynamic capabilities, which are required to support digital transformation projects, was difficult (Warner and Wäger, 2019). In the dynamic capabilities, it was and is essential that an organization sense and shape opportunities and threats, seize opportunity, and maintain competitiveness (Teece, 2007, p. 1319). The first two were related to portfolio management, where maintaining competitiveness was more related to the capability to deliver digital transformation projects.

In addition to the above digital and data resource capabilities, organizations also needed to develop process capabilities to make the resources work effectively and efficiently. Furthermore, organizations also needed to develop cultural capabilities to make resources work together and resolve issues and/or address challenges if and when they occurred (Orji, 2019).

9.6   Digital 2.0 – Data leadership

The chief data officer started off as a one-person band and gradually transformed into a chief data office, including a data governor and data quality managers (Kunisch et al., 2022). This increased head count enabled the chief data officer to further improve data quality and get basis reporting in place, as well as to start developing a data management tooling strategy to drive future data management improvements, also maintaining relationships with stakeholders, including representatives of the organization, the IT department, and the InfoSec team. This is helpful in order to better understand data requirements and to be involved in innovation and digital transformation projects from the beginning. Finally, the chief data officer also focused on the development, maintenance, and management of the data policies, which include processes and data qualification.

Chief data officers were also collaborating with chief digital officers, who were also mostly new in their role (Singh and Hess, 2020). The focus of both the chief data officer and the chief digital officer was on earning money by developing data-related products and services which generated new revenue (Treder, 2020). Initially, these new data-related products and services were powered with internal data as the experience with sharing data of partners was limited, and also the perceived commercial sensitivity was (too) high. As the internal data quality improved, so did the risks related to generating revenues from data-related products and services.

9.7   Digital 2.0 – Data analytics

The volume of data had a significant growth, and the data involved was beyond transactional data. The focus in data analytics is on predictive analytics, on training algorithms to forecast potential future outcomes. This also opened up opportunities to enrich products and services with data. This perfectly aligns with the digital transformation agenda. Most organizations still limited themselves to internal data, as the collaboration in ecosystems was still immature. Most organizations were concerned about jeopardizing their commercial interests or their contribution to public value.

In order to structure data analytics, most organizations centralized the data scientist, which in turn led to the introduction of artificial intelligence. The central team enabled a more structural approach to obtaining information from data analytics. This was where data-driven decision-making got started. But also this is where cyber security concerns started to grow.

Data analytics provided competitive intelligence (Ranjan and Foropon, 2021), which was achieved by the maturing of data-driven decision-making. This was driving additional funding for data analytics; this included attracting professionals, proving training, and making tooling available. Nevertheless, data analytics was still the domain of too few professionals and was in most organizations not embedded in the organization.

TATA CONSULTANCY SERVICES CASE STUDY: CARGOTEC GOES DIGITAL IN CARGO HANDLING

Rapid value delivery with cloud-based IoT platform on AWS and advanced analytics

Challenge

Cargotec aims to leverage digital services to transform cargo handling operations. New digital services provide huge opportunities for cargo handling industry. Cargotec's vision is to be the leader in intelligent cargo handling by 2020. It plans to connect its entire fleet and achieve comprehensive data analytics capabilities. The key aspects and considerations were:

- Geographical spread of equipment across the globe
- Diverse business units and operations across the organization
- Disparate equipment conforming to varied specifications and protocols
- Integration with existing legacy systems to migrate them to a unified AWS Cloud Platform
- Need for remote onboarding and diagnostics
- Secure end-to-end data and communication channel

Solution

TCS and Cargotec co-create an IoT platform to collect, store, and analyze sensory data. TCS leveraged its Sensor Data Analytics IoT Framework (SDAF) and modernized data lake using native services on AWS, to design and build a cloud-based platform for Cargotec. Our integrated solution enabled IoT-based, real-time data collection, management, and monitoring strategies. We provided a scalable solution using cloud Infrastructure as a Service, with secure data channels between the equipment and the cloud.

Key features

- Data Lake and Big Data platform, enabling storage and reporting of data in large quantities, algorithm-driven actions, business process automation, and data publication through APIs
- Web portals and Business Intelligence (BI)-based reports for KPIs, alerts, notifications, and performance-related metrics to support internal and external customers
- Cloud-based automation, leveraging advanced AWS Cloud PaaS services
- Provisioning for real-time and advanced analytics on equipment data

9.8 Conclusion

In Digital 2.0, many organizations scaled up and matured their digital transformation journey. Organizations improved on all levels, and the digital transformation started to get traction, while data and data analytics are playing a crucial role. In the following table, the characteristics are summarized.

TABLE 9.1 Characteristics of the second digital transformations phase – Digital 2.0

Characteristics	Digital transformation phase, Digital 2.0 – chief digital and chief data officer driven
	Chief digital officer and chief data officer-driven
Digital leadership	An external digital expert onboarded, which reports to management
Operating model[3]	Redesigning operating models for core services/products and managing individual digital transformations initiatives
Digital transformation model	Increasing the number of digital transformation projects and setting up portfolio management for digital transformation projects and implement agile ways of working (framework and processes)
Digital governance	Managed by steering committee that includes board of management members, senior business management, and innovation and technology leaders
Capabilities	Dedicated human resource management focus on attracting, retaining, and training digital and data professionals – including the setup of certification programs and career tracks
Data leadership	Chief data office in place including data governors and data quality managers and focus on improving the data quality, basic reporting, and develop a data management tooling strategy
Data analytics	Focusing on transaction data and internal data

Notes

1 Most organizations are embarking on Digital 3.0. Therefore, this chapter is written in the past tense.
2 See for additional insights in retention and talent management (Beulen, 2009).
3 To ensure this characteristic is applicable to both private and public sector organizations, we use "operating model" as a label. This can also be read as "business model."

10
DIGITAL 3.0
Preparing for digital transformation 2025

In Digital 3.0, organizations have embedded digital into the organizational DNA in order to avoid being disrupted. Digital initiatives are scaled up and business models are revamped. The contribution of data analytics is significant and includes large volume of external unstructured data. This requires ownership of both digital transformation and data analytics, which must be a seamless collaboration between management and digital and data leaders. Also, talent management is essential in this phase more than ever. Furthermore, organizations are fully converting to agile ways of working, which sets, despite agile frameworks such as SAFe and LeSS, some governance challenges. In the data domain, organizations must sort out data ownership and data management tooling in order to be in control of the continuously increasing data volumes, as data powers the digital transformation projects and enables the implementation of new business models.

10.1   Digital 3.0 – Digital leadership

Many organizations are on the brink of entering the third phase of the digital transformation. The organizations concluded that the core leadership skills remain the same, including the evaluation of change and investing, owning the transformation and talent management, and empowering employees. But organizations also realize that they need to supplement their leadership team's need to acquire new skills (Kane et al., 2019).

In the third digital transformation, the agile way of working has become the norm (Bresciani et al., 2021). This is setting a significant challenge for digital leadership; managing agile at scale implies that communicating targets is beyond sending a simple top-down message. Engaged leadership is needed to ensure that

DOI: 10.4324/9781003246770-13

the objectives are met. In the aftermath of the pandemic, (partly) remote working is still the norm in many organizations. Whether this is related to agile software development or to fostering innovations, remote working has presented some additional challenges.

On top of that, the platform economy is emerging. Digital leaders need to make sure that the infrastructure is integrated to facilitate a platform (Benitez et al., 2022). This is not only an information technology architecture challenge, but it is also an enterprise architecture challenge. The positioning of an organization toward a platform is challenging for deciding which platform(s) you would like to participate in, as well as initiating your own platform as an alternative. Obviously, the combination of participating in one or more platforms and initiating your own platform is also a viable option that needs to be explored. In short, the rise of platforms has added an additional challenge for digital leaders.

10.2 Digital 3.0 – Operating model

Subscription-based operating models are expanded to all products and services (Cheng and Wang, 2022). In the delivery of the products and the services, artificial intelligence is becoming more and more important. On the one hand, subscription-based operating models drive efficiencies for the organization, and reduces the risk profile. On the other hand, it drives additional insights for their clients, which creates additional value (Chen et al., 2021b). Public sector organizations create public value by collaborating with private sector organizations, typically social entrepreneurs, in public-private partnerships (Battisti, 2019).

An increasing number of subscriptions includes the collaboration with partners (Caputo et al., 2021). This increases the complexity of value chains and the complexity of collaboration. Sharing of data is becoming more complex; in the processes, the ownership of data needs to be agreed, as well as the cost and benefit allocation related to data sharing needs to be included in the contracts. The commercial interest of the partners and the client's interests need to be taken into account. As a consequence, the duration of the contracts is increasing.

The collaboration with partners and data sharing also increase the dependencies, especially in the context that organizations can be a partner in one market and at the same time a competitor in another market. For public sector organizations, the interests of the citizens drive their behavior (Battisti, 2019).

10.3 Digital 3.0 – Digital transformation model

The organization has evolved with greater maturity and agility, where all organization representatives, including information technology representatives, work seamlessly in agile digital transformation projects. Agility has fully expanded to the entire organization. This is why, for organizations that have adopted agile ways of working, business and information technology alignment as described by Henderson and Venkatraman is still relevant (1999). Portfolio management of digital transformation projects sets priorities for the different projects, where agile frameworks such as SAFe and LeSS set priorities within projects.

In addition to the frameworks, they need an agile architecture (Dragičević and Bošnjak, 2019). This is a bit of a balancing act, as an architecture provides structure and clarity on roles and responsibilities, and it also enables efficiencies. On the other hand, architecture limits the degrees of freedom of agility teams, which might hinder effectiveness. In this day and age, organizations are considering multiple technology stacks for their software development to address the needs and preferences of the information technology team and to avoid a vendor lock-in.

Finally, in innovating, leveraging ecosystems is also important. Collaborating with partners is an integral part of any digital operating model. Finding the right partners and maintaining relationships with partners is essential. The number of partners and the rate of change in partners is increasing. This makes setting up ecosystems much harder. There is also a need to be a network ecosystem fit in order to be successful in digital transformations (Xu and Koivumäki, 2019).

10.4　Digital 3.0 – Digital governance

Due to the growing number of digital transformation projects and the nearly 100% shift toward agile ways of working, digital governance has become even more important (Chen, 2017). The budgets related to the digital transformation projects have increased accordingly. Financial commitments need to be managed and organizations must adopt fast experimentation, including acceptance of failure (Beulen, 2018b). Also, organizations need to ensure their multidisciplinary teams are disciplined and cooperative in resolving issues, blockers, and dependencies.

Due to the increasing importance of ecosystems for digital transformation projects, digital governance is no longer based on closed organization boundaries, but rather is has permeable boundaries (Vaia et al., 2022). Digital governance has to be expanded on the strategic level of who our partners are and who our future partners will be, as well as on the tactical level of how issues with partners in the digital transformation project are dealt with (Green and Daniels, 2019).

Due to the number and size of the digital transformation projects portfolio, digital governance requires a dedicated steering committee with senior business managers, and innovation and technology leaders, supported by a project management office, preferably internally staffed, to manage the portfolio. Due to the importance of the digital transformation projects, this steering committee is supplemented by direct oversight of the board of management. Their governance ensures that there is a next level to ensure alignment with the strategy, to reflect and, if necessary, to respond quickly and serve as the escalation level.

10.5　Digital 3.0 – Capabilities

Due to the increase of digital transformation projects and the full adoption of agile ways of working, many organizations have a full focus on digital and data talent management. This means that in the recruiting process as well as in the assessment and performance reviews of staff, there is an expectation that, to a certain degree any employee has digital and data capabilities. Each year the expectation of these capabilities exceeds the expectation of the previous year. By raising the bar, organizations are working toward embedding digital and data capabilities in their DNA.

This requires a strategic renewal of organizational culture (Warner and Wäger, 2019, pp. 334–335). On the one hand, organizations require deep specialized knowledge to innovate, to add value, and to remain relevant, and on the other hand, it is also important for organizations to ensure that strategic objectives are met. This requires a lot of alignment and stakeholder management so that the organization continues to operate in a coherent way toward the strategic objectives. This is even more complicated as, due to the rise of ecosystems, collaboration with partners also needs to be managed. Managing the partnership is becoming a key and core capability of many organizations. Not many organizations are excelling in this capability (Beulen, 2022a).

10.6   Digital 3.0 – Data leadership

After the internal focus of the chief data officer, it is time to focus on the organization. It is important to ensure proper ownership of the data in the organization and to designate data stewards to support the data owners. The chief data officer has to orchestrate this and provide support to both the data owner and the data stewards. In addition, the chief data office focuses on the implementation of advance reporting and data management tooling. Advance reporting is established in close cooperation with data owners and data stewards. Information needs drive the setup and structure of the advanced reporting. For the implementation of data management tooling, the IT department and the InfoSec team are partners for the chief data office. The objective for data management tooling is to avoid human involvement; fully automated data processing is the ultimate goal.

The chief data officer has the objective of staying ahead of competition by leveraging data (Treder, 2020). This is quite a step up from generating additional revenue. Innovation and continued collaboration with the chief digital officer are needed and happening. Through improved data quality and growing experience with managing ecosystems and collaboration with partners, the reuse of data has become more feasible, but most organizations are still in the early stages.

By means of providing a perspective, in many organizations, the chief data officer is still not an established role (Kunisch et al., 2022), or the organization decides to position the role of the chief data officer on management level, e.g. director of data and data analytics or head of data and data analytics. Depending on the circumstances this might be justifiable, as C-level is not required in any organization.

10.7   Digital 3.0 – Data analytics

Data analytics is performed on all data, including external data (Amalina et al., 2019). As a consequence, the data volumes are unprecedented. The focus of data analytics is on prescriptive analytics, drawing specific recommendations from artificial intelligence algorithms. This makes a full focus on cyber security even more necessary – data management, tooling, access management, and data classification remains a top priority. But also, this opens up excellent opportunities to perform data analytics and gain insights and transform an organization into a data-driven organization (Hariri et al., 2019). Organizations need to think through their knowledge management. Due to the increased data literacy, the employees also have an increased responsiveness to knowledge (Ferraris et al., 2019). Furthermore, a natural outcome of increased data literacy is increased data democratization. This makes data management and data quality an imperative.

Organizations are also introducing machine learning, which sets requirements for ethical awareness, in addition to the revisions organizations need to make related to their data governance in ethical rule boards.

As a next step, following competitive intelligence as defined by Ranjan and Foropon (2022), organizations are using data analytics to provide ecosystem intelligence, which requires the sharing of data outside of the organization. This will be detailed in Chapter 12.

As a consequence, in combination with the growing pool of employees with data-analytic skills, data analytics is becoming part of the DNA in many organizations. Performing data analytics is no longer the exclusive domain of the central data science teams, many units in the organization also have their own data science teams. Furthermore, citizen data scientists work alongside these decentralized data science teams.

TATA CONSULTANCY SERVICES – GOOD PRACTICES AND ROADMAPS

Themis Michaelides – Tata Consultancy Services
Global head advisory and consulting for BTG – data and analytics

Good practices that help organizations head in the right direction are first and foremost the importance of understanding the data maturity perspective. How mature is an organization's data strategy? This is about understanding what you have at the moment, where do you want to go, and identifying the gaps to getting there. Themis Michaelides: "This is very important. Once there is a clear understanding of an organization's data maturity, then you're in a better position to make some decisions on the roadmap." Part of the maturity is having an organizational-wide data strategy in place that is aligned with the business strategy, vision, and goals and identifying what you are trying to achieve as an organization. This is part of the broader maturity journey which lays out the roadmaps to achieving organizational goals.

For roadmaps, it is good practice to be a bit pragmatic, not try to boil the ocean. This is especially true for large complex multinational organizations. Themis Michaelides:

> Start with a point of view that you can build on, which could be finding the right people to support you or finding the right kind of maturity in the organization, build from there and develop the right approach. These are the key components that are quite important to aligning analytics to organizational goals.

Looking for these capabilities, educating staff becomes a priority to achieving those goals. One strategy is educating your own people and bringing them up the ladder, which could be a very good strategy. The other is supplementing existing staff with the right profile, the right experience, and then use this to further mature. Themis Michaelides: "The pace of maturity in today's organizations favors the supplemental approach. Bring in the right skills where you need them and use those skills to educate your own." Building a strategy to educate everyone as a dependency to moving on with the roadmap is probably not going to give the velocity needed to achieve goals and keep the pace.

There are four good benchmarks for organizations to measure their maturity level and priorities, enabling them to develop a roadmap to address those priorities and aligning the roadmap to the business strategy. These four benchmarks are (1) governance, (2) leadership, (3) technology, and (4) incentives. Themis Michaelides also provides a sector perspective.

Governance

Governance builds the understanding of who is accountable and who is responsible, and that will drive to some extent where you are going to start – with business priorities. This is key because business professionals will always want to know what's in it for me, why am I doing this, why should I spend time? What does the business professional gain from taking ownership and accountability for data? Themis Michaelides:

> The concept of 'my data' is the correct kind of thinking. Understanding the data and what does good quality data look like is inherent in the business DNA to successfully run their business every day. Governance is just a way to formalize this business knowledge.

Depending on the size of the organization, governance models tend to be either centralized or federated. Large organizations tend to have more success with federated models. To be successful, a federated approach must have clear guidelines and policies for the varying business-driven governance models to stay aligned with the overall data strategy. Generally, a Center of Excellence (CoE) will be in control of the approach to driving data strategy and frameworks. While the constituent parts of the federated model will have their own capabilities to make their own decisions based on what works for that business, but within the guidelines and frameworks set by the CoE.

Leadership

Consensus from business leaders is another key indicator of maturity. Embarking on a journey to build out an analytics capability has to be led from the top. There have to be oversight and governance components to ensure analytics is focused on the right priorities, meeting the business needs, and the right controls are in place to ensure that results are accurate, trustworthy, and ethical. Themis Michaelides: "A clear vision, funding, and support from the top is critical to ensuring a successful analytics journey."

Support for the data analytics program must be part of the C-Suite agenda. The C-Suite is there to provide oversight and priority for the program, ensure it is progressing as planned, and empower the organization to make decisions at all levels, but not driving it in a dogmatic way. Themis Michaelides: "The best people to make decisions about data are the people who actually own, understand, and work with the data – that's where you find the edge in data-driven decision making." C-Suite support for federated models empowers the organization without dictating. Chief Data Officers are now joining the board as priority and focus for data analytics is morphing into various data flavors across the traditional roles – Chief Information Officer, Chief Financial Officer, Chief Digital Officers all have certain data elements to consider and manage. The Chief Data Officer is now a peer, setting data management standards for their organization.

Leaders need to clearly communicate so that people understand what the organization is trying to achieve and why these goals are in place. Having the right experts in place to execute these goals is crucial. Themis Michaelides:

> Anyone can Google and find ten different frameworks for data governance, but having the experience of implementing and executing any of the frameworks is what sets experts apart from amateurs. For example, a retail organization brought in new leadership for data governance and the first

thing they changed was the approach to the people. This breathed new life into the program, brought it in a new direction, and improved adoption. Every organization has a unique people culture, and the data governance approach must adapt to the culture.

Data-driven leadership at the highest levels of the organization sets the tone for creating data-driven organizations. Intuition is supplemented and backed up by analysis to make good decisions. Themis Michaelides:

> Creating data-driven organizations means you give people the data where they need it, when they need it, and with good quality, which reaps the benefits of improved data-driven decision-making from all levels of the organization with the increase of data democratization.

Technology

It is good to have an understanding of the various technologies in play and not be hesitant to experiment with emerging technologies. Themis Michaelides: "There are new technologies emerging all the time, and there is no one silver bullet to solve all data governance concerns." Best of breed technologies must be pieced together like a puzzle to solve for various business and data governance challenges. Often emerging technologies can provide new insights and new perspectives for elusive solutions.

One key emerging technology trend is data mesh and data fabric. Many organizations will begin looking at this technology over the next two to three years to further support data democratization. Understanding will grow that having data in a single data lake is not the answer to everything. Themis Michaelides: "Data mesh and fabric will enable accessing data, sharing data, and creating policies and procedures to govern the data – all at the source."

The emerging data mesh trend is another factor in the convergence of IT and business skills. Business professionals are gaining a greater understanding of the IT data perspective. It used to be IT's problem to create a report with a sliver of information and the business had to deal with it. Themis Michaelides: "Now more business professionals are involved in analyzing more data than ever before, asking their own multilayered questions and finding their own insights." There is a lot of convergence of analytics skills, which is linked to the benefits of data democratization. Data mesh and fabric technologies will only further enable business analytics over the next few years. Access to trustworthy data at source will bring analytics and data-driven decision-making into the everyday workspace. The convergence of data analytics skills will transform to become true business skills, achieving the "Data Citizen" status. Adoption of data mesh technologies promises to accelerate this transformation.

Incentives

The fourth good practice is to build incentives for people to use analytics in their day-to-day job. With data democratization, data analytics is no longer just in the data science or technology domain. Analytics now becomes part of every team's workspace to some extent. It is quite important to build the kind of culture of incentives for people to use data analytics as part of their day-to-day work.

Incentives for analytics usually come down to financials: either cost savings from synergies identified by the analytics or increased revenue from opportunities identified by the analytics. Depending on where a person is in the organization, if it is part of their job is to manage costs and/or increase revenues, then analytics becomes even more important. Enabling these business professionals with access to trusted data and training on analytics tools will incentivize them to incorporate analytics into their daily work practices. Themis Michaelides:

> From the executive level, analytics is incentivized by time-to-market for both cost savings and revenue initiatives – the ability to make good decisions in a faster way with trusted data will provide the edge to outperform the market, which is driving analytics at the top level.

Sector perspective

Financial Services is a bit more ahead of the game overall because purely from a compliance perspective, there is a carrot and stick kind of approach. This sector was forced to adapt. On the Retail Consumer Packaged Goods (CPG) side, especially retail, it's all about the customer. The marketing divisions are the earliest adapters of data analytics for analyzing customer preferences and defining product strategy. Digital transformation in Retail is all about an enhanced customer experience. If a retail organization does not have a digital strategy in place, they will not be able to reach customers through the customer journey. Improving the customer journey can mean the difference between success and failure.

Sectors that are a bit more behind include for example Manufacturing to some extent, as well as Travel/Hospitality, although you'd expect them to be more customer-centric. For the manufacturing sector, governing the avalanche of data from inventory management, supply chain optimization, demand forecasting, logistics, quality improvement, and countless other important metrics can be a heavy burden to bear.

For Hospitality, many organizations are embarking on analytics programs to improve the guest experience and are looking to other industries, such as retail, CPG, and banking for inspiration on building analytics cultures and programs. However, many organizations are struggling with sluggish implementations or are failing to see value from their efforts. Themis Michaelides: "Often it is because the organization fails to sufficiently plan for the data requirements because data exists in a myriad of proprietary and highly customized systems such as property management, CRM, and central reservations." Also, often data generated from the same vendor can look very different. This complex data infrastructure represents a huge barrier to success for the Hospitality analytics program.

10.8 Conclusion

In Digital 3.0, organizations have a full focus on digital transformation, and data and analytics are critical in the continuous innovation and advancing collaboration in ecosystems. Organizations improved further on all levels, and the digital transformation thrives on data and data analytics. In Table 10.1, the characteristics are summarized.

TABLE 10.1 Characteristics of the third digital transformation phase – Digital 3.0

Characteristics	Digital transformation phase, Digital 3.0 – board of management driven
Digital leadership	Board of management-driven Digital leadership embedded in DNA of the Board of management and the senior leadership team
Operating model[a]	Redesigning operating models for all services/products and managing portfolio of digital transformation initiatives
Digital transformation model	Scaling up the number of digital transformation projects and managing the digital transformation projects as a portfolio and converting fully to agile ways of working
Digital governance	Governed by the board of management and managed by senior business management and innovation and technology leaders
Capabilities	Full management focus on digital and data talent management
Data leadership	Data ownership in place and data stewards appointed, and focus on advanced reporting and the implementation of data management tooling
Data analytics	Focusing on all data – including external data

[a] To ensure this characteristic is applicable to both private and public sector organizations we use "operating model" as a label. This can also be read as "business model."

PART 4

Data sharing-centric digital transformations

Not so long ago, data sharing in most organizations was limited to sharing internal data. This is a good starting point, but it is not sufficient for achieving digital transformation success. In the context of the growing importance of ecosystems, data must be shared with partners. This is an additional requirement and is not straightforward. Many organizations are struggling with externally sharing the data and, as a consequence, with making partnerships work. The dynamics in many ecosystems do not make external data sharing easier.

To enable data sharing, organizations need to adjust their data management and governance. This provides the internal perspective on data sharing and is detailed in Chapter 11. Furthermore, there are competitive and sustainability, compliance, privacy, and ethical considerations. This provides the external perspective and is detailed in Chapter 12. In the last chapter of this part, the structuring of partnerships in ecosystems and the data sharing are detailed. The degree of exclusivity and the contractual relationships between partners in ecosystems are also detailed. This chapter provides guidance on how to make data sharing work.

DOI: 10.4324/9781003246770-14

PART 4

Data sharing-centric digital transformations

11

DATA MANAGEMENT AND GOVERNANCE IMPLICATIONS OF DATA SHARING

Data sharing in organizations is essential in digital transformations. This sets significant internal challenges for data management and governance. For data management, these challenges are not only data and identity & access management, but also data classification, as there are also competitive as well as compliance risks. Monitoring data usage has become more important than ever. The challenges in data governance are related to the expanded use of data, data analytics is no longer limited to a central team of data scientists. Organizations need to facilitate innovation, which often starts with sharing data. How can organizations structure data sharing in the early stages of establishing ecosystems? In short, organizations need to design their data sharing approach. Internal guidance is required, and this requires an update of the data strategy. Also, the concept of governing data prevails over data management (Vial, 2023), as this facilitates innovation in iterative governance mechanisms and has a focus on evaluation in context.

11.1 Identity and access

Organizations that innovate and collaborate, including sharing data, need to do so faster. This implies that properly working identity and access management is essential. Including external users presents additional challenges, predominantly in identity management. Organizations need to align with technical and security standards and protocols. In particular in international collaborations, due to multiple jurisdictions, this is not straightforward. By stacking requirements, sometimes it becomes no longer practical and might become a blocker for sharing data or even for setting up or continuing the collaboration.

DOI: 10.4324/9781003246770-15

Many organizations create a mutual domain where the partnering organizations process, store, and analyze data. Organizations typically outsource the hosting and management of a mutual domain to ensure that responsibilities and liabilities are clear.

Regarding access management, partnering organizations who share data need to map the roles of all partnering organizations and align on access rights. Furthermore, organizations need to align on the classification of the shared data,[1] and especially for data generated over time, this is complex. Data analytics will potentially impact the classification of shared data over time. As a consequence, partnering organizations that share data need to periodically review the mapping of roles and the mapping of the data classification. Not limited to partnering organizations that share data, deleting data is an important measure to avoid unwanted or not legitimate situations. The deletion of any data needs to be monitored and logged, as well as based on unambiguous and aligned policies and guidelines. This is doable, but it is not always as straightforward as an organization might think.

11.1.1   RBAC and ABAC

For identity and access management, many organizations have implemented a combination of role-based access controls (RBAC[2]) and Attribute-Based Access Controls (ABAC[3]). In identity management, many measures can be implemented such as biometrics, password, public-key infrastructure, single sign-on, token, smart card, and two/multifactor authentication. We must also consider organizations using Lightweight Directory Access Protocols (LDAPs) (Tsegaye and Flowerday, 2020). These network protocols detail how data from a directory service can be accessed, for example TCP/IP. For access management organizations can apply role-based, situation-based, attribute-based, discretionary, or mandatory rule sets (Tsegaye and Flowerday, 2020).

11.1.2   Emergency access controls

Emergency access controls are also relevant in the context of digital transformations and collaboration in ecosystem partnerships, and both result in unpredictable demands in terms of data sharing, data analytics, and users. As a consequence, emergency access controls are required to facilitate these dynamics (Nazerian et al., 2019). The dynamic can manifest itself as an emergency, which is an anticipated emergency situation. In this situation, policies can be pre-defined and, if not pre-defined, an organization has to deal with it as an exception. There are unanticipated emergency situations, where policies cannot be pre-defined (Nazerian et al., 2019). For improving security, the concept of Binding of Duty can be implemented to enforce security policies. This entails that an organization performing an action is bound to perform another action.

When initiating a partnership, the involved partners should be prepared for both emergency situations. For anticipated emergency situations, playbooks have to be prepared, whereas for the unanticipated emergency situations, scenarios and starting points have to be prepared. The playbooks as well as the scenarios have to be evaluated frequently as the context, including the competitive landscape, and applicable legislation and regulatory requirements might have changed. Typically, a semiannual review is sufficient.

11.2   Advanced data classification

Advanced data classification is needed to enable data sharing – partners need to operate off the same playbook. Individual organizations can have their own additional classifications, but the baseline set of classifications must be agreed across the ecosystem to eliminate friction points and ensure smooth data sharing. Furthermore, it also avoids data loss and includes procedural and technical controls; despite these controls, user awareness is important. The user needs to understand the sensitivity of the data and the implications of data analytics on the sensitivity of data. In particular, the latter is important for citizen data scientists; the data scientist typically has a better understanding of the sensitivity of data as they have more experience in data analytics. Nevertheless, this requires periodic programs, tailored to the specific data user groups of the partnering organizations. These programs can also include certification, which can be linked as a prerequisite to access and analyze the data.

The sensitivity of the data drives the risk level and sets the data classification. By data classification level, partnering organizations need to decide on the encryption level, type of storage, and transmittal requirements. This sets requirements for the enterprise and information technology architecture and the alignment of architecture between organizations that share data.

To set data classifications, there are several standards that can be applied, including the ISO 27001 & 27002 and the NIST special publication NIST 800-60 Volumes 1 and 2 – Guide for Mapping Types of Information and Information Systems to Security Categories. For ISO 27001 specifically, the control objective A.8.2 "Information Classification," and for ISO 27002 specifically, control objective 5.12 ("Classification of Information"), are relevant. The DLP technical controls are supportive in the implementation of data classification in partnership where data is shared outside the organization.

TATA CONSULTANCY SERVICES CASE STUDY: SCOTTISH NATIONAL DOG CONTROL DATABASE

Business context

The Scottish Government wants to establish a Scottish National Dog Control Database which will enable all 32 Local authorities and Police Scotland to seamlessly discover and exchange Dog Control Notice (DCN) data recorded within Scotland in a controlled environment. Currently, there is no Central Platform/ database to discover and access DCNs issued by local authorities.

What was done

An interactive prototype of a national database for dog control notices was developed as Proof of Concept with design thinking workshops during the discovery phase of the pilot.

- Conducted user interviews and workshops to identify key challenges
- Designed a prototype to demonstrate the user journeys and validated them with target users
- Ingest anonymized Dog Control Notice data and data structures used within the participating Local Authorities
- Identify reusable workflows and processes and inform the specification of a more permanent solution (including the development of a National Dog Control Database by the end of December 2021
- Build data pipelines to ingest DCN data and enabled dashboards and reporting through TCS Dexam
- Derive useful learning for the Improvement Service and for participating Councils

Value delivered

- Visibility of DCN data across Councils and Police Scotland
- DCN data easily searchable and discoverable to key internal and external stakeholders who need to be able to access this information if there is an incident
- Implemented the pilot requirements in a manner fully compliant with the DCN legislation in Scotland
- Created dashboards and heatmaps and visualized data about Dog Control Notices
- Dexam can be a strategic enabler for exchange of data to cater other use cases also other than DCN

11.2.1 Classification of open data

When sharing data, specific attention is required for open data, as in data analytics, open and restricted data can be used in conjunction. The insights coming from data analytics of hybrid data obligate participating organizations to decide how the insights will be classified. Will this be an expansion of the open data set? Nevertheless, by applying the FAIR principles (findable, accessible, interoperable, and reusable),[4] which originate from academic research, and making the new insights part of the open data set might have commercial or societal implications.

This sets requirements for implementing open data metrics, which needs to be responsible and evidence-based. Specifically for open data, it is important to ensure that supportive infrastructures and maintenance are in place, and for open data this is more complicated, as it needs to be provided by a neutral organization, where ecosystem and partnership agreements for allocating costs and providing support can be based on the anticipated added value for each of the involved organizations.

11.3 Monitoring data usage

Monitoring the data usage is important for ensuring compliance with data policies, security policies and cost allocation of data usage. Data policies focus on data identity and access management in the context of internal data users as well as data users from partners, whereas security policies focus on ensuring cyber resilience. The cost allocation of data usage is becoming more important due to increasing data volumes and frequency of running queries.

11.3.1 Data usage – Data policies

To enforce the data in line with data policies, organizations need to implement data management tooling and processes. If an organization has done a proper job on both accounts, the organization will be in control. However, the allocation of access rights will involve human interventions, including management approvals. This includes a "one-click" access removal of an off-boarded user from all systems. In data management and data discoverability, it is crucial to ensure that all systems can be automatically closed with "one click" of a human. Also, there can be abrupt changes required in the allocated rights, for example, when there are fraudulent suspicions toward an individual employee or employee of a partner, or toward a partner. Therefore, monitoring the access rights remains important and necessary. Monitoring is available 24/7 to quickly identify anomalies, as well as periodically to ensure that the rights of users related to data and specific data sets are in line with the data policies. Typically, the chief data office is involved in ensuring that 24/7 monitoring is in place, which is mostly outsourced, like cyber security monitoring. Also, the periodic reporting will typically be performed by the chief data office. Most organizations conduct a monthly check on the rights of the users.

11.3.2 Data usage – Security policies

In the context of cyber security, the classification of data is important, as this drives the measure an organization implements to protect their data. This includes monitoring data usage. In the context of cyber security, the monitoring of data is outsourced by many organizations, as this is a 24/7 responsibility. Most organizations are simply too small and/or lack the expertise to perform this task. Organizations typically employ a senior cyber security expert who will, in close collaboration with the chief data office, engage with the external monitoring service provider.

Furthermore, compliance has become more important for many organizations, for sector- or antitrust regulators, but also for more generic privacy regulators. Ensuring that data usage is compliant is therefore becoming more complex and will become even more complex due to anticipated increased regulatory compliance. This is where RegTechs can support organizations to be compliant.

11.3.3 Data usage – Cost allocation

Volumes of data and the query frequency are increasing at an unprecedented speed. As a consequence of that, required processing power and storage capacities are increasing accordingly. This will have a cost impact, despite the continuous decreasing unit prices for processing power and storage. Most data users are simply not aware of the costs associated with their data usages; in many organizations, the costs related to data usage are an integral part of the IT costs and are allocated by the number of employees or the revenue of an organization. This must change; organizations need to provide cost transparency related to data usage and chargeback models for individual organizational units to account for storage consumption. It is important to replace federated flat rate models, as data is just growing too quickly. Organizations should be aware of their consumption and the anticipated return on investment. This requires not only the implementation of tooling but also setting up awareness sessions to explain and guide users on how costs can be saved. This can also be used in the cost allocation between partners who collaborate in an ecosystem.

Furthermore, there are also architectural considerations that have to be taken into account. Most organizations are currently turning to cloud processing and cloud storage solutions. Uploading in the cloud does not trigger any charges from the cloud service provider, whereas downloading triggers charges. This is becoming more important, as most organizations currently have a dual or even multi-cloud strategy, e.g. Amazon Web Services, as well as Azure and potentially also Google, IBM, and/or Oracle cloud. The charging mechanisms impact how to build the application landscape on top of the cloud solutions.

11.4 Data-steering committee

Sharing data requires additional governance mechanisms. Organizations are beginning to implement a data-steering committee which ensures proper use of data in the organization, as well as in collaboration for data sharing with external partners; see, for example, data-steering committees in the medical sector in the European Union[5] or the data management committee of the University of Richmond in the US.[6] Furthermore the data management committee is branded as a data leadership committee by Tableau.[7] The basis for the data-steering committee is the data policy. Therefore, the chief data officer in close cooperation with the CIO is in the lead. Typically, (selected) data owners are also members of the data-steering committee to ensure that their interests are also safeguarded. The data-steering committee also creates support for data sharing. The data-steering committee can build on this trust by initiating an (external) audit on compliance of the data policy. Typically, a data-steering committee meets every quartile. In these meetings, not only are risks and compliance discussed and adjustments of data policies are approved and also opportunities in data analytics and data sharing are discussed and explored.

11.4.1 Data committee: Royal FloraHolland[8]

For over a hundred years, Royal FloraHolland (RFH) has been a cooperative in the floriculture market that represents the interests of growers. And it will continue to do so by creating and maintaining the best possible marketplace, as well as in our fast-changing global floriculture market.[9] The venue of RFH is €5.6b (2021). RFH has their Floriday trading platform, which in 2021 transacted over €1b of direct sales.[10]

RFH has established a data committee at the end of 2020 to discuss and evaluate the implementation of RFH's data and information policy. The data committee monitors compliance with the data and information policy. The data committee consists

---

DATA COMMITTEE ROYAL FLORAHOLLAND – EXTERNAL AUDIT[12]

As a platform, Floriday provides a secure environment for confidential grower and buyer data. That was the conclusion of the second independent audit conducted by Royal FloraHolland at the request of the data committee. The audit in 2021 had already confirmed the effectiveness of measures previously taken to ensure Floriday users' confidentiality of their information. The current audit re-examined this over a longer period and also tested its efficacy.

The audit involved looking at strictly confidential data in Floriday. This means the information to which only the relevant grower and buyer have access. Consider the price agreements in contracts and the consumer prices on the stickers. It has been established that strictly confidential data will not be shared outside of Floriday. It has also been established that the limited group of Royal FloraHolland employees, who have access to these data, can only view them on account of their position. Think of a Floriday support person. They must be able to support users when they need help.

Periodic audit of accounts – One of the recommendations from the audit is that growers and buyers should be reminded to periodically have their permissions checked in Floriday. From this fall, all main users will receive an email twice a year asking them to check which people have access to the Floriday account and with which permissions they have access. It also recently introduced the option for users to use two-factor authentication while logging in to increase account security.

Data Policy – https://www.floriday.io/en/data-policy

---

of the CIO, manager of Business Intelligence and data science, representatives from the growers, the buyers, the transporters, and an independent data expert.[11]

11.5 Conclusion

Data sharing has further complicated data management and data governance. This is where the chief data officer can help to structure and reduce the risk profile by setting and maintaining data policies and addressing the data aspects in security policies, as well as providing input to the enterprise architecture and information technology architecture.

Also, by implementing the data steering committee as an additional governance mechanism, organizations are able to better structure data sharing with their partners. Doing so will facilitate the communication, alignment between partners, and transparency.

Notes

1 This will be explored in more detail in the next paragraph, Section 11.2.
2 See NIST INCITS 359-2012 for a definition of RBAC: https://csrc.nist.gov/Projects/Role-Based-Access-Control.
3 See NITS for a definition of ABAC: https://www.nist.gov/publications/guide-attribute-based-access-control-abac-definition-and-considerations-1.
4 See also https://www.go-fair.org/fair-principles/.
5 https://www.ema.europa.eu/en/documents/scientific-guideline/guideline-data-monitoring-committees_en.pdf.
6 https://itgovernance.richmond.edu/data-management/index.html.
7 https://www.forbes.com/sites/tableau/2021/05/26/how-to-create-a-data-leadership-committee-and-get-everyone-on-the-same-page/.
8 As an independent member, Erik Beulen is a member of the data committee of Royal Flora Holland. This section is based on information available on the website.
9 https://www.royalfloraholland.com/en/about-us/our-cooperative-company - accessed 20 December 2022.
10 https://np-royalfloraholland-production.s3-eu-west-1.amazonaws.com/8-Over-ons/Documenten/Royal-FloraHolland-Annual-Report-2021.pdf.
11 https://www.royalfloraholland.com/en/news-2022/week-49/audit-of-confidential-data-in-floriday-was-again-completed-successfully.
12 https://www.royalfloraholland.com/en/news-2022/week-49/audit-of-confidential-data-in-floriday-was-again-completed-successfully.

12

DATA SHARING – COMPETITIVE AND SUSTAINABILITY, COMPLIANCE, PRIVACY, AND ETHICAL IMPLICATIONS

Sharing data in ecosystems and value chains demands well-considered decisions to ensure the competitive position of the organization is not jeopardized. It is important to understand that most organizations participate in multiple ecosystems and value chains and that, over time, there will be changes in the ecosystems and value chains in which organizations choose to participate. Adding value applies to both private and public sector organizations. On top of that, data sharing outside the organizations might have sustainability, compliance, privacy, and ethical implications. This chapter details approaches and good practices to fuel digital transformation by data sharing across ecosystems and value chains.

To start, data sharing also addresses societal challenges (BCG, 2021a). There are five ways to generate value from data sharing: (1) create trust – establish a single source of truth and provide timely transparency; (2) facilitate coordination – streamline logistics, align incentives, and create new business models; (3) raise awareness, make distant challenges visible, and provide an understanding of their magnitude, (4) validate the hypothesis, understand the cause and effect more quickly and accurately, thereby using fewer resources; and (5) enable innovation, enrich data through aggregation, and match data with innovators. The use of tooling for data sharing mitigates three risks (BCG, 2021b): data breaches, data mis-sharing and misuse, and data quality risks related to validation and authentication. Nevertheless, three challenges require attention of organizations: (1) dark data/aggregation complexity; (2) barriers to interoperability, which can be addressed by RESTful APIs to securely exchange information on the internet; and (3) barriers to transfer, which can be resolved by transfer and streaming tools (BCG, 2021b).

DOI: 10.4324/9781003246770-16

12.1 Competitive implications

The competitive implications of data sharing are not limited to private sector organizations. Competitive implications are about adding value for both private and public sector organizations. Many organizations are expanding their data sharing. Data related to products, services, markets, and customers or citizens is shared to add value. This information also enables the organizations involved to make more informed decisions. Organizations should be aware that sharing data might impact their future ability to add value, as they can potentially be disintermediated in a value chain. Organizations can also have conflicting interests as they might participate in different ecosystems and value chains. This increases the complexity of making decisions on data sharing.

However, in addition to increased added value and also improved efficiency and effectiveness of supply-chain processes, data sharing also supports risk management and disruption mitigation, and it creates resilience (Colicchia et al., 2019).

12.1.1 Agreeing on data-sharing permissions and obligations

In data sharing, it is key to agree on the format of data. This includes anonymizing and/or masking and setting different levels of confidentiality. Also, aggregation levels and time lags need to be agreed on. Finally, the data life cycle, and if and when shared data must be disposed, needs to be agreed on. This also includes clear obligations on data removal when an organization decides to discontinue the collaboration and as a consequence, will not receive shared data in future. All these techniques can be deployed to protect the interests of the participating organizations.

Typically, the shared data is analyzed, which results in additional insights for the analyzing organization. The participating organizations need to decide whether these additional insights have to be shared back or if these are solely beneficial to the analyzing organization.

Also, agreement is required on the ownership of the shared data. Are receiving organizations allowed to reshare or even sell the shared data with other organizations? For obvious reasons, this is rarely allowed. Nevertheless, the situation becomes more complex when receiving organizations conduct analysis on the shared data and reshare or sell their analysis.

Finally, organizations also need to agree on and assure meeting compliance obligations and the security of the data, especially if the shared data is sensitive data, such as privacy or medical data, but also commercially sensitive data in the context of antitrust legislation. The cost and governance related to these obligations can be significant, as can be the exposure when these risks materialize.

TATA CONSULTANCY SERVICE CASE STUDY: GOVERNMENT OF INDIA – SUPPLY-CHAIN ECOSYSTEM FOR SCALING UP INDIGENIZATION OF DIAGNOSTICS TEST KITS

Client needs

- Centre for Cellular and Molecular Platforms (C-CAMP) wanted to scale up indigenous Covid-19 diagnostic test-kit production capacity to a million test kits a day
- Objective is to build a robust, scalable supply-chain ecosystem of Indian Micro, Small and Medium Enterprises (MSMEs) capable of producing large quantities of reagents and other components needed for diagnostic test kits for COVID-19

What was done

TCS developed and deployed a dynamic digital supply-chain platform which is powered by TCS Dexam solution that allows medium- and small-scale enterprises to embrace new ecosystem-based business models, giving them the ability to bridge information gap and bring efficacies and scale across the entire value chain
The solution facilitates

- Easy self-service onboarding of Suppliers and Manufacturers
- Product and WANT publishing
- Transaction capability with unlimited price negotiation
- Advanced Search and discovery
- Interactive Analytics and Visualization
- Dashboards for all stakeholders
- Insights on registered products, manufacturers, and quality analysis

The project entails eliminating supply-chain bottlenecks and handholding MS-MEs to help them bridge capability gaps, meet necessary quality standards, and expand capacities to be able to indigenously produce a million test kits a day.

Impact

- Witnessed 190+ Members (Manufacturers, suppliers, service providers, etc.) onboarded and 370+ products registered
- Visibility on supplier-specific quality levels, capacities, and inventories across the ecosystem
- The cost for a RTPCR kit to manufacturers, which was INR 1800 in June 2020 has reduced to INR 50 by June 2021
- C-CAMP eyeing InDx as Strategic enabler to Integrate with international Marketplaces & Exchanges

12.1.2 Agreeing on data-sharing costs or pricing

Collaborating and sharing data in ecosystems and value chains is also not free and requires investments, as well as proper governance. In the context of dynamics and collaborations, it is important to distinguish between the initial investment, such as setting up databases and parameterized software, and related commitments and the operating costs, such as with community clouds. Preferably, the cost allocation is linked to volumes of data shared and unit transfer pricing. Uncertainty related to volumes can be an argument to agree on periodic cost allocations. Also, the cost allocation is not necessarily aligned with the achieved benefits. Often, dominant and larger organizations accept a larger part of the costs to make it attractive for other, smaller organizations to be part of an ecosystem and/or value chain – cross-subsidizing. Furthermore, agreement on the implications of exiting the collaboration is important. The exit clause details what costs are owed. Furthermore, remaining organizations might need to adjust the allocation of the operating cost of the data sharing. To manage the data exchange and the cost allocation, participating organizations need to set up a governance structure to ensure that collective interests are protected and decisions are made.

As an alternative to sharing costs and benefits, one of the participating organizations might decide to offer data sharing as a service. Typically, this organization is in direct contact with the consumer or citizen, and the charges are subscription-based and/or unit pricing. The insights from the consumer or citizen are of value for the partners that are more upstream in the value chain. Contractual agreements detail the charging and mutual obligations. This alternative is more straightforward and is more equipped to respond to changes in participating organizations, as well as market dynamics.

12.2 Sustainability implications

The sharing of sustainability data is becoming increasingly important and subject to legislation. Understanding the contribution to the carbon footprint, as well as ensuring that your organization and the partners in ecosystems and value chains contribute to sustainability and meet sustainability goals, has also become more important for many organizations.

The most recent disclosure requirements include those of the Securities and Exchange Commission (SEC), which announced new environmental, social, and governance (ESG) disclosure requirements for companies in 2022.[1] Public companies must enhance and standardize climate and climate risk-related disclosures. This potentially includes logging these risks in the risk register. The European Union established the Corporate Sustainability Report Directive[2] to also achieve standardized reporting on company environmental and social impact activities, starting from the fiscal year 2023 onwards. Furthermore, the United Nations principles of responsible investments play an important role in achieving sustainability goals: approximately 3,750 financial institutions have signed up on these principles (KPMG, 2021). Nevertheless, ESG reporting is globally maturing; the concerns and issues related to the reporting are detailed in the next paragraph.

12.2.1   *Standardized ESG disclosure as a business imperative*[3]

Materiality has and will always be applicable to any financial report. Implicit inclusion of ESG disclosure is not good enough (Sustainalytics, 2020). Only a handful of companies had proactively self-identified pandemic risks as a material factor in the S1 and 8-K form (Waters Technology, 2020a). A global non-financial report standard for integral ESG disclosure is needed (XBRL, 2020), as regulators are enforcing ESG disclosure to increase transparency and improve sustainability. In this matter, the European regulators are in the lead. Shareholders and investors need ESG disclosures and include ESG data in their portfolios to hedge risks and find alpha (Waters Technology, 2020b). Organizations should embrace the opportunities of ESG disclosure; in addition to doing good, this creates value (McKinsey, 2020c).

Unfortunately, there is still no true golden ESG standard – current examples of standards are SASB,[4] CDP,[5] CSDB,[6] GRI,[7] and IIRC[8] (KPMG, 2021). Furthermore, many organizations generate self-reporting ESG data, which lacks transparency and comparability (Hoepner and Schneider, 2018). On top of this, it is challenging to analyze the ESG properly due to a lack of historic data, with data sets running only 5–10 years back (Waters Technology, 2020b), which is further complicated by definitions that have changed and been revised over time, as well as significant consolidation of the selling market, e.g. Morningstar/Sustainanalytics and Dow Jones Index/Robeco SAM. There are two issues with the reports of these rating agencies: black-boxing (Waters Technology, 2020c), which hinders a data-centric approach; and unrelated ESG disclosure of different rating agencies, as the correlation of five ratings agencies was on average 0.61 – compared to a 0.99 correlation of Moody's and S&P credit rating (Berg, 2019). Also, EGS data is confronted with signal behavior. Society and regulators have adjusted metrics and weightings of metrics over time – E, S, and G – and within categories (Clayton, 2020; McKinsey, 2020c). In addition back testing is difficult or even impossible, as ESG has been differently priced by the market over the years (Water Technology, 2020b). Finally, there is still a lot of greenwashing (Nemes et al., 2022).

12.3   Compliance implications

Organizations that share data should be knowledgeable on the compliance obligations of the sector and the jurisdictions involved. In particular, data sharing between organizations operating in different countries might run into different, and sometimes even conflicting, compliance requirements. Involvement of legal subject matter experts, compliance and risk managers is needed to avoid organizations being not compliant. As compliance regulations are subject to change, the legal involvement is not limited to the initiation of the data sharing; over time, legal checkpoints are required to ensure compliance. Also, involving RegTechs across an ecosystem will ensure compliance of the ecosystem and the partners involved in the ecosystem.

In the context of compliance, the ownership of data is important to ensure high quality data. Poor data quality of shared data might result in noncompliance. Monitoring the data quality of shared data is important. The quality of the transaction data is typically high. The focus related to data quality should be on the non-transaction data that are shared, where a further focus on the data quality of sensitive data is required. Attention to data quality is becoming even more important when partners apply data analytics to the shared data, as data analytics triggers decision-making and therefore an increased risk of impact due to poor quality of shared data. This stresses the importance of management attention to compliance in data sharing. As part of the data-sharing agreement and the data-sharing governance, liability needs to be detailed and captured in the governance. This requires involvement of the chief data office.

In addition to compliance rulings and legislation that reduces and/or hinders data sharing, there is also legislation that enforces data sharing. Open banking is the most prominent example of enforced data sharing. This will be detailed shortly in Section 12.3.1.

Finally, transparency is also an important concept that promotes data sharing. Politically, this was advocated nearly a decade ago by the G20's anti-corruption working group (ACWG) – open data was expected to advance public sector transparency and integrity. The workgroup detailed this in six principles (G20, 2014). In Section 12.5, additional ethical implications are detailed.

12.3.1 Open banking

In the context of digital transformation and data sharing, open banking is a good example of compliance implications. The Payment Services Directive (PSD2) of the European Union gives customers more control over their personal account data. PSD2 entered into force on 12 January 2016, and EU Member States had until 13 January 2018 to transpose it into national law.[9] Basically, the customer can request their financial institution to share their personal account data with a competing financial institution to transact with the competitor. Fintech benefits from this legislation, where this legislation exposes the exclusive ownership of the client. This exclusive ownership, combined with the high barriers to switching from one financial institution to another financial institution, has protected this regulated market for a long time.

The possibility that customers could request to share their personal account data boosted innovation and set requirements for financial service providers to adopt application program interfaces (APIs). Traditional financial service providers are struggling to keep up, as they have legacy technology stacks and typically significant technical debt. The competitive services of fintechs can potentially disrupt these traditional financial service providers.

12.4 Privacy implications

Privacy implications are not only a European matter. The United States is moving forward with data privacy and protection. Nevertheless, the United States has a different approach. Their legislation is captured predominantly in state and, to a lesser extent, federal laws, and there is no general data privacy protection or all-encompassing legislation, as there is in Europe. However, the United States is progressing by introducing the Consumer Online Privacy Rights Act in 2019 and the Setting an American Framework to Ensure Data Access, Transparency, and Accountability Act (the Safe Data Act) in September 2020. This legislation is supplementing legislation, for example, the California Consumer Privacy Act (2018) and California Privacy Rights Act (2020).[10]

The European Union has implemented the General Data Protection Regulation (GDPR), which replaced the Data Protection Directive. This regulation protects the data privacy of EU citizens. Organizations must provide an adequate level of privacy protection. If not adequate, these can be supplemented by Binding Corporate Rules, for privacy protection within the organization, or Standard Contract Clauses (SCCs), Article 49 derogations, and international trade agreements to transfer personal data (Calia, 2022). The GDPR is challenged serval times (Schrems I and II). In the first challenge, the Safe Harbor route was blocked by the Court of the Justice of European Union. The rationale was that the annual self-certification, including compliance with seven basic data protection and privacy principles, was not sufficient to address the concerns over US government surveillance implications for the privacy of EU citizens. This was repaired by an improved international trade agreement, the EU-US Privacy Shield Framework. This framework included an "ombudsperson mechanism" (article 29). This agreement was invalidated. The route for data transfer to the United States is Standard Contractual Clauses (SCCs). The European Commission introduced two new SCCs for use between controllers and processors and for the transfer of personal data to third countries. Data localization is suggested and challenged as a possible solution. The opponents argue that localization neither solves the problem of foreign surveillance nor enhances personal privacy while undermining other values embraced by the European Union (Chander, 2020, p. 771). Data privacy continues to be a sensitive topic related to the transfer of personal data from the European Union to the United States.

12.5 Ethical implications

When sharing data, organizations need to be very aware of potential ethical implications and implement ethical principles.[11] The ethical implications for external data sharing are obviously bigger, but also internal data-sharing organizations, need to take into account the ethical implications of data sharing. There is criticism on the big data industry as coined by Martin; nevertheless, selling data is not wrong but requires governance (2020). Important in this matter is to obtain guidance from the software manufacturers and consulting organizations involved. These can support your organization (Beulen et al., 2022). Microsoft, followed by Amazon and IBM, made a bold move by not being willing to sell facial recognition technology to US police departments on ethical grounds. To put things bluntly, they had no confidence that US police departments would use their products ethically (Forbes, 2020). Other vendors might have a different view and might be willing to sell this technology to the US police department; nevertheless, the responsible use of facial recognition technology remains with the government.

In the accountable organization, one should be mindful for upstream as well as downstream accountability. Organizations need to consider what can be done with the data; data analytics will generate new insights. Organizations need to be confident that potential insights can still be considered ethical. If organizations share for a longitudinal period, this will become harder. Additional agreements are required on the usage of data and the data life cycle.

Furthermore, organizations need to be mindful that ethical norms are constantly changing and are contextual. This must be taken into account in data-sharing decisions and might result in an adjustment in or pausing data sharing and a periodic review of the ethical norms is necessary.

Finally, governments need to consider the ethical implications of sharing and analyzing data gathered by mass surveillance. The implications of mass surveillance can be serious and possibly nasty. For individual citizens living in and organizations operating in these countries, there is not much room to maneuver. International public sector organizations such as the United Nations, public sector organizations, and activists might consider expressing their concerns, but not much more can be done. In democratic countries, citizens and activists might consider initiating litigation.

12.6 Conclusion

Data sharing is needed and required, but for many organizations, it is still the early days. Data sharing in the context of compliance requires additional standard setting, where data sharing in ecosystems as well as value chains requires trust, courage, and experimentation. All data-sharing learnings will ultimately create value. Advancing technologies and maturing tooling supports data sharing and reduces the risks of data sharing.

The compliance and privacy requirements will further increase over time, as will the demands from ethical considerations. Data sharing will become not only more difficult but also more needed, as data sharing continuous to be an integral part of doing business. As a consequence, organizations need to build capabilities in this area and adjust their data policies, as well as their security policies, accordingly.

Driven by both compliance and privacy requirements, ethical demands, and the need to create value, organizations must step up.

Notes

1 See https://www.sec.gov/news/press-release/2022-46.
2 See https://finance.ec.europa.eu/capital-markets-union-and-financial-markets/company-reporting-and-auditing/company-reporting/corporate-sustainability-reporting_en.
3 This section is largely based on online webinar of XBRL Europe – 2 November 2020 – Erik Beulen – "Tackling globally standardized ESG disclosure is a business imperative."
4 https://www.sasb.org/.
5 https://www.cdp.net/en.
6 https://www.cdsb.net/.
7 https://www.globalreporting.org/.
8 https://www.integratedreporting.org/.
9 See https://www.ecb.europa.eu/paym/intro/mip-online/2018/html/1803_revisedpsd.en.html.
10 Also in Colorado, Connecticut, Utah, and Virginia.
11 For ethical principles, see https://aiethicslab.com/big-picture/.

13
PARTNERING IN ECOSYSTEMS[1] – HOW TO STRUCTURE COLLABORATION?

No organization can do without partnering in ecosystems. Both private and public sector organizations need to collaborate with ecosystem partners in multiple value chains to develop their product and service offerings. In addition, the dynamics in markets and ecosystems are increasing at an unprecedented rate. Identifying the most beneficial value chains and finding the right ecosystem partners is a challenge for many organizations. The identification and initiation of ecosystem partnerships can be very costly and do not guarantee returns. On top of this are the challenges to maintain partnerships and continuously innovate value creation. The wider context of partnering in ecosystems is a combination of continuous technology innovation, stricter (global) legislation, and cyber security threats. All of the above make partnering in ecosystems an even greater challenge.

Partnering in ecosystems powers digital transformations. The creation of ecosystem partnering requires proper governance. In addition to formal contracts with partners in value chains, relational contracting and psychological contracts are essential, as it is difficult to capture all details in formal contracts, as well as make the contractual commitments accessible and comprehensible for the large number of stakeholders involved in ecosystem partnering. To be successful in partnering in ecosystems, organizations must also continually keep up their partnering capabilities, including retaining and attracting the right talent.

In this chapter, the results of a global survey (N = 82) will be presented.

First, the context for partnering in ecosystems and value chains is detailed. Next, the selection of ecosystem partners and value chains is discussed, followed by a deep dive into ecosystem capabilities in conjunction with digital transformation. Then, contracting in ecosystems addresses the dilemma of short-term versus long-term contracting as well as the contracting exclusivity predicament. Subsequently, data sharing across value chains is detailed. This

DOI: 10.4324/9781003246770-17

includes upward and downstream data sharing and data analytics with the goal of increasing value creation and strengthening partnerships.

13.1   Introduction to ecosystems and value chains

A value chain is a business model that describes the full range of activities needed to create a product or service that typically involves multiple organizations. Organizations collaborate in ecosystems across value chains. In this section, four topics are addressed. The first topic is the number of value chains in which organizations are operating. For organizations to create value through ecosystem partnerships, they need to understand how many value chains they are operating in, which value chains provide the most value, and in which value chains they should or want to be operating. This understanding is not limited to the number of value chains, as quantity does not necessarily equal quality. Ecosystem partnership is very different from a commercial business-to-business contractual relationship. In ecosystem partnering, collaboration with the end-client in mind is the starting point for value creation. Think of classic examples such as Philips' and Douwe Egberts' Senseo collaboration to increase sales by portion-packed consumption[2] and Walmart and Shopify creating Walmart's Marketplace[3] to compete with Amazon.

The second topic is the value chain integration. Integration strategies, e.g. forward as well as backward integrations, determine value creation. A perfect example is Ideal for online payments in the Netherlands.[4] It was founded by ABN Amro, ING Bank, Postbank, and Rabobank; Ideal sets the standard and ensures interoperability. Also, organizations need to identify what investments are required to initiate and maintain operation in value chains. Initiating value chains can be costly and return on investment must be evident.

Funding is the third topic, which is a balancing act, requiring a well-considered strategy and strong operational discipline. A good example is the Randstad Tech & Touch strategy that includes the Randstad Investment Fund.[5]

Finally, as the fourth topic, competitive position requires attention. Competitive positions change over time. The competitive position will increase by improving the conditions with ecosystem partners and/or by increasing the exclusivity in the ecosystem, e.g. remove alternative partners from the ecosystem. Organizations need to ensure that their positions are improving rather than deteriorating over time and might consider focusing on the creation of intellectual property to improve their competitive position within value chains.

13.1.1   Number of value chains

Most organizations operate in multiple value chains in parallel. The organizations which operate in up to five value chains are predominantly in the non-profit sector. Operating in +10 value chains are mostly global organizations with revenues of +1,000m euro. Most organizations gradually expand the number of value chains, and also in many cases continue participation in a value chain for a period of five years or more. This stability can be explained by the effort required to initiate and participate in a value chain.

13.1.2 Value chain integration

Nineteen organizations are expanding their presence in value chains forward, where about one-third of the organizations are expanding their presence forward and backward in value chains. Only four organizations are expanding their presence only backward. The concern is with the 26 organizations that are not expanding their presence in value chains. These 26 organizations are predominantly organizations with revenues under 1,000m euro and in the governmental sector. Organizations in the banking and financial sector are underrepresented. Only 1 of the 11 organizations in the banking and financial sector is not expanding its presence in the value chains.

13.1.3 Funding value chains

Organizations might consider funding the participation of key partners, typically smaller or specialized organizations or start-ups. The participation of these key partners will create a network effect that is beneficial for all partners. It increases access to resources and markets and improves competitive positions. Nearly 70% of the organizations fund value chains. Over two-thirds of organizations (N = 40) fund less than 20% of their value chains, of which 30% of organizations (N = 12) fund for more than 12 months. There are also 15 organizations which fund more than 20% of value chains. This major cross-subsidizing results in significant IP creation. Also, there are 25 organizations that never funded their value chains. These organizations are typically smaller organizations, < 250m euro revenue, and create no (N = 7) or minimal IP (N = 13).

13.1.4 Competitive position

Improving competitive position is important for both profit and non-profit organizations. Just over one-third of the organizations improved their competitive position compared to 36 months ago, whereas just under 60% of the organizations (N = 48) neither improved nor deteriorated their competitive position. Only four organizations reported a deterioration of their competitive position compared to 36 months ago. Successful organizations are predominantly focused on forward integration, sometimes combined with backward integration. Furthermore, these organizations are mainly involved in value chains for +60 months, but they are also active in participating in new value chains initiated less than 18 months ago. The survey data does not indicate that size matters, nor is there a differentiation by sector for the successful organizations. As expected, the creation of IP positively relates with the competitive position. Finally, funding value chains has a higher adoption in successful organizations.

INTELLECTUAL PROPERTY IN ECOSYSTEMS

Creating intellectual property (IP) in ecosystems requires partners to have trust in the network. To foster trust, transparency combined with proper govern-ance and fair contractual commitments are crucial. The creation of IP is also important, as this is a solid indicator of innovation and reassures trust with other partners, while also improving competitive advantage in the value chain. Our research shows that 80% of the responding organizations create IP in ecosys-tems, where 41% of the responding organizations create substantial IP in eco-systems, while just over 20% of the participating organizations that created no IP; see Figure 13.1). Not surprisingly, most of the participating organizations that create substantial IP in ecosystems operate predominantly in the business-to-business market (66%). As the differentiation in sectors is too scattered, the data do not allow for a deep dive into sectors. Furthermore, our survey data does not provide evidence of the contribution of increased IP creation into success for organizations which improved their competitive position in most value chains compared to 36 months ago, versus organizations which did not improve their competitive position. However, as expected, IP creation is positively related to the number of value chains: nearly 40% of the participating organizations with a significant IP creation participate in +25 value chains, whereas only 13% of the participating organizations with no IP creation participate in +25 value chains.

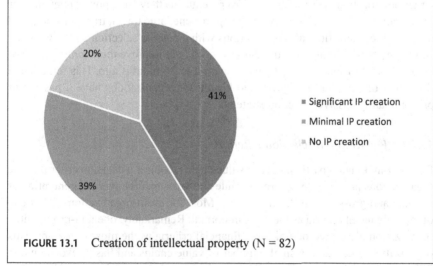

20%

41%

39%

- Significant IP creation
- Minimal IP creation
- No IP creation

FIGURE 13.1   Creation of intellectual property (N = 82)

13.2 Selection of partners

Ecosystems start with the selection of value chains. Organizations need to manage this as a portfolio. In assessing the potential of partnering in an ecosystem, organi-zations have to identify market synergies, including increased volumes, market

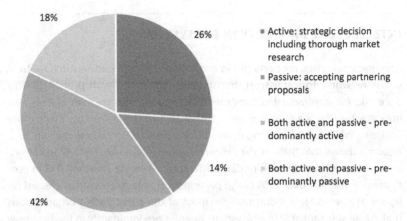

FIGURE 13.2   Selection strategies for value chains (N = 82)

penetration, and contribution to brand awareness, as well as operational synergies e.g. more efficient creation of products or services.

In the survey, except for one organization in travel, transportation, and hospitality, no organizations with an active or predominantly active selection of value chains based on strategic decisions and underpinned with a thorough market research experienced deterioration of their competitive position in value chains compared to 36 months ago. As expected, these organizations are predominantly the larger organizations with +1,000m euro revenue, as they have power over smaller organizations in value chains. Also, except for one large travel, transportation, and hospitality organization, all organizations with a passive selection strategy, by accepting partnering proposals, deteriorated or did not improve their competitive position in most of their value chains compared to 36 months ago. It is remarkable that 7 out of the 11 life sciences and healthcare organizations have a passive or predominantly passive selection strategy.

13.2.1   Participation selection criterion

Decision-making on participating in value chains requires a decision criterion. The organizations preferred long-term revenue and gross margin over the generation of revenue and gross margin from the start. Most for-profit organizations listed one of these financial criteria as the most important. Remarkably, one non-profit Dutch organization also listed one of these financial criteria as the most important. This organization operates in a small number of value chains and has a revenue under 250m euro. Similarly, two large Dutch governmental organizations have listed one of these financial criteria as most important.

Interesting is that 34 organizations indicated an indirect financial decision criterion for participating in value chains: exposure/prestige; leverage and extended skills and capabilities; or accelerate innovations and time to market.

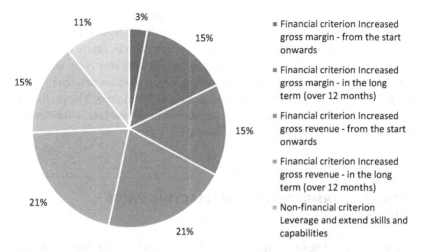

11% 3%
15%
15%
15%
15%
21%
21%
21%

- Financial criterion Increased gross margin - from the start onwards
- Financial criterion Increased gross margin - in the long term (over 12 months)
- Financial criterion Increased gross revenue - from the start onwards
- Financial criterion Increased gross revenue - in the long term (over 12 months)
- Non-financial criterion Leverage and extend skills and capabilities

FIGURE 13.3   Participation primary selection criteria – financial criteria and non-financial criteria (N = 82)

Eleven organizations indicated exposure/prestige as the most dominant decision criterion, and this includes over 50% governmental organizations (N = 6). Between five and ten other organizations indicated capabilities as the most dominant decision criterion. Leverage and extended skills and capabilities were mostly mentioned by Dutch organizations with a revenue up to 250m euro. Larger global organizations might have fewer difficulties in getting access to capabilities due to their footprint and/or size. Finally, eight other organizations indicated accelerated innovation and time to market as the most dominant decision criterion. Most likely due to the small data set, no common characteristics were identified of these eight organizations, including their ability and success in creating IP.

13.2.2   Compliance considerations in selecting ecosystem partners

Ethical and compliance considerations are of increasing importance for any organization. Both topics are frequently and at length discussed by managers and executives. Globally, ethical awareness and consciousness are rising and compliance obligations are more strict, and they will continue to be even more strict in the future. Organizations must take both ethical and compliance considerations into account when selecting ecosystem partners.

The ethical considerations are detailed in the text frame. In compliance, there is an increasing focus on privacy but also on antitrust legislation. In the context of ecosystem partnering, the latter is extremely important. For just under 30% of the organizations, there is no need to closely monitor the antitrust legislation; different from what we expected, this includes only four non-profits and a mix of global and

Dutch organizations, as well as mix of small and large organizations, whereas the organizations which require closely monitored antitrust legislation are typically large, for-profit organizations. With regard to anticipation of future legislation, we conclude with surprise that 44% of the organizations only reactively anticipate on future legislation. The profile of organizations which have no anticipation are, as expected, Dutch organizations with revenues up to 250m euro. The profile of the organizations that do anticipate future legislation in all markets is foreseeable as the opposite – global and large organizations.

ETHICAL CONSIDERATIONS IN SELECTING VALUE CHAINS

Ethical considerations should not be abstract and should align with corporate guidance that defines what is within the norms and values of the organization and what is not. Examples of ethical considerations are informed consent, voluntary participation, do no harm, or only assess relevant components. For further reference, see the European Union framework for ethics in artificial intelligence: https://digital-strategy.ec.europa.eu/en/library/ethics-guidelines-trustworthy-ai.

Given the increased awareness and consciousness, we would expect that nearly all organizations would indicate ethics as a knock-out criterion in selecting value chains, but only one-third indicated ethics as a knock-out criterion; see Figure 13.4. What is even more remarkable is that 12 organizations in "sensitive" sectors did not indicate ethics as a knock-out criterion: five governmental, four life sciences and healthcare organizations, and three financial services organizations. By expanding the responses to 5 and higher (1–7 Likert scale), we see predominantly the larger organizations, +1,000m euro revenue. Studying the lower end of the spectrum, there are scores of three and lower for five organizations.

We observe that most of the organizations scoring a four or lower are active in ≤ 10 value chains. The implication of being active in a smaller number of value chains might be that organizations hold strong, long-term ties with their business partners. However, the data does not clearly indicate a longer duration of the partnerships for organizations with a lower number of value chains. As expected, most organizations scoring a four or less operate in the B2B sector. To be clear, ethics are also important in the B2B sectors, but to a lesser degree than for the B2C and governmental and non-profit organizations. In the B2B sector, transparency and pressure from public opinion are less direct.

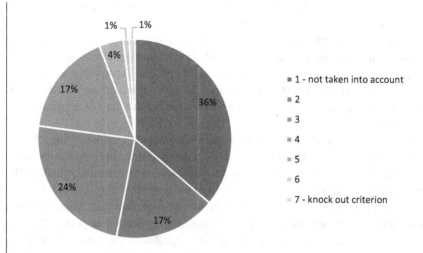

FIGURE 13.4   Degree ethical considerations are taken into account when selecting value chains (1–7 Likert scale, 1 = not taken into account and 7 = knock out criterion) (N = 82) (Beulen, 2022a)

13.3   Ecosystem capabilities

To be successful in ecosystem partnering, organizations need to have a data-driven strategy, in which data analytics are crucial. Especially in ecosystem partnering, organizations have limited control, many stakeholders are involved, and markets, society, and legislation are continuously in motion. This is even more difficult for smaller organizations, as smaller organizations can have less impact on value chains, making their position in ecosystem partnering less competitive. However, smaller organizations can also inherently bring more risk into the value chain – value chains are as strong as their weakest link. In addition to scale, stable management also contributes to the success of ecosystem partnering. Organizations with a large number of management changes are perceived as fundamentally unstable and difficult to deal with, since trust needs to be maintained on an organizational as well as personal level. These management changes impact trust levels, in addition to potential changes in strategy, resulting in possible changes in ecosystem partnering.

Furthermore, the collaboration has to be anchored in the top of an organization. Doing so ensures aligned objectives in ecosystem partnering, which is more straightforward for national than for international organizations. It is important to assign an owner to each value chain who has a sufficient mandate in their own organization. These partner executives have a management profile, with significant operational experience, as well as market knowledge. This profile will ensure that partner managers are fully-fledged counterparts within their own organization as well as for the business partners. The ecosystem capabilities are not limited to the strategic layer of organizations but also on the tactical and operational layers of the organization's ecosystem capabilities, mainly in monitoring the ecosystem partnerships and creating value by working with partners. The capabilities in the latter are distinctly different capabilities required for more transactional relationships. In ecosystem partnering, there is a more collective mindset and responsibility for value creation.

In addition, organizations need to create a governance structure to align the involvement and objectives of all value chains. On top of that, this governance structure also facilitates value chain portfolio management to ensure continuity. The structure and objectives are not different from the governance structures which organizations have implemented for their supplier management. The learned lessons from supplier management can be applied to managing ecosystem partnership, but the complexity and impact are of much more significant magnitude. In addition to this internal governance, external governance, together with the business partners, has to be implemented. This implementation is detailed in Section 13.4 – contracting in ecosystems.

13.3.1 Partnering capabilities

In ecosystem partnering, it is important that all partners have equal partnering capabilities to ensure a smooth and seamless collaboration. In our survey, 51% of the respondents had equally mature partnering capabilities, and only 20% of the organizations had a difference of > 2, in a 1–7 Likert scale, in partnering capabilities. Therefore, about 80% of the survey organizations met this ecosystem partnering key performance indicator. However, just under one-third of the survey participants have a partner capability maturity > 5 for both their own and their partner's capabilities (1–7 Likert scale), so there is still room for improvement.

Remarkably, the respondents assessing their partnering capabilities as less mature than the capabilities of their business partners outnumber the respondents assessing their partnering capabilities as more mature. There is no distinct survey participant profile (sector, organization size, or geographical spread) for each of the three partnering capability profiles.

Respondents in the low maturity quadrant (e.g. < 3 for both partnering capabilities, on a 1–7 Likert scale) are predominantly smaller Dutch organizations, 9 out of the 14 organizations are non-Dutch, and only five organizations have a revenue +1,000m euros. The respondents in the high maturity quadrant (e.g. > 5 for both partnering capabilities, in a 1–7 Likert scale) are predominantly international organizations, however, the size of these organizations lacks a distinct profile and ranges from organizations with the revenue of 25m to +10,000m euro.

To collaborate with business partners, supporting processes and tooling are important. The survey results show that the partnering capabilities and the maturity of

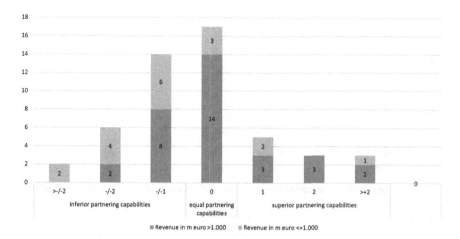

FIGURE 13.5 Mapping the delta for the partnering capabilities to manage business partners of the own organization and their business partners by revenue, both
1–7 Likert scales, 1 = inferior partnering capabilities and 7 = superior
partnering capabilities (N = 67) (Beulen, 2022a)

the supporting processes and tooling are aligned; organizations with a mature business partnering capability have mature supporting processes and tooling, where
organizations with an immature business partnering capability have immature supporting processes and tooling.

Just over 50% of the organizations report partnering capabilities and the maturity for the supporting processes with an equal or difference of one on a 1–7
Likert scale, and when comparing the partner capabilities of their business partners
and their support processes, these capabilities score similarly. The overlap of both
percentages is over 65%. For tooling, the percentages are similar; however, there
are no scores of 7 for the tooling of their own organization or the business partner
organizations.

The differences in the Likert score (1–7) between the maturity of the partnership capability and the supporting process maturity are detailed in Figure 13.6. In
Figure 13.7, the differences between the partnership capacity and the tooling are
detailed.

Remarkably, the organizations in highly regulated sectors (N = 17 which equals
50% of the highly regulated sector) such as government and public services, life
sciences and healthcare, banking and financial services, insurance, and telecommunications do not have a high maturity in supporting processes. For tooling, the
maturity for the organizations in highly regulated sectors is only slightly better. In
support processes, only 21% of organizations from highly regulated sectors have a
5 or higher (1–7 Likert scale, N = 7), where for tooling, only 17% of the organizations from highly regulated sectors has a maturity score of 5 or higher (1–7 Likert
scale, N = 6).

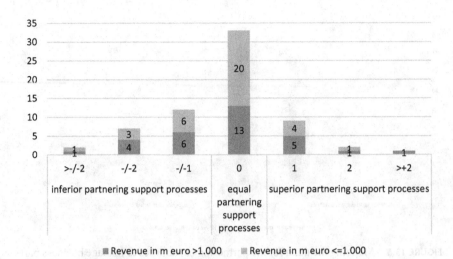

FIGURE 13.6 Mapping the delta for the partnering support processes of the own organization and their business partners by revenue, both 1–7 Likert scales, 1 = inferior partnering capabilities and 7 = superior partnering capabilities (N = 66) (Beulen, 2022a)

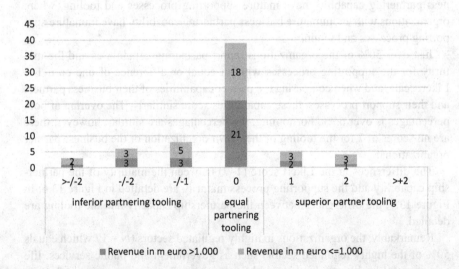

FIGURE 13.7 Mapping the delta for the partnering tooling of the own organization and their business partners by revenue, both 1–7 Likert scales, 1 = inferior partnering capabilities and 7 = superior partnering capabilities (N = 65) (Beulen, 2022b)

13.4   Contracting with ecosystem partners

Transparency is important in contracting when considering the objectives of an organization. Transparency will increase trust levels between business partners in ecosystems. In addition to formal governance, informal governance is also important, as detailed in the text box. Organizations also benefit from implementing a psychological contract that includes a simple outline of objectives and starting points, in addition to the formal contract. A psychological contract is extremely helpful; contracting in ecosystems is extremely difficult, as not all stakeholders, managers, and involved staff see the big picture. A psychological contract may be of help.

Furthermore, it is important that all business partners in an ecosystem get their fair share. Engaging in an ecosystem has to be favorable for all ecosystem partners. This requires the implementation of a governance structure throughout the value chain. In this governance structure, partner managers frequently monitor and, if required, adjust the ecosystem and the underlying agreements to ensure the ecosystem continues to be favorable for all involved business partners. For the larger ecosystems, this implies weekly or at a minimum, monthly meetings, in addition to daily operational meetings. For smaller ecosystems, a lower meeting frequency suffices.

Finally, ecosystem partners might consider investing in onboarding new ecosystem partners to ensure that these new ecosystem partners gain enough from participating in the ecosystem. Obviously, this subsidizing needs to be temporary. If permanent subsidizing is required, the ecosystem partners need to consider alternatives, such as the acquisition of the business partner or building up capabilities within one or more ecosystem partners to replace the subsidized ecosystem partner.

ECOSYSTEM GOVERNANCE

In any contracting, it is difficult to document every detail and accommodate all possible future circumstances. Incomplete contracts are a reality that organizations and their business partners in ecosystems have to deal with. Therefore, including objectives in a formal contract is a good practice. These objectives can be used to discuss and agree on any topic which is not fully described in the contract – relational governance. Adding relational governance to formal governance is good practice in contracting. Most organizations combine formal and relational contractual governance (N = 37), whereas there are 23 organizations that predominantly rely on formal contractual governance. There is no evident difference in the improvement in their competitive positions between organizations relying on both types of contractual governance, compared to

36 months ago, as detailed in Figure 13.8. There is also a distinctly different profile between organizations of the two different types of contractual difference. There are only four organizations which predominantly rely on informal contract governance; none of the four organizations have a revenue +1,000m euro revenue, and three out of four have a revenue under 250m euro.

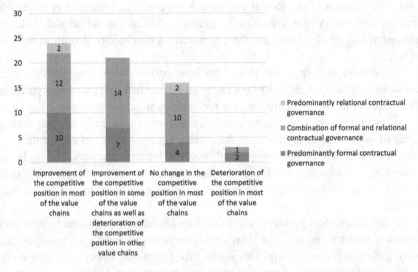

FIGURE 13.8   Contractual governance grouped by competitive position compared to 36 months ago (N = 64) (Beulen, 2022a)

13.4.1   Exclusivity and pricing commitments

Exclusivity in commitments in ecosystem partnerships is a big challenge in the dynamics that most organizations are facing. On the other hand, the investments required to successfully participate in ecosystems are significant. The organizations offering a limited exclusivity, where less than 25% of revenue is related to exclusive value chains, represent a mix of smaller and larger organizations, where due to their market dominance, predominantly larger organizations were expected (N = 22).

Similar for the organizations which are characterized as significant exclusivity, we observed a mix of smaller and larger organizations; however, these profiles only include five organizations. These organizations combine exclusivity with long-term price commitments and benefit sharing. The other organizations have either pricing commitments up to and including 12 months or pricing commitments over 12 months combined with benefit sharing, where the degree of exclusivity is positively related to the latter.

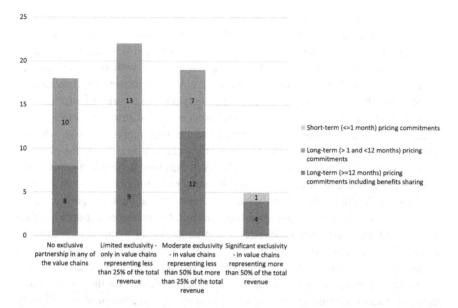

FIGURE 13.9   Exclusivity in ecosystem partnerships grouped by pricing commitments (N = 64) (Beulen, 2022a)

In the distinction for the pricing commitments, we observe no difference in size of the organization, nor is any sector over- or underrepresented. Both pricing commitment and benefits sharing can be instrumental in not only building ecosystems but also maintaining and expanding ecosystems, as they remove uncertainties for the involved organizations. The downside of pricing commitments in dynamic markets is, of course, that due to price increases, the pricing commitments are no longer competitive or even cause for loss. This is where objectivity in formal contracts and relational contractual governance is important. Ecosystem partners can revise agreed pricing commitments including the agreement on benefits sharing.

13.5   Data sharing in ecosystems

Data sharing is essential for value creation in ecosystem partnering. However, organizations have significant challenges in sharing data across value chains. These challenges are not limited to their own organization. They also include challenges for their business partners. Multi-party computation (MPC) is an emerging solution to preserve privacy and confidentiality. MPC makes use of secret sharing protocols, which do not disclose the shared data of individual partners, but only the outcome of the protocol, which is needed for all participating partners, as sharing all data of individual partners is not always necessary, practical, or wise in ecosystems.

As expected, for their own organization, the survey responses included challenges related to data quality. Data quality concerns were predominantly directed toward unstructured data. In general, low data quality negatively impacts the value that data analytics can add. Furthermore, the survey responses include data governance, privacy and information architecture in combination with the maintenance of interfaces (APIs), and the use of data in conjunction with new technologies such as Robotica. However, concerns about the environment were also reported, as (large-scale) data processing, including data analytics, has a carbon footprint. One of the respondents listed cultural and social aspects and indicated challenges in the internal collaboration between business and technology representatives. Another respondent put forward an additional architectural challenge related to the platform of choice, with data storage and data analytics in the cloud definitely a compliance challenge that needs to be addressed in ecosystem partnering.

The data sharing and data analytics challenges for the business partners echo many of the challenges of their own organization. Business partner-specific data sharing and data analytics challenges are predominantly about standardization of data formats, which is related to data sharing and data analytics. Furthermore, the ability to share large volumes of data has been indicated as a challenge. Access to data lakes and databases of business partners set challenges for their own organization as well as for business partners. These challenges are not limited to identity and access management (IAM); they also significantly increase the risk profile in terms of confidentiality and security risks.

As expected, most organizations share data equally with their business partners in ecosystems (82%). There are six organizations that share more data than their business partners share with them, this is a mix of smaller and larger organizations, including two large life sciences and healthcare organizations with revenues of +10,000m euro. Furthermore, there are five organizations which share less data than their business partners share with them, surprisingly these are also a mix of organizations, including two large organizations with revenues of +10,000m euro, and three smaller organizations.

In our study, we differentiated between data ranging from transaction data only to transaction data supplemented by additional insights, meaning no aggregation or anonymizing. Any organization needs to be aware of the increasing strength of artificial intelligence and machine learning, and generating insights from aggregated and anonymized data is continuously becoming more feasible. In ecosystem partnering, all organizations need to take this into account when agreeing on sharing data with ecosystem partners.

ALTERNATIVES TO DATA-SHARING TECHNOLOGY

Data sharing across an ecosystem requires technology. There are three technology alternatives, data sharing by a platform, a trust framework, and centralized technologies. The platform is an independent organization that connects partners and provides data-sharing services as a transaction. Typically, platforms are used in ecosystems with a large number of non-exclusive partners, processing standard transactions, and where transactions with a relatively small value and costs are combined with data sharing. Platforms can deal with any ecosystem dynamic and new partners can be easily onboarded. Second, trust frameworks can be used, e.g. the European Union's trust framework electronic identification and trust services eIDAS or DIGiD in the Netherlands. These trust frameworks do not share the actual identity but only confirm the identity. Trust frameworks enable electronic transactions of any kind and are not limited to B2C transactions. These trust frameworks can be an integral part of platforms as well as centralized technologies. Centralized technology provides the functionality to more stable and long-term ecosystem partnerships. The nature of the transactions is more bespoke and complex and typically represents a large monetary value and costs. Investment in implementing and maintaining centralized technology solutions are known problems, which can only be overcome by larger organizations processing the abovementioned transaction type.

13.5.1 Data quality in ecosystems

Data sharing in ecosystems sets additional requirements for data quality, which is still a challenge in many organizations. Among the organizations, 61% rate data quality as low to moderate – < 4 score in a 1–7 Likert scale. There is no distinct profile of organizations and their shared data quality rating, nor for their current competitive position compared to 36 months ago; see Figure 13.10.

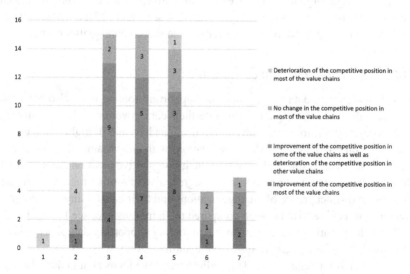

FIGURE 13.10   Data quality of shared data, 1–7 Likert scale (1 = deficient and 7 = excellent), grouped by competitive position compared to 36 months ago (N = 61) (Beulen, 2022a)

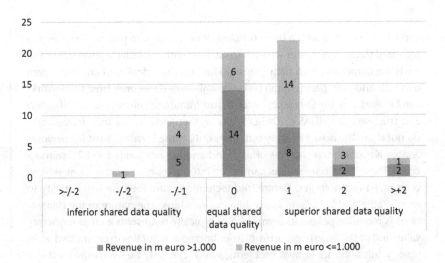

FIGURE 13.11 Mapping the delta for the quality of the shared data of the own organization and their business partners by revenue, both 1–7 Likert scales, 1 = deficient shared data quality and 7 = excellent shared data quality (N = 60) (Beulen, 2022a)

The delta in data quality of the shared data score indicates that the data quality of the shared data is higher for the surveyed organizations than their scores for data quality of the shared data of their business partners. The data quality of the shared data of the larger organizations, over 1,000m euro revenue, is lower than the data quality of shared data of smaller organizations – see Figure 13.11. There is no distinct profile of organizations and the delta in the shared data quality rating.

13.5.2 *Data governance in ecosystems*

As for data quality, data governance and supporting tooling have also been rated low. Two-thirds of the organizations rate their data governance low to moderate (< 4 score); furthermore, only seven organizations have a 6 or higher data governance score on a 1–7 Likert scale. Organizations with an immature data governance are extremely vulnerable, not only from their competitive position but also from a compliance perspective and, to a lesser degree, also in terms of ethical disregard. There is no distinct profile of the organizations and their data quality rating, nor for their current competitive position compared to 36 months ago; see Figure 13.12.

The delta in rating data governance and tooling supporting data sharing is limited, and 77% of the organizations have a similar rating, whereas 21% of the organizations have a delta of one. This indicates that the focus area in data sharing is data quality over data governance and support tooling.

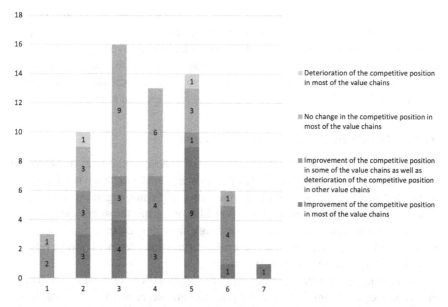

FIGURE 13.12   Rating data governance and tooling supporting data sharing, 1–7 Likert scale (1 = deficient and 7 = excellent), grouped by competitive position compared to 36 months ago (N = 63) (Beulen, 2022a)

13.6   Successful operating in ecosystems

There are three ground rules for ecosystem partnership: explore business models, be transparent toward ecosystem partners, and focus on maximizing added value for the ecosystems over added value for individual partners. Designing ecosystems is all about exploring business models. What business model is attractive to all partners? Answering this question and others, while ensuring long-term value creation, sets the first ground rule: full transparency from the start. Obviously, even in ecosystem partnering, there are conflicting commercial interests for involved partners; however, this can go hand in hand with full transparency. This is particularly important for ensuring long-term value creation, and as a consequence, partners need to commit to the ecosystems in which they are participating.

Partnering in ecosystems also requires that partners keep each other honest. Evaluating how collaboration and value creation evolve over time for all involved partners is the second ground rule. Again, here transparency is important. In the governance of ecosystem partnerships, organizations need to discuss the value creation by pre-set parameters. These discussions have to take place regularly to ensure that the interests of all partners are taken care of.

This results in the third ground rule. Involved partners have the obligation to adjust the business model and underlying commercial agreements in order to ensure that participation in the ecosystem is beneficial for all partners. However, if in ecosystems one or more partners no longer create value, more fundamental discussions need to be held. Potentially, ecosystems will be dismantled, or partners will be swapped. Partners must initiate these changes with caution and should avoid opportunism.

In order to successfully operate in ecosystems, there are four areas that require action: partnering, contracting, data sharing, and compliance and ethics. The remainder of this section includes good practices for these four areas.

13.6.1   Ecosystem good practices – Partnering

Developing partnership capabilities is essential. These capabilities are centered around defining and updating the partner strategy, managing individual partnerships, and managing a portfolio of partnerships. Typically, organizations appoint analysts to continuously monitor the portfolio of partnerships and explore new opportunities and partner managers to manage individual partnerships. The focus of partner managers is external and internal. Partner managers will also be responsible for value creation in the ecosystem.

For managing a portfolio of partnerships, organizations appoint executives to ensure strategic alignment across the portfolio and serve as the escalation level. Furthermore, these executives are the custodians of the three ecosystem partnering ground rules. They also consolidate and review the new opportunities identified by the analysts and initiate additional new opportunities. Usually, all opportunities will be presented to management by the executives responsible for the portfolio of ecosystem partnerships.

13.6.2   Ecosystem good practices – Contracting

Despite trust being the center of ecosystems, contracting remains important. Partnerships are designed by trust and are managed by contracts. In contracting, terms and conditions need to be attractive to all partners. Contracting is not only limited to formal contracts but also to relational governance, including a psychological contract that explains the contracting starting points to stakeholders who are not directly involved. For successful contracting in ecosystem partnering, rigorous governance is a must.

The focus of governance is on both monitoring and change management procedures. The dynamics in ecosystems and/or the market will impact ecosystem partnership. Partners must collectively understand this impact. Proper change management procedures enable partners to adjust contracting and ensure that participation in the ecosystem remains attractive to all partners. In case this is no longer feasible, the partners need to agree on modifications in the ecosystem, again following the change management procedures including clear parameters, such as minimal volume products or services and/or (indexed) price level thresholds. This will protect all partners from being negatively impacted by opportunistic behavior from one or more partners in the ecosystem.

13.6.3 Ecosystem good practices – Data sharing

As in any collaboration, also in ecosystem partnerships, sharing data is exciting and risky. Partners may have the feeling that they will jeopardize their competitive position and give up any intellectual property rights. In fact, to mitigate potential risks, organizations should/need to start small with data sharing and expand over time. It is important to have a controlled expansion that includes benefit tracking, which is an integral part of contractual governance. Organizations need to decide on the transparency of the shared data, e.g. anonymized, aggregated, or real time versus time lag. Organizations must take into account the growing impact of advancing technology such as artificial intelligence and machine learning. Over time, partners might decide to make changes to the agreed transparency of the shared data, meaning reducing the data transparency to protect the interest of partners in the ecosystem. To monitor the shared data, organizations need to implement proper tooling across the participating organizations. This tooling also helps to improve the quality of the data.

Furthermore, data sharing does not necessarily mean that the data changes. Data ownership must be clear at all times. This will also improve data quality, as the data owner holds the responsibility for data quality.

Due to monetization, data becomes more complex due to diffused data ownership. If data is enriched and included as an embedded part in a service or product by a partner that is not the data owner, how will benefits be shared between partners? This requires a good understanding of the efforts and contributions of all partners to the value creation, as this ultimately drives the distribution of profits. In monetization data, there is a specific challenge in sharing customer experience data with all partners. The ultimate customer experience is relevant for all partners but typically owned by the last link of the value chain, which is for sure not the sole partner that created this value. Therefore, partners specifically need to align on sharing customer experience data in ecosystem partnerships. There is a distinct need to build a feedback loop on customer experience that goes back up the value chain to all ecosystem partners.

TATA CONSULTANCY SERVICE CASE STUDY: EMBRACING INDUSTRIAL IOT

The data analytics culture is transforming processes and improving efficiencies at Tata Chemicals' mother plant

Tata Chemicals (TCL) is among the largest soda ash companies in the world with a global capacity of about 5.5 million tons per annum. Its Mithapur plant in Gujarat, India, alone has the capacity to manufacture 900,000 tonnes of soda ash per annum.

Even though the soda ash segment has been growing, the business is facing increased pricing pressures. To stay competitive, TCL recognized the need to drive operational excellence and embarked on a digital journey.

Early shoots

In 2017, TCL partnered with Tata Consultancy Services (TCS) to conduct a Discovery Value Assessment (DVA) at its Mithapur plant. "Increasing efficiency was set as one of the key business objectives," recollects N Kamath, plant head, Tata Chemicals, Mithapur. "And the team set out to identify use cases to deliver the objectives."

Analysis of six months' operational data of the carbonation towers and high-pressure boilers indicated high process variance as a key issue, resulting in loss of efficiency and yield.

"When you reduce variation, you ensure steady efficiency," says Mr Kamath, adding, "And once you achieve steady efficiency, you can find ways to improve it. The carbonation towers were at 67.8 percent efficiency; we set a target of 70 percent." Even one percent improvement in yield, adds as much as $400,000 to the annual margin.

This was an ideal 'digital twin' use case for carbonation towers and boilers, both of which are critical assets. "In the true spirit of agile, three towers and two boilers were identified as part of the proof-of-value pilot. Our approach was to demonstrate results early and then scale-up to the rest of the towers and boilers," says Sayantan Roy from TCS who has been spearheading these efforts with Tata Chemicals.

While the team was building a business case, there was skepticism if this was 'just another technology project.' The project needed to deliver the key performance indicators (KPI) improvements as well as financial savings. This skepticism, in hindsight, became a driver for the results-oriented approach.

An eye-opening field trip

In 2018, a field visit was organized for Tata group companies; from Tata Chemicals, its MD & CEO, Mr Mukundan, led a cross-functional team. The objective was to learn how Industry 4.0 is being implemented to deliver the KPI improvements as well as financial savings.

Importance of historical data

"Even though we had started the DVA earlier, the field visit made two things happen," Mr Kamath says, adding, "We got a boost from the senior management, and we returned with the belief that analytics could indeed add value to the plant." The plant has data from over 32,000 sensors, stored in multiple decision support systems (DCS), to provide a single view to the operator on how the plant is running. The operator changes certain parameters on the equipment to get the right output.

While the DCS does store historical data, it goes back only a couple of months. Decision support systems require operational data of the equipment going back 12–18 months. The first step was getting the historical data in place and an historian implementation was initiated. In parallel, the value assessment exercise was completed for carbonation towers and boilers.

Carbonation towers

Carbonation is a critical process in soda ash production and it determines the yield of soda ash. Any process variation results in lower yield. A single operator monitors 15 carbonation towers and adjusts control loops based on quality of the results and upstream process variation to get the best possible yield. Since the process is highly complex, even with sophisticated control systems in place, it was not possible to analyze the data manually and act in real time.

With the historian in place, a prescriptive analytics system was developed for the carbonation towers. The new solution didn't just report data, as was the case earlier, but also recommended actionable insights to the operator. The plant operator is now enabled with advisory to change the temperature, pressure, or flow to a very specific value.

These new insights were integrated within the single-pane-of-glass in the control room itself. The operator would execute the prescribed action and change the parameters, using the existing DCS screen. With the digital twin of the carbonation towers, the operator knows exactly what parameters to change and by how much so that the towers work at peak efficiency.

With three towers going live in September 2019 and the remaining 11 in May 2020, the AI-led actionable insights are enabling proactive measures in real time. There are fewer process inconsistencies, average efficiency has improved, standard deviation has substantially reduced, and the average yield has improved by 0.5%.

Boilers

The performance and reliability of the power plant are critical in reducing process variations and maximizing output. When boilers operate at sub-optimal efficiencies, they consume more fuel.

A low steam-to-fuel ratio also affects the boiler adversely, which in turn affects its availability since maintenance processes have to be run more frequently. All of this increases the operating costs and impacts the profit margins.

To improve the power plant's boiler efficiency, a digital twin was developed. The AI-driven algorithm generates set points on real-time basis which enables operators to correct the processes and thereby improve the boiler's efficiency. Like with the carbonation towers, these algorithms work in the background, and the operator gets actionable insights which in the earlier world were entirely dependent on their tacit knowledge.

In April 2020, the implementation was completed for two boilers. The new insights have brought down the rate of increase in the boiler stack temperature and reduced fuel consumption; thus, operators are able to maintain a high steam-to-fuel ratio.

Big learnings come from challenges

The most important building block of an effective data model is clean data across a duration of 12–24 months at least. It was decided to build the data model for boilers first. The team found that data for a longer duration was unavailable as the DCS had the capacity to store data for just a month or two. "We quickly shifted our focus from boilers to the carbonation towers where such data was available," says Prasanna Wadke, technology evangelist at Tata Chemicals. If this decision had not been taken, it would have caused a six-month delay in realizing outcomes.

To implement the decision support system on the carbonation towers and boilers, the two pieces of equipment had to be independently connected to a local area network. This was not possible as they shared the same IP address with other assets connected to the various distribution control systems across the plant. "But changing the IP addresses of two of the most critical assets required them to be powered down, which would have taken six months. We worked with our IT teams to find a solution that required no down time. This was a breakthrough that helped save time," says Mr Wadke.

From the business side change management was crucial. Workers on the plant floor were given adequate training on the new ways of working and the benefits thereof. "The biggest takeaway is when you're positioning a technology-led transformation with business, you have to quantify savings in cold rupee terms. Most projects fail because they are unable to define that. The Digital Value Assessment approach enabled the upfront quantification of benefits. This made change management easier," he adds.

Like Tata Steel, Tata Chemicals also faces challenges in hiring talent due to Mithapur's remote location. Tata Chemicals worked with TCS as its strategic partner. "Even though we didn't have talent in AI and machine learning (ML), a lot of our managers have Six Sigma certification," Mr Wadke says. "This helped because they could appreciate this kind of an improvement initiative. We also created key roles such as data scientist in-house."

The cross-functional team from TCL and TCS did not just include AI and ML experts but also those who had worked on boilers for ten years and knew the vagaries of running one. The team also had chemical engineers who had run process plants. "Cross-functional teams don't just bring diversity of expertise, they also ease communication and increase your chances of success," Mr. Wadke says.

Driving sustained results

"To sustain the program, you need to constantly revalidate the mathematical and data model that has been built. You need experts who understand these models," he says. TCL has retained a core team, led by a digital advisor, for engaging with the plant managers to ensure operator adoption is smooth and to monitor outcomes. They also plan new use cases for future implementation.

Our connected future

Tata Chemicals is already seeing the benefits. The digital twins for carbonation towers and boilers are delivering savings of approximately Rs. 5.2 crore per year. As a result, there is strong buy-in of how digital can create an impact, which otherwise would not have been possible.

"We are now looking at digital to offer solutions to many of our problems," Mr Kamath says. Whether it is using ISRO satellites to analyze the color of the condensers across the unmanned 36,000 acres of salt works or using camera imaging to do a headcount at an assembly point during a drill, digital is offering answers to questions no one thought of asking earlier. "As part of our next project, we are looking to improve the throughput of the cement plant by minimizing the variation in clinker quality and reducing unplanned downtime of critical equipment," he adds.

13.6.4 Ecosystem good practices – Compliance and ethics

Compliance and ethics are two distinct but closely related topics. Any organization has to adhere to legislation, and compliance is the minimum threshold. Ethics goes beyond legislative adherence; ethical principles and policies are determined and driven at the organizational level and need to be aligned throughout the value chain. In addition, organizations need to be on top of their compliance set and maintain their ethical standards.

Regarding compliance, it is important that organizations anticipate upcoming legislation. The volume and impact of upcoming legislation is and will increase significantly. For ecosystem partnering, upcoming legislation related to antitrust and privacy regulations are the dominant forms of legislation to watch. Anticipation is important as legislation might impact the business models and/or agreed processes and procedures. Partners need time to adjust their arrangements, followed by adjusting the underlying processes and procedures.

With regard to ethics, aligning on norms and values in the partnership design and over the duration of the ecosystem partnerships is crucial. This requires that partners maintain their ethical guidelines, as norms and values continuously influx. To maintain ethical standards, specific governance must be implemented. In addition to an ethical rule board with diverse members, an algorithm rule board also must be installed. The rule board reviews the data sets and algorithms in use to avoid unethical decision-making.

13.7   Conclusion

Organizations recognize the need to improve in ecosystem partnerships, but they are still in preparation mode. This is a concerning observation. Increased management attention is required for increased value creation by better partnering with the ecosystem.

Most organizations still operate in traditional customer/supplier relationships. For over a decade platforms have structured many markets. The business model of the platform is different, but in essence, the platforms provide only a marketplace. Transforming business models in ecosystems requires a different mindset. Trust is crucial in building ecosystems but it needs to be backed by contracts. Ecosystem partners must have the long-term perspective but they also need to be mindful of opportunistic behaviors from ecosystem partners and their own executives.

In addition to developing partnering capabilities and applying adequate contracting mechanisms, the real challenges are in data sharing, ensuring compliance, and safeguarding ethical behavior. The latter two are conditional for successful ecosystem partnering. The implication is not that compliance and ethics are simple and straightforward. Both have a very dynamic nature, increasing numbers of upcoming legislation and continuously changing ethical norms. These topics require continuous management attention and need to be included in any decision-making as an integral part of the norms and values of any organization.

Data sharing is the binding factor in ecosystem partnerships, as data fuels value creation. Data also impacts competitive relations, creates dependencies between partners, and in some cases even creates intellectual property. Data-sharing concepts are at the heart of ecosystem partnership design, as well as in managing partnerships, and enabling data analytics. Management requires a continuous alignment between partners and the willingness of partners to adjust the collaboration and underpinning agreements to foster continuous value creation for all partners involved. In the ever-growing dynamics and globalization of markets, this is the ultimate challenge for executives in the next decade.

Notes

1 This chapter is based on HPDO report Excelling in the Digital World – Ecosystem Partnering (Beulen, 2020b).
2 See https://www.senseo.us/.
3 See https://marketplace.walmart.com/.
4 See https://www.ideal.nl/en/ideal-information/.
5 See https://www.randstad.com/about-randstad/randstad-innovation-fund/.

PART 5

Aligning at the crossroads of data analytics and digital transformations

To stay ahead of the curve, organizations need to continuously innovate. A digital transformation is not a one-off project. Analyzing data for digital transformations never stops, and insights from analyses and new and generated data are input for more advanced analyses providing new insights and/or improving data-driven decision-making. Therefore, organizations need to develop and implement strategies; these are built on the phases detailed in Part 3. These strategies are different for organizations within public and private sectors. Chapter 14 details a scenario for four types of organizations. Beyond these strategies and scenarios, the bigger aims for 2030 are detailed in Chapter 15. There are many uncertainties, but organizations can be assured that technology will move faster than expected and, that ecosystems will be more dynamic than ever, while compliance will continue to be more stringent, and the threat of cybercrime will be more significant. In short, there will be a lot of opportunities for organizations that set the right strategies, are responsive, and are able to attract, retain, and train their employees, as the demand for digital and data capabilities will continue to grow.

DOI: 10.4324/9781003246770-18

14

IDENTIFYING GOOD PRACTICES AND ROADMAPS FOR ALIGNING ANALYTICS AND DIGITAL ORGANIZATIONAL GOALS

In this chapter, scenarios for four types of organizations are detailed. These scenarios include "good practices" and are based on Chapter 10, as well as follow to detail the same seven characteristics. The four types of organizations are central government (public sector), local government (public sector), private sector organizations providing services, and private sector organizations providing services as well as products. The central government and private sector organizations providing services will be fully described, where for the local government only the differences with the central government, and for private sector organizations with services and products only the difference with private sector organizations with services will be described. In this chapter also the impact of size and geographical spread will be addressed. Obviously, there are also differences per region, but these are too specific to address in this book.

14.1 Good practices and roadmaps for central public sector organizations

Central public sector organizations must balance between supporting G2B and G2C digital transformation and data analytics initiatives. Supporting one will positively impact the other. Focusing on core themes will increase the digital and data analytics savviness of the inhabitants. A good example of bold moves is e-voting, as this increases the involvement of the citizens. Estonia started a blockchain that allows e-voting in 2005 and has conducted +10 nationwide elections (Ehin et al., 2022). Countries implementing e-voting must be aware of the digital divide, but must also use e-voting to reduce the digital divide and ensure digital inclusion by actively increasing the savviness of their citizens. Another example is Know Your Customer (KYC) legislation and regulations, as this prevents criminal and fraudulent

DOI: 10.4324/9781003246770-19

financial transactions. However, there is room for improvement in many countries. First, KYC requires significant efforts from financial institutions including management attention, resources, and investments in adjusting internal processes and tooling. Second, KYC is not efficient, as it is conducted in every individual financial institution. Finally, KYC is not very customer friendly, customers experience delays in the execution of financial transactions and they have to provide information multiple times. Similar to the case for e-voting, blockchain could be a technology that can address these three KYC challenges. The introduction of a blockchain-based self-sovereign identity also addresses privacy concerns (Schlatt et al., 2022). In the legislation and regulations, central public sector organizations must embrace innovative technologies to achieve their objective, namely, preventing criminal and fraudulent financial transactions.

As digital and data analytics become more important and an integral part of doing business and of our lives, it is essential that central public sector organizations police violation of legislation, regulations, and ethical standards. Policing violations will generate trust. The policing of violations by the central government impacts both externally, toward businesses as well as citizens, and internally, toward central public sector organizations. Central organizations need to lead by example.

For external violations, the focus of public sector organizations must be on ensuring online trust and cyber resilience. Especially in Europe, many laws are and will come into place. First, there is the Digital Service Act package, which consists of the Digital Service Act focusing on improving the mechanisms for the removal of illegal content and the effective protection of users' fundamental rights online, and the Digital Markets Act, ensuring that large online platforms, i.e. gatekeepers, behave in a fair way online. Second, there are, related to cyber resilience, the NIS2 Directive, the AI Act, the Cybersecurity Act, the Digital Operational Resilience Act, and the Cyber Resilience Act. Some of these are proposed, while others are adopted, or applicable,[1] but these are all to come. The legislation is going beyond the digital space. For example, the Cyber Resilience Act focuses on cyber security for all products with digital components and sets obligations for the manufacturers, including enforcing cyber security by design, providing clear and understandable instructions, documenting cybersecurity risks, reporting obligations of actively exploited vulnerabilities and incidents, handling vulnerabilities effectively and providing security updates. This legislation will improve cyber security and cyber resilience. Central public sector organizations must actively police violations of online trusts and cyber security legislation and regulations, as this will increase the trust of businesses and citizens and their willingness to engage in digital transformation and apply data analytics.

In addition to external violations, central governments also need to police internal violations. The pandemic has been a challenge for many central governments. Tracking software has been used extensively to alert citizens; this practice has raised privacy and ethical concerns in many countries. However, the pandemic was unprecedented and unanticipated. Central governments need to plan and develop strategies on how to better handle this in the future. A more clear-cut example that amplifies the need for central public sector organizations to anticipate better is Cambridge Analytica in 2016, which was hired by Leave. EU and the UK Independence Party. The democratic process was manipulated, as personal data from millions of Facebook users was collected without consent.[2] Another example in artificial intelligence is the Dutch government using data and algorithms in fraud detection. The Dutch government deployed artificial intelligence to handle childcare benefit applications that disproportionately denied benefits to ethnic minorities and charged them with fraud. As a consequence, the Dutch cabinet resigned in January 2021. In response to this and other data and privacy issues, the Dutch government launched an improvement program, which has increased the focus on data quality and responsible data analytics names "Open Op Orde."[3]

External and internal policing requires strong governance. Central public sector organizations need to establish authorities to deal with data protection and privacy. An example in the European Union is the European Data Protection Board, which is composed of representatives of the national data protection authorities, and the European Data Protection Supervisor. Furthermore, there is the OECD initiative on enforcement of privacy legislation including recommendations – see Action Plan for the Global Privacy Enforcement Network (2012/2013).[4]

14.1.1 Roadmap – Digital leadership for central public sector organizations

In achieving the next level, the digital leaders of central public sector organizations need to get connected with supranational organizations and exchange lessons learned related to digital transformations and data analytics. Good examples in this context are the United Nations Development Program[5] and the Organization for Economic Co-operation and Development (EOCD).[6] There are similar connections with compliance, as digital leaders must ensure compliance with existing and upcoming legislation and regulations. In addition to connecting with the regulators, digital leaders must consult legal, compliance, and risk managers, as well as technology advisers, and build a knowledge ecosystem to ensure a timely anticipation.

All this networking and knowledge management is also input for updating the digital strategy and the data analytics strategy. External input and validation prepare central public sector organizations for entering the next phase of digital transformation.

14.1.2 Roadmap – Operating model for central public sector organizations

Central public sector organizations should update the operating model and strengthen the operating model by increasing data analysis and adding data in order to increase the value creation. The emphasis on data analytics and adding data must be done by design. Therefore, involvement of enterprise and IT architects in addition to the chief data office is required.

Central public sector organizations need to develop an operating model which provides insight to businesses and citizens, 'sharing back' is the central theme of the next digital transformation phase. The format of the data needs to support usability, and the sharing of these insights needs to be transparent. Businesses can use the insights in doing business and create added value for their clients, and citizens should benefit from an even more convenient interaction with the central government.

14.1.3 Roadmap – Digital operating model for central public sector organizations

Agile ways of working have already been fully adopted in Digital Transformation Phase 3.0, and this includes fully embracing agile frameworks such as SAFe and LeSS. The next level is to document and share priorities with politicians, business, and citizens. By adopting this approach, a central public sector organization provides full transparency, potentially followed by involvement and participation in priority setting. Just to be clear, this will not be easy, nor straightforward and requires a mature organization with a strong agile governance. Many central public sector organizations are not there yet, but if you do proper stakeholder management and the decision-making and processes are unambiguous, this provides a good opportunity to participate.

14.1.4 Roadmap – Digital governance for central public sector organizations

The focus of many central public sector organizations in the digital transformation phase 3.0 was still on budget-driven governance, simply because this is how many central public sector organizations have operated since their establishment. Focus on setting priorities and managing digital and data analytics initiatives must be converted towards generating maximum public value. As a consequence, an additional budget is needed for digital transformations. This change means steering the available budget from the opportunities that generate the most public value in order to allocate the budget towards any opportunity that generates sufficient public value. This will result in the shift of traditional budgets to digital transformation and data analytics budgets.

14.1.5 Roadmap – Capabilities for central public sector organizations

The most important change central public sector organizations need to make in talent management is changing the capability perspective to a sourcing perspective.

One of the pain points of central public sector organizations is the large number of self-employed contractors. The explanation for this phenomenon is that the compensation packages of central public sector organizations are restricted to civil servants. Contracting is providing additional room to maneuver; nevertheless, most countries also have a maximum hourly/day rate in place. In the sourcing perspective, central organizations need to either offer the self-employed contract employment or replace them with talent that is motivated to contribute to the creation of public value and accepts the compensation packages. Alternatively, central public sector organizations contract with service providers. This strategy enables central public sector organizations to agree on output obligations and volume discounts. Furthermore, the dependency from self-employed contractors is reduced, as service providers are committed to replacing their staff if and when required (Beulen and Ribbers, 2021).

14.1.6   Roadmap – Data leadership for central public sector organizations

Maturing the data stewards and having 100% automated data management tooling in place elevates central public sector organizations to the next digital transformation phase. The maturing of the data stewards is important as the volumes of the data sets are growing, as well as the number of data consumers. Typically, not only the seniority of the data stewards' advances, but also the number of data stewards increases. If necessary, organizations also might decide to appoint additional data owners by splitting data sets across multiple data owners. This will make the role of the data owner more manageable, as this is a key role. The increased use and reuse of data also sets requirements for the data management tooling. Any manual intervention could jeopardize data quality.

14.1.7   Roadmap – Data analytics for central public sector organization

Focusing on getting insights from unstructured external data will bring central public sector organizations to the next digital transformation phase. Unstructured external data sets set additional requirements for the onboarding and classification of data, as well as the allocations of rights to use the data. Furthermore, the verification of algorithms applied on data sets including external unstructured data sets is more complex. This sets requirements and raises the bar for central public sector organizations.

In this next digital transformation phase, central public sector organizations also need to look for potential additional data sets that can increase public value. Balancing data volumes and having data life cycle management in place protects against becoming data obese, which also contributes to sustainability objectives.

14.2 Good practices and roadmaps for local public sector organizations

Local public sector organizations have similar but different challenges as central public sector organizations. For starters, the scale of most local public sector organizations is smaller. This will affect data analytics and their digital transformations. Local public sector organizations should consider collaborating with other local public sector organizations by implementing shared technology and service centers (SSCs). This helps local organizations to build at scale, and as a consequence, to introduce new technologies and innovate (Richter and Bruehl, 2020). An important success factor in implementing and managing SCCs is managerial involvement and no political involvement. The electoral motives and whims for politicians are not helpful for digital transformations and data analytics success.

The primary good practice of the central government that will apply to a smaller degree to local public sector organizations is the supporting role in policing violations of legislation and ethical standards, where this is the primary responsibility of the central public sector organizations. This will be detailed in Section 14.2.1 – structuring collaboration between local public sector organizations, and Section 14.2.2. – sharing digital and data analytics resources between local public sector organizations.

The other three good practices of central public sector organizations (focus on critical processes, balance between G2B and G2C digital and data analytics initiatives, and lead by example) also apply to local governments, but they are not different from the good practices for central governments.

Most of the seven characteristics for central governments are not different for local governments; this includes operating models, digital operating model, digital governance, digital leadership, and data analytics. The distinct differences for the local public sector organizations are in the characteristics of digital leadership and capabilities. These are detailed in the following subsections.

14.2.1 Roadmap – Digital leadership for local public sector organizations

In addition to the good practices to set up shared service centers, local public sector organizations must connect with central public sector organizations to share lessons learned and insights, as well as budget allocation related to digital transformations and data analytics. This is similar to the central public sector organizations connecting with supranational organizations; it facilitates knowledge management. Also, as national legislation and regulations typically are prepared and implemented by central public sector organizations, connecting with them ensures local public sector organizations are prepared for upcoming legislation and regulations.

14.2.2 Roadmap – Capabilities for local public sector organizations

In setting up shared services centers with other local public sector organizations, staffing requires management attention. Many local public sector organizations are constrained in their abilities to make nonperforming civil servants redundant. Furthermore, many local public sector organizations also do not have a performance-driven culture. This increases the risk that participating local public sector organizations use the SSC as an opportunity to transfer their nonperforming civil servants into the SSC. This will resolve a problem in their organization but create a problem in the SSC. The onboarding of civil servants requires significant management attention from all participating local public sector organizations. Only with capable staff can a SCC successfully support the participating local public sector organization in the next digital transformation phase.

14.3 Good practices and roadmaps for private sector organizations providing services

In the act of monetizing, data producing organizations face fierce competition. In this competition, significantly increased insights are expected at the same or even slightly reduced charges. This presents challenges for private sector organizations providing services in entering the next digital phase. As an example, financial institution organizations need to go beyond dashboarding, and they need to provide insights into competitors and sector developments, as well as investment advice, based on open data, anonymized, and masked data, in order to avoid commercially sensitive data being shared. In addition, private sector organizations providing services shift from risk protection to risk prevention (Bain, 2023). Think about the use of health apps, in return for reduced insurance fees, or installing an app to monitor driving behavior, in return for a reduced car insurance fee.

Similar to public sector organizations, private sector organizations must also anticipate upcoming regulations and legislation. They need to make sure that they are ready and compliant. Furthermore, private sector organizations need to consider going beyond the compliance requirement. This is not limited to benefiting from a responsible and social image but also avoids continuously playing catch-up. It offers the opportunity to lead by example and potentially contribute to social discussions.

14.3.1 Roadmap – Digital leadership for private sector organizations providing services

In achieving the next level, the digital leaders of private sector organizations need to get connected with their peers and exchange lessons learned related to digital transformations and data analytics.

Also, for compliance, connecting with peers is important. This ensures compliance with existing and upcoming legislation and regulations. In addition to connecting with the supranational and central public sector organizations, digital leaders must consult legal, compliance, and risk managers as well as technology advisers and they must build a knowledge ecosystem to ensure timely anticipation of legislation and regulatory changes.

All this networking and knowledge management is also an input for updating the digital strategy and the data analytics strategy. External input and validation prepare private sector organizations for the next digital transformation phase.

14.3.2   Roadmap – Operating model for private sector organizations providing services

Private sector organizations must advance monetization by increasing data analytics and adding data. This will provide additional insights and, therefore, will result in increased value creation. Analytics by design is required, and immediate involvement of the enterprise and IT architects, in addition to the chief data office is essential.

Private sector organizations must develop operating models that provide insights to the ecosystem partners; "sharing back" is the central theme of the next digital transformation phase. The format of the data needs to support usability, and the sharing of these insights needs to be transparent and not jeopardize the commercial interest and ethical value of any of the ecosystem partners.

14.3.3   Roadmap – Digital operating model for private sector organizations providing services

Private sector organizations have already fully adopted agile ways of working in the digital transformation phase 3.0, this includes fully embracing agile frameworks such as SAFe and LeSS. The next level is to document and share priorities with stakeholders and ecosystem partners while avoiding commercial conflicts of interest. By adopting this approach, a private sector organization provides full transparency, potentially followed by involvement and participation in priority setting. Just to be clear, this will not be easy nor straightforward and requires a mature organization with a strong agile governance. Many private sector organizations are not there yet, but if you do proper stakeholder management and the decision-making and processes are unambiguous, this provides a good opportunity to strengthen the partnerships and basis for collaboration and innovation.

14.3.4   Roadmap – Digital governance for private sector organizations providing services

In most private sector organizations, governance has already transformed from budget-driven to generating added value. In the next phase of the digital transformation, digital governance is more decentralized, in addition to embracing agile ways of working, business will be able to align better and faster with the continuously changing demands and requirements. This is furthermore increasing the involvement of employees, as due to the decentralized governance additional managers are mandated to prioritize innovative ideas, which drives innovation. As a consequence, budgets should be allocated at a lower level in the organization. The challenge for private sector organizations is to align all decentralized digital transformation and data analytics budgets with enterprise objectives. This requires a balancing act, since strict monitoring and managing of the decentralized initiatives will demoralize employees and stifle innovation, and too little monitoring and managing will jeopardize the achievements of organizational objectives.

14.3.5   Roadmap – Capabilities for private sector organizations providing services

The most important change that private sector organizations make in talent management, is turning the capability and sourcing perspective into a full sourcing perspective. Different from public sector organizations, employment packages are typically not a problem in private sector organizations, although large organizations and some sectors, e.g. financial services, provide more attractive employment packages than other private sector organizations.

The pain points for private sector organizations are the large number of IT professionals from different service providers, as well as the large number of self-employed contractors. The explanation for this phenomenon is that the growth in demand in the last decade was simply too large to acquire enough qualified employees. The most important step in sourcing is vendor consolidation. By reducing the number of service providers, the vendor management effort reduces, and the potential volume discount is on the horizon, along with transforming contracts from best effort contracts to output contracts (Beulen and Ribbers, 2021). Also, from the sourcing perspective, private sector organizations need to either offer the self-employed contract employment or replace them with fresh talent.

14.3.6   Roadmap – Data leadership for private sector organizations providing services

This characteristic of private sector organizations is quite similar to that of public sector organizations. Also, for private sector organizations, maturing the data stewards and having 100% automated data management tooling in place is important to enter the next digital transformation phase. This is important, as the volumes of the data sets are growing, as are the number of data consumers; basically, each employee is a citizen data scientist, and therefore the seniority of the data stewards advances as the number of data stewards increases. Also, additional data owners must be appointed as data sets are split and allocated to multiple new data owners. This sets additional challenges for digital governance.

Unlike public sector organizations, most private sector organizations have already fully automated their data management tools.

14.3.7 Roadmap – Data analytics for private sector organizations providing services

In addition, the roadmap for data analytics for private sector organizations is quite similar to the roadmap for public sector organizations. The focus must be on getting insights from unstructured external data, unlike public sector organizations, many private sector organizations buy the unstructured external data. These procured data sets are either stored or accessed directly via an API. This still results in additional requirements for the onboarding and classification of data, as well as the allocations of rights to use the data. Also, the verification of algorithms applied to data sets, including external unstructured data sets, is more complex and has an increased risk profile due to the large volumes of procured unstructured external data. This sets requirements and raises the bar for private sector organizations.

14.4 Good practices and roadmaps for private sector organizations providing services and products

Private sector organizations that manufacture products and provide services have the same challenges as private sector organizations that provide only services. They need to provide significantly increased insights at the same or even slightly reduced charges. In addition, they have to decide in how they would like to invest, as products also require investments, in addition to investments in services. It is difficult to make trade-offs, as the products also generate revenue streams.

With regard to anticipating upcoming regulations and legislation, there is not much of a difference. What is discriminating is the size of an organization. For larger organizations, it is easier to stay informed, and where larger organizations might struggle to implement changes due to legacy constraints and technical debt, smaller organizations might face difficulties in allocating sufficient and qualified resources to implement the change.

Most of the seven characteristics for private sector organizations providing service only are not different for private sector organizations providing services and products, but this also includes digital leadership, digital operating models, digital governance, capabilities, and data analytics. The distinct differences are in the operating model and in data leadership. These are detailed in the below subsections.

14.4.1 Roadmap – Operating model for private sector organizations providing service and products

While provision of services and manufacturing products, the operating model has to be transformed into a 100% services model with usage-based subscription fees. This increases the risk profile but is necessary to meet the expectations of clients. Private sector organizations need to be mindful that innovation is not slowed down due to outdated products. Service demands set the pace and might result in writing off manufactured but outdated products. Furthermore, upcoming legislation, e.g. the Cyber Resilience Act, related to product-related cyber security obligations further increases the risk related to products.

14.4.2   Roadmap – Data leadership for private sector organizations providing services and products

The change in the operating model also impacts the profile of the data stewards. The data stewards related to products need to change as the operating model has changed from a hybrid operating model addressing products as well as services, into an operating model with solely services. The new data stewards need to be trained and integrated in with the existing data stewards. Typically, there are no changes to the data owners, as the data owners related to the product do not change when the product is not changing.

14.5   Conclusion

Despite the distinct difference between the four types of organizations, there are a lot of similarities. Any organization needs to set their strategy, adjust if and when required, and push as hard as they can to remain relevant. The most important changes, regardless of the type of organization, are the increasing applicable legislation as well as the full focus on services in any operating model. The context of continuously growing data sets and dynamics creates opportunities for any organization to improve and increase added value.

Notes

1 For more insights, see https://www.europarl.europa.eu/news/en/headlines/security/20221103STO48002/fighting-cybercrime-new-eu-cybersecurity-laws-explained.
2 See for more context https://www.theguardian.com/news/series/cambridge-analytica-files
3 See https://www.rijksoverheid.nl/documenten/rapporten/2021/04/06/open-op-orde-generiek-actieplan-informatiehuishouding-rijksoverheid - in Dutch.
4 See for more details https://www.privacyenforcement.net/content/home-public.
5 See https://digitalstrategy.undp.org/.
6 See https://www.oecd.org/digital/.

15

2030 PERSPECTIVE ON LEVERAGING DATA ANALYTICS IN ACHIEVING DIGITAL TRANSFORMATION SUCCESS

In Chapter 10, we looked back as well as ahead to the short term, and we defined digital transformation phases. For the mid-term, we detailed a scenario for four types of organizations in Chapter 14. The focus of this chapter is on the long term. What should organizations do today to ensure they are relevant in 2030? The focus is on the potential impact of emerging technologies, such as quantum computing and the metaverse, as well as how to anticipate on upcoming legislation and the growing emphasis on ethics.

15.1 Leveraging data analytics

There are five challenges related to data analytics: being in control of the data, increasing engagement with RegTechs and ensuring cyber resilience, increasing data sharing in ecosystems, ensuring adequate processing power, and increasing rigor of ethical assessments of algorithms.

Organizations have successfully improved their data quality by assigning data owners and data stewards. The next challenge is to control data, by means of relevance, as well as volumes and usage. Relevance can be improved by data set certification. This provides good guidance to data consumers in selecting data sets in the service catalog for performing data analytics. Being in control of volumes and usage ensures cost control and contributes to sustainability as well as reduces compliance risks and cyber security risks.

With regard to managing the compliance risks, organizations need to increase the use of RegTechs. The increasing legislation and regulations make building up an in-house capability very difficult and is not always cost-effective. For most organizations, it will already be a challenge to build up and maintain the capability to manage RegTechs and compliance advisers. The cyber security risk is expected to

DOI: 10.4324/9781003246770-20

continue to increase. Data analytics is an important tool for cyber security specialists in monitoring cyber security to ensure cyber resilience.

An additional challenge is to increase data sharing in ecosystems combined with making the shared data also available for citizen data scientists, instead of only for the data scientists. This sets additional requirements for governance but ultimately creates value by stimulating innovation.

Technological development is ongoing; this is related to traditional processors, including base frequency, maximum turbo speed and hyper-threading, and innovative technologies such as quantum computing. For many organizations, quantum computing is a promise for the foreseeable future; nevertheless, organizations need to continuously explore new innovative technologies. There is skepticism that quantum computing is suitable for data analytics (Beulen, 2020a).

As algorithms have become more complex, the number of data scientists and citizen data scientists has increased. On top of that, ethical awareness is growing significantly, and what is considered as ethical is changing rapidly. This sets requirements for advancing the rigor of the ethical assessment of algorithms. Audit firms are offering frameworks and consulting services to perform this type of assessment. These are still the early days, but in the foreseeable future, audit firms will be able to provide some type of ethical algorithm assurance (Beulen et al., 2022).

15.2   Achieving digital transformation success

There are three challenges related to digital transformations: investing in talent and partners, focusing on sustainability, and empathizing in connecting.

Organizations need to invest in talent and partners. Digital transformations are a capability play, and technology is important, but access to talent is more important. Organizations need to balance between training their employees and recruiting, outsourcing, and partnering. The distinction between outsourcing and partnering is not always clear. In outsourcing, the service provider provides services, whereas partnerships collaborate and co-create services. Outsourcing services are typically standard services, whereas partnership services are more innovative.

Furthermore, sustainability is getting more and more important. Many organizations have embraced the United Nations Sustainability Development Goals. These provide good guidance on how sustainability can be achieved and can be used to explore partnerships and promote the organization in retaining and recruiting employees. In addition, as these goals are widely adopted, organizations can use the goals to position and profile their organization. To be clear, sustainability is not limited to environmental themes; social themes such as inclusion are also becoming more and more important in digital transformations.

Finally, organizations need to include empathy in connecting. This is with employees, contractors, service providers, and partners, as well as with customers for private sector organizations, regardless of whether the organization operates in a B2B or B2C market, and citizens and business for public sector organizations. This is becoming more important as online communication matures from portals and online video chat to more immersive communication on, for example, the metaverse. This is a new era and requires a more personal and inclusive approach, which is not straightforward in a global setting with different and blending cultures, norms and beliefs.

TATA CONSULTANCY SERVICES – 2030 PERSPECTIVES

Themis Michaelides – Tata Consultancy Services
Global head advisory and consulting for BTG – Data and analytics

While it may seem that 2030 is a long way off, when looking back and thinking about what was happening in data 8 years ago, it was mostly traditional business intelligence. Data governance and data-driven decision-making were just beginning to emerge into the mainstream, following the early adopters driven mostly by compliance initiatives. Now, data-driven decision-making is in every industry including the governmental sector. Themis Michaelides: "We should expect and plan for the same level of dramatic change in the next eight years, especially in productizing data, data ethics and data sharing." Furthermore, organizations should keep an eye on tooling. Organizations have to invest in tooling to get better insights from their data. Themis Michaelides: "Finally organizations need to ensure they are compliant in regards to the data they keep and respect privacy legislation at all times. Also this is and will be a moving target."

Productizing data

We expect to see more data marketplaces, brokering deals between data consumers and data providers. Data becomes a commodity across industries and ecosystems, to be traded, bartered, priced, indexed, exchanged, and derived. Themis Michaelides:

> You'll be able to give data to someone else and they can reciprocate with some of their data. That is the whole course of data democratization, data sharing, and data monetization and commoditization. Imagine if you could tie passenger information or profile avatars within the tourist or travel industry – from airlines to car rentals to hotels to restaurants.

Artificial Intelligence (AI)/Machine Learning (ML), analytics, and ethics will drastically mature over the next decade. Today data scientists are still struggling to find the right data, in the right quantity, at the right time – this will become seamless, as well as accessing the data in the right place with the right ethics.

Ethics

Ethics is a challenging topic to predict. When you are doing a Google search and moments later Facebook is prompting you with advertising on the same topic, that can be unnerving for those not comfortable with that kind of data sharing and immediate targeted marketing. But then again, it's nice to see notifications of things you might like. Themis Michaelides: "So it's a double edge sword." There's a whole generation growing up with and born into this kind of targeted AI-based marketing, and there is nothing unnerving about it – it is just typical marketing. Unfortunately, but understandably, governments are far behind in the development of regulations and policies requiring ethics in AI. Themis Michaelides: "Governments tend to be reactive rather than proactive. Industry experts will need to work with governmental agencies to bring policies in line with technology advancements."

Data sharing

The true value of data sharing is outside the organization. Naturally, there is value in internal data sharing, but if you really want to expand data sharing, organizations must think about it in a wider, cross-organizational context. Themis Michaelides: "When we think about ecosystems, and also in the context of digital transformation, we must think about the commercial confidentiality and guardrails around data sharing across organizations." The data mesh approach promises centralized data access, ownership, and clear guidelines, procedures, and policies with security layered on top of it. What someone can and cannot do with the data needs to be very clearly defined. In addition to clearly defined ethical guidelines, governance processes need to be in place.

Tooling

What is needed to support a setup of the data mesh and fabric is primarily technology and process. Organizations must select best-of-breed technologies. Many organizations have a scattered, diverse landscape of technologies with a lot of custom interfaces, where uniformity is far on the horizon. Themis Michaelides: "For example, one organization has four different MDM tools, four different vendors, six different reporting platforms, and multiple clouds – they are integrating platforms without having a strategy in place." Data mesh promises a virtual layer across all these environments so that as environments continue to expand, the data mesh technology will scale with the evolving technology architecture. Organizations may have to just accept that, especially for multinationals, there will always be an element of many tools in use, multiple environments, multiple licenses, that integration and consolidation efforts will always be the laggard and never come to full fruition. Themis Michaelides: "Try to eliminate too many tools doing the same job, but also understand that some will still exist. We are now trending towards implementing a common layer." Organizations should focus on a common architecture that provides a quality communication protocol, quality layer, for these tools to communicate with each other in a usable way. Nevertheless, this is still a big challenge.

Compliance and privacy

With data and digital transformation, highly regulated compliance and privacy obligations are a constant theme. Any kind of change in architecture needs to account for compliance and data privacy, which can be an inhibitor for change and frustrating for organizations wanting to change. Themis Michaelides: "But it is not really a choice – compliance and privacy are a constant no matter the change in strategic or technology or business direction." A provocative position to consider is Facebook as an example; do they consciously make decisions to not always comply with the rules and assume the risk for the advancement of their business strategy? It is all about data sharing, connecting the world, if the compliance and privacy regulations have not caught up with technological strategies for the greater good, do they take the risk and move forward anyway, anticipate the challenges, make the case, and expect the rules can and will adjust to accommodate their greater good objectives?

Themis Michaelides: "The questions come down to who owns the data – what are the owners red lines and is it flexible enough for owners to control and adjust their own red lines to suit their needs and preferences?" Some may not want their data shared by Facebook without permission, while others will be ok with it. Some may not want their data shared with Cambridge Analytica for political purposes but may be ok with sharing their data with Walmart and Target so that they can receive coupons and discounts. Data owners set their own parameters for data sharing, opt in/out, on top of a common layer of standard regulatory compliance and privacy policies and rules. Themis Michaelides:

> Put the power in the hands of the people, where data owners also reap the benefits of data sharing, participate in the economics of data sharing, and receive a share of the profits for data sharing. This is already apparent in power consumption, individual homes with solar rooves selling extra electricity back to the grid This is the future of data sharing as well.

15.2 Closing words

This book details our perspective on the combination of data analytics and digital transformations. In short, we believe that the journey has just begun. Also, after 2030, new technologies and continuously increasing data volumes will set new challenges and will elevate organizations to the next level, whereas other organizations will be disrupted or become no longer relevant. We trust that you are as excited as we are to experience what this journey will look like and how we all can contribute and shape it. Exciting times are ahead, indeed!

REFERENCES

Abraham, R., Schneider, J., & Vom Brocke, J. (2019). Data governance: A conceptual framework, structured review, and research agenda. *International Journal of Information Management*, *49*, 424–438.

Accenture. (2019). Closing the data value gap. https://www.accenture.com/_acnmedia/PDF-108/Accenture-closing-data-value-gap-fixed.pdf#zoom=50. Accessed 20 August 2022.

Achar, S. (2022). Cloud computing forensics. *International Journal of Computer Engineering and Technology*, *13*(3), 1–10.

Adamik, A. (2016). The mechanism of building competitiveness through strategic partnering. *Management*, *20*(1), 292.

Adams, M. A., & Bennett, S. (2018). Corporate governance in the digital economy: The critical importance of information governance. *Governance Directions*, *70*(10), 631–639.

Ahmad, Z., Shahid Khan, A., Wai Shiang, C., Abdullah, J., & Ahmad, F. (2021). Network intrusion detection system: A systematic study of machine learning and deep learning approaches. *Transactions on Emerging Telecommunications Technologies*, *32*(1), e4150.

Ajagekar, A. (2020). Quantum computing for process systems optimization and data analytics. Graduate School of Cornell University.

Akhtar, P., Frynas, J. G., Mellahi, K., & Ullah, S. (2019). Big data-savvy teams' skills, big data-driven actions and business performance. *British Journal of Management*, *30*(2), 252–271.

Alhassan, I., Sammon, D., & Daly, M. (2019). Critical success factors for data governance: A theory building approach. *Information Systems Management*, *36*(2), 98–110.

Almeida, F., & Calistru, C. (2013). The main challenges and issues of big data management. *International Journal of Research Studies in Computing*, *2*(1), 11–20.

AlNuaimi, B. K., Singh, S. K., Ren, S., Budhwar, P., & Vorobyev, D. (2022). Mastering digital transformation: The nexus between leadership, agility, and digital strategy. *Journal of Business Research*, *145*, 636–648.

Amalina, F., Hashem, I. A. T., Azizul, Z. H., Fong, A. T., Firdaus, A., Imran, M., & Anuar, N. B. (2019). Blending big data analytics: Review on challenges and a recent study. *IEEE Access*, *8*, 3629–3645.

Amankwah-Amoah, J., & Adomako, S. (2019). Big data analytics and business failures in data-Rich environments: An organizing framework. *Computers in Industry, 105*, 204–212.

Anagnostopoulos, I. (2018). Fintech and regtech: Impact on regulators and banks. *Journal of Economics and Business, 100*, 7–25.

Andrews, K., Steinau, S., & Reichert, M. (2021). Enabling runtime flexibility in data-centric and data-driven process execution engines. *Information Systems, 101*, 101447.

Anthony Jnr, B. (2021). Managing digital transformation of smart cities through enterprise architecture – A review and research agenda. *Enterprise Information Systems, 15*(3), 299–331.

Anthony, S. D., Viguerie, S. P., Schwartz, E. I., & Van Landeghem, J. (2018, February). *2018 Corporate longevity forecast: Creative destruction is accelerating*. INNOSIGHT Holdings, LLC.

Arner, D. W., Barberis, J., & Buckey, R. P. (2016). FinTech, RegTech, and the reconceptualization of financial regulation. *Northwestern Journal of International Law and Business, 37*, 371.

Atwal, H. (2020). The dataops factory. In *Practical DataOps* (pp. 249–266). Apress.

Aubert, B. A., Kishore, R., & Iriyama, A. (2015). Exploring and managing the "innovation through outsourcing" paradox. *The Journal of Strategic Information Systems, 24*(4), 255–269.

Axelsen, H., Jensen, J. R., & Ross, O. (2022). DLT compliance reporting. *arXiv preprint arXiv:2206.03270*.

Bain. (2023). Customer behavior and loyalty in insurance: Global edition 2023. https://www.bain.com/insights/customer-behavior-and-loyalty-in-insurance-global-edition-2023/. Accessed 26 February 2023.

Batini, C., Cappiello, C., Francalanci, C., & Maurino, A. (2009). Methodologies for data quality assessment and improvement. *ACM Computing Surveys (CSUR), 41*(3), 1–52.

Battisti, S. (2019). Digital social entrepreneurs as bridges in public–private partnerships. *Journal of Social Entrepreneurship, 10*(2), 135–158.

BCG. (2021a). Sharing data to address our biggest societal challenges. https://www.bcg.com/publications/2021/data-sharing-will-be-vital-to-societal-changes. Accessed 10 July 2021.

BCG. (2021b). The new tech tools in data sharing. https://www.bcg.com/publications/2021/new-data-sharing-tools-helping-companies-find-value. Accessed 10 July 2021.

Beck, K., Beedle, M., Van Bennekum, A., Cockburn, A., Cunningham, W., Fowler, M., … Thomas, D. (2001). Manifesto for agile software development. https://www.agilealliance.org/wp-content/uploads/2019/09/agile-manifesto-download-2019.pdf. Assessed 6 August 2023.

Bederna, Z., & Szadeczky, T. (2020). Cyber espionage through Botnets. *Security Journal, 33*(1), 43–62.

Benfeldt, O., Persson, J. S., & Madsen, S. (2020). Data governance as a collective action problem. *Information Systems Frontiers, 22*, 299–313.

Bengio, Y., Goodfellow, I., & Courville, A. (2017). *Deep learning* (Vol. 1). Cambridge, MA: MIT Press.

Benitez, J., Arenas, A., Castillo, A., & Esteves, J. (2022). Impact of digital leadership capability on innovation performance: The role of platform digitization capability. *Information & Management, 59*(2), 103590.

Berg, F. (2019). Are you sure you're investing ethically? MIT Sloan, 10 December 2019. https://mitsloan.mit.edu/sustainability-initiative/welcome. Accessed 20 July 2022.

Berman, S. J. (2012). Digital transformation: Opportunities to create new business models. *Strategy & Leadership, 40*(2), 16–24.

Berman, S., Baird, C. H., Eagan, K., & Marshall, A. (2020). What makes a chief digital officer successful? *Strategy & Leadership, 48*(2), 32–38.

Bertsimas, D., & Kallus, N. (2020). From predictive to prescriptive analytics. *Management Science, 66*(3), 1025–1044.

Beulen, E. (2004). Governance in IT outsourcing partnerships. In: Wim van Grembergen (ed.), *Strategies for information technology governance* (pp. 310–342). Igi Global.

Beulen, E. (2007, March). The management of global sourcing partnerships: Implications for the capabilities and skills of the IS function. In *1st Information systems workshop on global sourcing: Services, knowledge and innovation*, Val d'Isère, France.

Beulen, E. (2008). The enabling role of information technology in the global war for talent: Accenture's industrialized approach. *Information Technology for Development, 14*(3), 213–224.

Beulen, E. (2009). The contribution of a global service provider's Human Resources Information System (HRIS) to staff retention in emerging markets: Comparing issues and implications in six developing countries. *Information Technology & People, 22*(3), 270–288.

Beulen, E. (2011). Contract renewal decisions in IT outsourcing: "Should I stay or should I go". *Journal of Information Technology Management, 22*(4), 47–55.

Beulen, E. (2018a). Information management leads top line information technology initiatives and contributes to bottom line targets: The chief information officer is a technical innovator and custodian of the IT architecture. Tilburg University Press.

Beulen, E. (2018b). High Performance Digital Organisations—Challenges and journeys, white paper. https://itexecutive.nl/wp-content/uploads/2020/06/Whitepaper-HPDO2-DEFlr.pdf. Accessed 9 July 2021.

Beulen, E. (2019). Implementing and contracting agile and devops: A survey in the Netherlands. In *Digital Services and Platforms. Considerations for Sourcing: 12th Global Sourcing Workshop 2018, La Thuile, Italy, February 21–24, 2018, Revised Selected Papers 12* (pp. 124–146). Springer International Publishing.

Beulen, E. (2020a). High Performance Digital Organisations – Thriving in the data economy. https://hpdo.nl/thriving-in-the-data-economy/. Accessed 11 July 2021.

Beulen, E. (2020b). High Performance Digital Organisations – Demonstrating data driven leadership. https://itexecutive.nl/hpdo/demonstrating-data-driven-leadership/. Accessed 11 July 2021.

Beulen, E. (2022a). High Performance Digital Organisations – Value creation by improved ecosystem partnering. https://itexecutive.nl/data-governance/hpdo-paper-value-creation-by-improved-ecosystem-partnering/. Accessed 25 May 2022.

Beulen, E. (2022b). Cloud Journey, achieving business performance. https://itexecutive.nl/cloud-journey/cloud-journey-paper-achieving-business-performance/. Accessed 13 August 2022.

Beulen, E., & Bode, R. (2021). An information technology and innovation committee to guide digital transformations. *Corporate Board: Role, Duties and Composition, 17*(2), 38–53.

Beulen, E., Plugge, A., & van Hillegersberg, J. (2022). Formal and relational governance of artificial intelligence outsourcing. *Information Systems and e-Business Management, 20*(4), 719–748.

Beulen, E., & Ribbers, P. (2002, January). Managing complex IT outsourcing-partnerships. In *Proceedings of the 35th Annual Hawaii International Conference on System Sciences* (pp. 10–pp). IEEE.

Beulen, E., & Ribbers, P. (2003, January). IT outsourcing contracts: Practical implications of the incomplete contract theory. In *Proceedings of the 36th Annual Hawaii International Conference on System Sciences* (pp. 10–pp). IEEE, Big Island, HI, USA, pp. 1–10.

Beulen, E., & Ribbers, P. M. (2010). *Managing IT outsourcing* (2nd ed.). Routledge.

Beulen, E., & Ribbers, P. M. (Eds.). (2020). *The Routledge companion to managing digital outsourcing*. Routledge.

Beulen, E., & Ribbers, P. M. (2021). *Managing information technology outsourcing* (3rd ed.). Routledge.

Beulen, E., & Tiwari, V. (2010). Parallel transitions in IT outsourcing: Making it happen. In *Global Sourcing of Information Technology and Business Processes: 4th Global Sourcing Workshop 2010, Zermatt, Switzerland, March 22-25, 2010, Revised Selected Papers 4* (pp. 55–68). Springer Berlin Heidelberg.

Beulen, E., Tiwari, V., & Van Heck, E. (2011). Understanding transition performance during offshore IT outsourcing. *Strategic Outsourcing: An International Journal, 4*(3), 204–227.

Beulen, E., Van Fenema, P., & Currie, W. (2005). From application outsourcing to infrastructure management: Extending the offshore outsourcing service portfolio. *European Management Journal, 23*(2), 133–144.

Binjubeir, M., Ahmed, A. A., Ismail, M. A. B., Sadiq, A. S., & Khan, M. K. (2019). Comprehensive survey on big data privacy protection. *IEEE Access, 8*, 20067–20079.

Birch, K., Cochrane, D. T., & Ward, C. (2021). Data as asset? The measurement, governance, and valuation of digital personal data by Big Tech. *Big Data & Society, 8*(1), 20539517211017308.

Borgogno, O., & Colangelo, G. (2019). Data sharing and interoperability: Fostering innovation and competition through APIs. *Computer Law & Security Review, 35*(5), 105314.

Bova, F., Goldfarb, A., & Melko, R. G. (2021). Commercial applications of quantum computing. *EPJ Quantum Technology, 8*, 2.

Bramson, A. L. (2020, June). Toward universal data interoperability in networked belief models. In *2020 13th International Conference on Human System Interaction (HSI)* (pp. 124–129). IEEE.

Brenneman, K. (2018). What a chief data officer needs to know. *Information Management, 52*(5), 44–45.

Bresciani, S., Ferraris, A., Romano, M., & Santoro, G. (2021). Digital leadership. In *Digital transformation management for agile organizations: A compass to sail the digital world* (pp. 97–115). Emerald Publishing Limited.

Brosseau, D., Ebrahim, S., Handscomb, C., & Thaker, S. (2019, May). The journey to an agile organization. *McKinsey & Company, 10*, 1–10.

Brownlow, J., Zaki, M., Neely, A., & Urmetzer, F. (2015). Data and analytics-data-driven business models: A blueprint for innovation. *Cambridge Service Alliance, 7*, 1–17.

Brynjolfsson, Erik and McElheran, Kristina Steffenson, Data in Action: Data-Driven Decision Making in U.S. Manufacturing (January 01, 2016). US Census Bureau Center for Economic Studies Paper No. CES-WP-16-06, Rotman School of Management Working Paper No. 2722502, Available at SSRN: https://ssrn.com/abstract=2722502 or http://dx.doi.org/10.2139/ssrn.2722502.

Busse, R., & Weidner, G. (2020). A qualitative investigation on combined effects of distant leadership, organisational agility and digital collaboration on perceived employee engagement. *Leadership & Organization Development Journal, 41*(4), 535–550.

Butler, T., & O'Brien, L. (2019). Understanding RegTech for digital regulatory compliance. In: Theo Lynn, John G. Mooney, Pierangelo Rosati and Mark Cummins (eds.) *Disrupting finance: FinTech and strategy in the 21st century* (pp. 85–102), Palgrave McMillan.

Calia, D. (2022). Schrems II: The EU's influence on US data protection and privacy laws. *Washington University Global Studies Law Review, 21*, 247.

Cappiello, C., Caro, A., Rodriguez, A., & Caballero, I. (2013). An approach to design business processes addressing data quality issues. ECIS 2013 Completed Research. 216. http://aisel.aisnet.org/ecis2013_cr/216.

Caputo, A., Pizzi, S., Pellegrini, M. M., & Dabić, M. (2021). Digitalization and business models: Where are we going? A science map of the field. *Journal of Business Research, 123*, 489–501.

Carmel, E., & Beulen, E. (2005). Managing the offshore transition. In: Eran Carmel and Paul Tjia (eds.), *Offshoring information technology: Sourcing and outsourcing to a global workforce* (pp. 130–148). Cambridge University Press.

Carlo, B., Daniele, B., Federico, C., & Simone, G. (2011). A data quality methodology for heterogeneous data. *International Journal of Database Management Systems, 3*(1), 60–79.

Castro, A., Machado, J., Roggendorf, M., & Soller, H. (2020). How to build a data architecture to drive innovation—today and tomorrow. 3 June. https://www.mckinsey.com/business-functions/mckinsey-digital/our-insights/how-to-build-a-data-architecture-to-drive-innovation-today-and-tomorrow. Accessed 20 November 2021.

Cavaliere, F., Mattsson, J., & Smeets, B. (2020). The security implications of quantum cryptography and quantum computing. *Network Security, 2020*(9), 9–15.

Chander, A. (2020). Is data localization a solution for schrems II? *Journal of International Economic Law, 23*(3), 771–784.

Chanias, S. (2017). Mastering digital transformation: The path of a financial services provider towards a digital transformation strategy. In Proceedings of the 25th European Conference on Information Systems (ECIS), Guimarães, Portugal, June 5–10, 2017. ISBN 978-989-20-7655-3 Research Papers. http://aisel.aisnet.org/ecis2017_rp/2

Chen, D. Q., Zhang, Y., Xiao, J., & Xie, K. (2021a). Making digital innovation happen: A chief information officer issue selling perspective. *Information Systems Research, 32*(3), 987–1008.

Chen, L., Jordan, S., Liu,Y.-K., Moody, D., Peralta, R., Perlner, R., & Smith-Tone, D. (2016). NISTIR 8105 report on post-quantum cryptography. https://csrc.nist.gov/publications/detail/nistir/8105/final. Accessed 25 July 2021.

Chen, Y., Visnjic, I., Parida, V., & Zhang, Z. (2021b). On the road to digital servitization–The (dis) continuous interplay between business model and digital technology. *International Journal of Operations & Production Management, 41*(5), 694–722.

Chen, Y. C. (2017). *Managing digital governance: Issues, challenges, and solutions.* Routledge.

Cheng, C., & Wang, L. (2022). How companies configure digital innovation attributes for business model innovation? A configurational view. *Technovation, 112*, 102398.

Cichy, C., & Rass, S. (2019). An overview of data quality frameworks. *IEEE Access, 7*, 24634–24648.

Clayton, J. (2020). https://www.sec.gov/news/public-statement/clayton-amac-opening-2020-05-27. Accessed 30 October 2022.

CNBC. (2022). https://www.cnbc.com/2022/12/20/amazon-reaches-settlement-with-eu-on-antitrust-case.html. Accessed 24 December 2022.

Colicchia, C., Creazza, A., Noè, C., & Strozzi, F. (2019). Information sharing in supply chains: A review of risks and opportunities using the systematic literature network analysis (SLNA). *Supply Chain Management: An International Journal, 24*(1), 5–21.

Colson, E. (2019). Why data science teams need generalists, not specialists. *Harvard Business Review*. https://hbr.org/2019/03/why-data-science-teams-need-generalists-not-specialists

Cong, L. W., & He, Z. (2019). Blockchain disruption and smart contracts. *The Review of Financial Studies, 32*(5), 1754–1797.

Cover, T. M., & Ordentlich, E. (1996). Universal portfolios with side information. *IEEE Transactions on Information Theory, 42*(2), 348–363.

Cunliffe, K. S. (2021). Hard target espionage in the information era: New challenges for the second oldest profession. *Intelligence and National Security, 36*(7), 1018–1034.

Curry, E., & Sheth, A. (2018). Next-generation smart environments: From system of systems to data ecosystems. *IEEE Intelligent Systems, 33*(3), 69–76.

DAMA. (n.d.). DAMA DMBOK. https://www.dama.org/cpages/body-of-knowledge. Accessed 14 April 2021.

DAMA International. (2017). *DAMA-DMBOK data management body of knowledge* (2nd ed.). New Jersey: Technics Publications.

Dasoriya, R., Kotadiya, P., Arya, G., Nayak, P., & Mistry, K. (2017, July). Dynamic load balancing in cloud a data-centric approach. In *2017 International Conference on Networks & Advances in Computational Technologies (NetACT)* (pp. 162–166). IEEE.

Dasu, T., & Johnson, T. (2003). *Exploratory data mining and data cleaning.* John Wiley & Sons.

Datnow, A., & Park, V. (2014). *Data-driven leadership* (Vol. 12). John Wiley & Sons.

Davidson, S., Giesen, E., Harmer, M., & Marshall, A. (2018). How industry leaders enhance the value of ecosystems. *Strategy & Leadership, 46*(2), 26–33.

de la Vega, A., Chang, L. J., Banich, M. T., Wager, T. D., & Yarkoni, T. (2016). Large-scale meta-analysis of human medial frontal cortex reveals tripartite functional organization. *Journal of Neuroscience, 36*(24), 6553–6562.

De Langhe, B., & Puntoni, S. (2021). What leaders get wrong about data-driven decisions. *Mit Sloan Management Review, 62*(3), 14–16.

Deloitte. (n.d.-a). RegTech is the new FinTech. https://www2.deloitte.com/content/dam/Deloitte/tw/Documents/financial-services/tw-fsi-regtech-new-fintech.pdf. Accessed 10 October 2022

Deloitte. (n.d.-b). RegTech universe 2023. https://www2.deloitte.com/lu/en/pages/technology/articles/regtech-companies-compliance.html. Accessed 7 February 2023.

De Mauro, A., Greco, M., Grimaldi, M., & Ritala, P. (2018). Human resources for Big Data professions: A systematic classification of job roles and required skill sets. *Information Processing & Management, 54*(5), 807–817.

Demchenko, Y., De Laat, C., & Membrey, P. (2014, May). Defining architecture components of the Big Data Ecosystem. In *2014 International Conference on Collaboration Technologies and Systems (CTS)* (pp. 104–112). IEEE.

Denning, S. (2018a). How major corporations are making sense of Agile. *Strategy & Leadership, 46*(1), 3–9.

Denning, S. (2018b). *The age of agile: How smart companies are transforming the way work gets done.* Amacom.

Denning, S. (2019). Lessons learned from mapping successful and unsuccessful Agile transformation journeys. *Strategy & Leadership, 47*(4), 3–11.

D'Ignazio, C. (2017). Creative data literacy: Bridging the gap between the data-haves and data-have nots. *Information Design Journal, 23*, 6–18.

Dignum, V. (2018). Ethics in artificial intelligence: Introduction to the special issue. *Ethics and Information Technology, 20*(1), 1–3.

Dragičević, Z., & Bošnjak, S. (2019). Agile architecture in the digital era: Trends and practices. *Strategic Management, 24*(2), 12–33.

Dremel, C., Wulf, J., Herterich, M. M., Waizmann, J. C., & Brenner, W. (2017). How AUDI AG established big data analytics in its digital transformation. *MIS Quarterly Executive, 16*(2), 81–100.

Dryer, R. L., & Stroud, S. S. (2015). Automatic license plate readers: An effective law enforcement tool or big brother's latest instrument of mass surveillance? Some suggestions for legislative action. *Jurimetrics, 2*, 225–274.

Duan, C., Kotey, B., & Sandhu, K. (2021). Ecosystem strategies for transnational digital entrepreneurship: A conceptual framework of three ecosystems. In: Carson Duan, Bernice Kotey and Kamaljeet Sandhu (eds.), *Disruptive technology and digital transformation for business and government* (pp. 1–23). IGI Global.

Dwivedi, Y., et al. (2021). Artificial Intelligence (AI): Multidisciplinary perspectives on emerging challenges, opportunities, and agenda for research, practice and policy. *International Journal of Information Management, 57*, 101994.

Dwivedi, Y. K., Rana, N. P., Jeyaraj, A., Clement, M., & Williams, M. D. (2019). Re-examining the unified theory of acceptance and use of technology (UTAUT): Towards a revised theoretical model. *Information Systems Frontiers, 21*(3), 719–734.

Dwork, C., & Minow, M. (2022). Distrust of artificial intelligence: Sources & responses from computer science & law. *Daedalus, 151*(2), 309–321.

Earley, S. (2017). The role of the chief data officer: Managing expectations. *IT Professional, 19*(3), 66–69.

Eberl, J. K., & Drews, P. (2021). Digital leadership–mountain or molehill? A literature review. In *Innovation through information systems: Volume III: A collection of latest research on management issues* (pp. 223–237). Wirtschaftsinformatik 2021 Proceedings. 5. https://aisel.aisnet.org/wi2021/HDigitaltransformation17/Track17/5

EDM Council. (2020). DCAM framework. https://edmcouncil.org/frameworks/dcam/. Accessed 14 April 2021).

Egon Zehnder. (2019). https://www.egonzehnder.com/cdo-decoded. Accessed 23 June 2021.

Ehin, P., Solvak, M., Willemson, J., & Vinkel, P. (2022). Internet voting in Estonia 2005–2019: Evidence from eleven elections. *Government Information Quarterly, 39*(4), 101718.

Ehrlinger, L., & Wöß, W. (2022). A survey of data quality measurement and monitoring tools. *Frontiers in Big Data, 5*, 850611.

Eisenberg, I. W., Bissett, P. G., Zeynep Enkavi, A., Li, J., MacKinnon, D. P., Marsch, L. A., & Poldrack, R. A. (2019). Uncovering the structure of self-regulation through data-driven ontology discovery. *Nature Communications, 10*(1), 1–13.

El Morr, C., & Ali-Hassan, H. (2019). Descriptive, predictive, and prescriptive analytics. In *Analytics in healthcare* (pp. 31–55). Springer.

Ereth, J. (2018). DataOps-towards a definition. *LWDA, 2191*, 104–112.

Eskandarpour, R., Ghosh, K. J. B., Khodaei, A., Paaso, A., & Zhang, L. (2020). Quantum-enhanced grid of the future: A primer. *IEEE Access, 8*, 188993–189002.

Espinosa, R., Garriga, L., Zubcoff, J. J., & Mazón, J. N. (2014, October). Linked open data mining for democratization of big data. In *2014 IEEE International Conference on Big Data (Big Data)* (pp. 17–19). IEEE.

European Commission. (n.d.) The digital services act package. https://digital-strategy.ec.europa.eu/en/policies/digital-services-act-package. Accessed 10 July 2021.

European Commission. (2020). Anti-trust – Press release. https://ec.europa.eu/commission/presscorner/detail/en/ip_20_2077. Accessed 11 July 2021.

Fadler, M., & Legner, C. (2022). Data ownership revisited: Clarifying data accountabilities in times of big data and analytics. *Journal of Business Analytics*, 5(1), 123–139.

Fensel, D., Şimşek, U., Angele, K., Huaman, E., Kärle, E., Panasiuk, O., ... Wahler, A. (eds.) (2020a). Introduction: What is a knowledge graph? In *Knowledge graphs: Methodology, tools and selected use cases* (pp. 1–10), Springer.

Fensel, D., Simsek, U., Angele, K., Huaman, E., Kärle, E., Panasiuk, O., ... Wahler, A. (2020b). *Knowledge graphs*. Springer International Publishing.

Fernandez, J. A., David, E. M., & Chen, S. (2022). Agile organizational norms and systems. In *Innovative to the core: Stories from China and the world* (pp. 153–172). Emerald Publishing Limited.

Ferraris, A., Mazzoleni, A., Devalle, A., & Couturier, J. (2019). Big data analytics capabilities and knowledge management: Impact on firm performance. *Management Decision*, 57(8), 1923–1936.

Forbes. (2020). IBM, Microsoft and Amazon not letting police use their facial recognition technology. 12 June. https://www.forbes.com/sites/larrymagid/2020/06/12/ibm-microsoft-and-amazon-not-letting-police-use-their-facial-recognition-technology/?sh=23cb3c4a1887. Accessed 22 December 2022.

Forrester. (2019). The future of machine learning is unstoppable. Research report. 25 April.

Frank, M., & Walker, J. (2016). Some key challenges for data literacy. *The Journal of Community Informatics*, 12(3), 232–235.

G20. (2014). Introductory note to the G20 anti-corruption open data principles. http://www.g20.utoronto.ca/2015/G20-Anti-Corruption-Open-Data-Principles.pdf. Accessed 23 February 2022.

Gartner. (n.d.-a). https://www.gartner.com/en/information-technology/glossary/digitization. Accessed 7 July 2021.

Gartner. (n.d.-b). Gartner glossary. Definition digitization. https://www.gartner.com/en/information-technology/glossary/digitization. Accessed 7 July 2021.

Gartner. (n.d.-c). Gartner glossary. Definition quantum computing. https://www.gartner.com/en/information-technology/glossary/quantum-computing. Accessed 24 July 2021.

Gartner. (2017). Artificial intelligence will create more jobs than it eliminates. 13 December. https://www.gartner.com/en/newsroom/press-releases/2017-12-13-gartner-says-by-2020-artificial-intelligence-will-create-more-jobs-than-it-eliminates. Accessed 25 July 2021.

Gartner. (2021a). Gartner top 10 data and analytics trends for 2021. Contributor K. Panetta. February 22, 2021. https://www.gartner.com/smarterwithgartner/gartner-top-10-data-and-analytics-trends-for-2021/. Accessed 17 July 2021.

Gartner. (2021b). Decision assessment model. https://www.gartner.com/smarterwithgartner/would-you-let-artificial-intelligence-make-your-pay-decisions. Accessed 25 July 2021.

Gartner. (2021c). 12 Actions to improve your data quality, ID G00744046, April 1.

Gasser, U., & Almeida, V. (2022). Futures of digital governance. *Communications of the ACM*, 65(3), 30–32.

Ghasemaghaei, M., & Calic, G. (2019). Does big data enhance firm innovation competency? The mediating role of data-driven insights. *Journal of Business Research*, 104, 69–84.

Ghasemaghaei, M., Ebrahimi, S., & Hassanein, K. (2018). Data analytics competency for improving firm decision making performance. *The Journal of Strategic Information Systems*, 27(1), 101–113.

Gill, M., & VanBoskirk, S. (2016). The digital maturity model 4.0. In *Benchmarks: Digital transformation playbook*. http://forrester.nitro-digital.com/pdf/Forrester-s%20Digital%20Maturity%20Model%204.0.pdf

Gobble, M. M. (2018). Digitalization, digitization, and innovation. *Research-Technology Management, 61*(4), 56–59.

Gong, C., & Ribiere, V. (2021). Developing a unified definition of digital transformation. *Technovation, 102*, 102217.

Goodhue, D. L., Wybo, M. D., & Kirsch, L. J. (1992). The impact of data integration on the costs and benefits of information systems. *MIS Quarterly*, 293–311.

Greasley, A. (2019). *Simulating business processes for descriptive, predictive, and prescriptive analytics*. De Gruyter.

Green, J., & Daniels, S. (2019). *Digital governance: Leading and thriving in a world of fast-changing technologies*. Routledge.

Greenstein, S. (2010). Digitization and value creation. *IEEE Micro, 30*(4), 4–5.

Griffin, J. (2008). The role of the chief data officer. *Information Management, 18*(2), 28.

Grobman, S. (2020). Quantum computing's cyber-threat to national security. *Prism, 9*(1), 52–67.

Grover, L. K. (1996, May). A fast quantum mechanical algorithm for database search. In *Proceedings of the 28th Annual ACM Symposium on Theory of Computing*, Philadelphia, PA.

Gruber, T. R. (1993). A translation approach to portable ontology specifications. *Knowledge Acquisition, 5*(2), 199–220.

Gruska, J. (1999). *Quantum computing* (Vol. 2005). London: McGraw-Hill.

Guarino, N., Oberle, D., & Staab, S. (2009). What is an ontology? International handbooks on information systems. In Staab, S., & Studer, R. (Eds.), *Handbook on ontologies* (pp. 1–17). Springer.

Gupta, I., Singh, A. K., & Singh, N. (2019). Layer-based privacy and security architecture for cloud data sharing. *Journal of Communications Software and Systems, 15*(2), 173–185.

Gupta, S., & Gupta, A. (2019). Dealing with noise problem in machine learning data-sets: A systematic review. *Procedia Computer Science, 161*, 466–474.

Haenlein, M., & Kaplan, A. (2019). A brief history of artificial intelligence: On the past, present, and future of artificial intelligence. *California Management Review, 61*(4), 5–14.

Hamilton, J. (2019). How to transform and stay secure. *ITNOW, 61*(2), 40–43.

Hariri, R. H., Fredericks, E. M., & Bowers, K. M. (2019). Uncertainty in big data analytics: Survey, opportunities, and challenges. *Journal of Big Data, 6*(1), 1–16.

Härting, R. C., Reichstein, C., & Jozinovic, P. (2017). The potential value of digitization for business. *INFORMATIK, 2017*, 1647–1656.

Helfat, C. E., & Raubitschek, R. S. (2018). Dynamic and integrative capabilities for profiting from innovation in digital platform-based ecosystems. *Research Policy, 47*(8), 1391–1399.

Hemon, A., Lyonnet, B., Rowe, F., & Fitzgerald, B. (2020). From agile to DevOps: Smart skills and collaborations. *Information Systems Frontiers, 22*(4), 927–945.

Henderson, J. C., & Venkatraman, H. (1999). Strategic alignment: Leveraging information technology for transforming organizations. *IBM Systems Journal, 38*(2.3), 472–484.

Hey, T. (1999). Quantum computing: An introduction. *Computing & Control Engineering Journal, 10*(3), 105–112.

Hinterhuber, A. (2022). Digital transformation, the Holy Grail, and the disruption of business models: An interview with Michael Nilles. *Business Horizons, 65*(3), 261–265.

Hoepner, A., & Schneider, F. (2018). Debate: Can self-reporting be effective for investors? https://www.environmental-finance.com/content/market-insight/debate-can-self-reporting-be-effective-for-investors.html. Accessed 13 October 2022.

Holbeche, L. (2019). Designing sustainably agile and resilient organizations. *Systems Research and Behavioral Science, 36*(5), 668–677.

Hood, C. (1991). A public management for all seasons? *Public Administration, 69*, 3–19.

HP. (2019). Beyond the qubit: Quantum computing, near-term alternatives, and Memory-Driven Computing, November. https://www.labs.hpe.com/pdf/Beyond_the_qubit.pdf. Accessed 5 September 2022.

Humby, C. (2013). Tech giants may be huge, but nothing matches big data, editor C. Arther. 23 August. https://www.theguardian.com/technology/2013/aug/23/tech-giants-data. Accessed 17 July 2021.

Hunt, J. P., Stanton, R., & Wallace, N. (2012). US residential-mortgage transfer systems: A data-management crisis. http://faculty.haas.berkeley.edu/stanton/pdf/Mortgage_Transfer.pdf

Hyysalo, J., Kelanti, M., Sauvola, T., Liukkunen, K., & Sauvola, J. (2019). Fenix: A platform for digital partnering and business ecosystem creation. *IT Professional, 21*(1), 74–81.

IDC. (2021). Data creation and replication will grow at a faster rate than installed storage capacity, according to the IDC Global DataSphere and StorageSphere Forecasts. 24 March 2021. https://www.idc.com/getdoc.jsp?containerId=prUS47560321#:~:text=Driven%20by%20the%20steady%20growth,storage%20capacity%20across%20the%20globe. Accessed 17 July 2021.

Ifenthaler, D., & Egloffstein, M. (2020). Development and implementation of a maturity model of digital transformation. *TechTrends, 64*(2), 302–309.

Indu, I., Anand, P. R., & Bhaskar, V. (2018). Identity and access management in cloud environment: Mechanisms and challenges. *Engineering Science and Technology, an International Journal, 21*(4), 574–588.

Inghirami, I. (2021). Taming corporate data. https://boa.unimib.it/retrieve/e39773b8-677e-35a3-e053-3a05fe0aac26/Taming%20Corporate%20Data.pdf

Janeček, V. (2018). Ownership of personal data in the Internet of Things. *Computer Law & Security Review, 34*(5), 1039–1052.

Ji, S., Pan, S., Cambria, E., Marttinen, P., & Philip, S. Y. (2021). A survey on knowledge graphs: Representation, acquisition, and applications. *IEEE Transactions on Neural Networks and Learning Systems, 33*(2), 494–514.

Jin, G. Z., & Wagman, L. (2021). Big data at the crossroads of antitrust and consumer protection. *Information Economics and Policy, 54*, 100865.

Jin, J., Ma, L., & Ye, X. (2020). Digital transformation strategies for existed firms: From the perspectives of data ownership and key value propositions. *Asian Journal of Technology Innovation, 28*(1), 77–93.

Jones, T. M., & Gautschi, F. H. (1988). Will the ethics of business change? A survey of future executives. *Journal of Business Ethics, 7*, 231–248.

Kale, V. (2017). *Agile network businesses: Collaboration, coordination, and competitive advantage.* CRC Press.

Kane, G. C., Phillips, A. N., Copulsky, J., & Andrus, G. (2019). How digital leadership is (n't) different. *MIT Sloan Management Review, 60*(3), 34–39.

Kaplan, A., & Haenlein, M. (2019). Siri, Siri, in my hand: Who's the fairest in the land? On the interpretations, illustrations, and implications of artificial intelligence. *Business horizons, 62*(1), 15–25.

Kar, A. K., Ilavarasan, V., Gupta, M. P., Janssen, M., & Kothari, R. (2019). Moving beyond smart cities: Digital nations for social innovation & sustainability. *Information Systems Frontiers, 21*(3), 495–501.

Karpen, S. R., White, J. K., Mullin, A. P., O'Doherty, I., Hudson, L. D., Romero, K., ... Larkindale, J. (2021). Effective data sharing as a conduit for advancing medical product development. *Therapeutic Innovation & Regulatory Science, 55*(3), 591–600.

Keplinger, K. (2018). Is quantum computing becoming relevant to cyber-security? *Network Security, 2018*(9), 16–19. See also: Mosca, M. (2018). Cybersecurity in an era with quantum computers: Will we be ready? *IEEE Security & Privacy, 16*(5), 38–41.

Khatri, V., & Brown, C. V. (2010). Designing data governance. *Communications of the ACM, 53*(1), 148–152.

Khin, S., & Ho, T. C. (2018). Digital technology, digital capability and organizational performance: A mediating role of digital innovation. *International Journal of Innovation Science, 11*(2), 177–195.

Kietzmann, J., Lee, L. W., McCarthy, I. P., & Kietzmann, T. C. (2020). Deepfakes: Trick or treat? *Business Horizons, 63*(2), 135–146.

Kirchmer, M. (2018). Enterprise architecture enabling process governance for agility, compliance and more. *CIO Review, Enterprise Architecture Special, 5.* https://www.researchgate.net/profile/Mathias-Kirchmer/publication/325387229_Enterprise_Architecture_enabling_Process_Governance_for_Agility_Compliance_and_more/links/5b09e84b0f7e9b1ed7f7d351/Enterprise-Architecture-enabling-Process-Governance-for-Agility-Compliance-and-more.pdf

Kluegl, P., Toepfer, M., Beck, P. D., Fette, G., & Puppe, F. (2016). UIMA Ruta: Rapid development of rule-based information extraction applications. *Natural Language Engineering, 22*(1), 1–40.

Kosmarski, A. (2020). Blockchain adoption in academia: Promises and challenges. *Journal of Open Innovation: Technology, Market, and Complexity, 6*(4), 117.

Kotarba, M. (2018). Digital transformation of business models. *Foundations of Management, 10*(1), 123–142.

KPMG. (2021). Closing the disconnect in ESG data. https://assets.kpmg.com/content/dam/kpmg/xx/pdf/2021/10/closing-the-disconnect-in-esg-data.pdf. Accessed 12 June 2022.

Kraus, S., Palmer, C., Kailer, N., Kallinger, F. L., & Spitzer, J. (2019). Digital entrepreneurship: A research agenda on new business models for the twenty-first century. *International Journal of Entrepreneurial Behavior & Research, 25*(2), 353–375.

Kunisch, S., Menz, M., & Langan, R. (2022). Chief digital officers: An exploratory analysis of their emergence, nature, and determinants. *Long Range Planning, 55*(2), 101999.

Kwon, H., Chatarasi, P., Pellauer, M., Parashar, A., Sarkar, V., & Krishna, T. (2019, October). Understanding reuse, performance, and hardware cost of DNN dataflow: A data-centric approach. In *Proceedings of the 52nd Annual IEEE/ACM International Symposium on Microarchitecture* (pp. 754–768), October 12–16, 2019, Columbus, OH, USA. ACM, New York, NY, USA, 15 pages. https://doi.org/10.1145/3352460.3358252

Ladley, J. (2019). *Data governance: How to design, deploy, and sustain an effective data governance program.* Academic Press.

Larriva-Novo, X. A., Vega-Barbas, M., Villagrá, V. A., & Rodrigo, M. S. (2020). Evaluation of cybersecurity data set characteristics for their applicability to neural networks algorithms detecting cybersecurity anomalies. *IEEE Access, 8*, 9005–9014.

Lasla, N., Al-Sahan, L., Abdallah, M., & Younis, M. (2022). Green-PoW: An energy-efficient blockchain proof-of-work consensus algorithm. *Computer Networks, 214*, 109118.

Leal, G. D. S. S., Guédria, W., & Panetto, H. (2019). An ontology for interoperability assessment: A systemic approach. *Journal of Industrial Information Integration, 16*, 100100.

Lee, I. (2020). Internet of Things (IoT) cybersecurity: Literature review and IoT cyber risk management. *Future Internet, 12*(9), 157.

Lenzerini, M. (2018). Managing data through the lens of an ontology. *AI Magazine, 39*(2), 65–74.

Leonardi, P. M., & Treem, J. W. (2020). Behavioral visibility: A new paradigm for organization studies in the age of digitization, digitalization, and datafication. *Organization Studies, 41*(12), 1601–1625.

Leon-Urrutia, M., Taibi, D., Pospelova, V., Splendore, S., Urbsiene, L., & Marjanovic, U. (2022). Data Literacy: An essential skill for the industry. In: Bojan Lalic, Danijela Gracanin, Nemanja Tasic and Nenad Simeunović (eds.), *Industrial innovation in digital age* (pp. 326–331). Springer.

Lepenioti, K., Bousdekis, A., Apostolou, D., & Mentzas, G. (2020). Prescriptive analytics: Literature review and research challenges. *International Journal of Information Management, 50*, 57–70.

Levallet, N., & Chan, Y. E. (2018). Role of digital capabilities in unleashing the power of managerial improvisation. *MIS Quarterly Executive, 17*(1), 4–21.

Lewrick, M., Link, P., & Leifer, L. (2018). *The design thinking playbook: Mindful digital transformation of teams, products, services, businesses and ecosystems.* John Wiley & Sons.

Li, H., Ota, K., & Dong, M. (2018). Learning IoT in edge: Deep learning for the Internet of Things with edge computing. *IEEE Network, 32*(1), 96–101.

Li, X., Xiong, H., Li, X., Wu, X., Zhang, X., Liu, J., ... Dou, D. (2022). Interpretable deep learning: Interpretation, interpretability, trustworthiness, and beyond. *Knowledge and Information Systems, 64*(12), 3197–3234.

Liu, Y., Hassan, K. A., Karlsson, M., Pang, Z., & Gong, S. (2019). A data-centric Internet of Things framework based on azure cloud. *IEEE Access, 7*, 53839–53858.

Lucas Jr, H. C. (1978). Empirical evidence for a descriptive model of implementation. *MIS Quarterly, 2*(2), 27–42.

Lyon, D., & Zureik, E. (eds) (1996). Surveillance, privacy, and the new technology. In *Computers, surveillance, and privacy* (pp. 1–18), University of Minnesota Press.

Machado, I. A., Costa, C., & Santos, M. Y. (2022). Data mesh: Concepts and principles of a paradigm shift in data architectures. *Procedia Computer Science, 196*, 263–271.

Mahanti, R., & Mahanti, R. (2021). *Data governance and compliance* (pp. 109–153). Springer Singapore.

Malgieri, G., & Custers, B. (2018). Pricing privacy–the right to know the value of your personal data. *Computer Law & Security Review, 34*(2), 289–303.

Martin, K. E. (2020). Ethical issues in the big data industry. In: Robert D. Galliers, Dorothy E. Leidner and Boyka Simeonova (eds.), *Strategic information management* (pp. 450–471). Routledge.

Martínez, P. L., Dintén, R., Drake, J. M., & Zorrilla, M. (2021). A big data-centric architecture metamodel for Industry 4.0. *Future Generation Computer Systems, 125*, 263–284.

Martínez-Gutiérrez, A., Díez-González, J., Ferrero-Guillén, R., Verde, P., Álvarez, R., & Perez, H. (2021). Digital twin for automatic transportation in industry 4.0. *Sensors, 21*(10), 3344.

Mateescu, A., Brunton, D., Rosenblat, A., Patton, D., Gold, Z., & Boyd, D. (2015). Social media surveillance and law enforcement. *Data Civil Rights, 27*, 2015–2027.

Matt, C., Hess, T., & Benlian, A. (2015). Digital transformation strategies. *Business & Information Systems Engineering, 57*(5), 339–343.

Matzler, K., von den Eichen, S. F., Anschober, M., & Kohler, T. (2018). The crusade of digital disruption. *Journal of Business Strategy, 39*(6), 13–20.

Maynard-Atem, L. (2019). The data series – Data democratisation. *Impact, 2019*(1), 10–11.

McAfee, A., Brynjolfsson, E., Davenport, T. H., Patil, D. J., & Barton, D. (2012). Big data: The management revolution. *Harvard Business Review, 90*(10), 60–68.

McCausland, T. (2021). Innovating for Sustainability. *Research-Technology Management, 64*(4), 59–63.

McComb, D. (2019). *The data-centric revolution: Restoring sanity to enterprise information systems*. Technics Publications.

McDaniel, M., Storey, V. C., & Sugumaran, V. (2018). Assessing the quality of domain ontologies: Metrics and an automated ranking system. *Data & Knowledge Engineering, 115*, 32–47.

McGilvray, D. (2021). *Executing data quality projects: Ten steps to quality data and trusted information (TM)*. Academic Press.

McKinsey. (2018). *AI, automation, and the future of work: Ten things to solve for.* https://www.mckinsey.com/featured-insights/future-of-work/ai-automation-and-the-future-of-work-ten-things-to-solve-for. Accessed 25 July 2021.

McKinsey. (2020a). A game plan for quantum computing. February 6. https://www.mckinsey.com/business-functions/mckinsey-digital/our-insights/a-game-plan-for-quantum-computing. Accessed 24 July 2021.

McKinsey. (2020b). Designing data governance that delivers value. https://www.mckinsey.com/capabilities/mckinsey-digital/our-insights/designing-data-governance-that-delivers-value. Accessed 23 July 2022.

McKinsey. (2020c). The ESG premium: New perspectives on value and performance. 12 February 2020. https://www.mckinsey.com/capabilities/sustainability/our-insights/the-esg-premium-new-perspectives-on-value-and-performance. Accessed 23 July 2022.

Mehta, S., Dawande, M., Janakiraman, G., & Mookerjee, V. (2021). How to sell a data set? Pricing policies for data monetization. *Information Systems Research, 32*(4), 1281–1297.

Mell, P., Grance, T., & Information Technology Laboratory (National Institute of Standards and Technology). Computer Security Division. (2011). The nist definition of cloud computing (Ser. Nist special publication, 800–145). Computer Security Division, Information Technology Laboratory, National Institute of Standards and Technology.

Micheli, M., Ponti, M., Craglia, M., & Berti Suman, A. (2020). Emerging models of data governance in the age of datafication. *Big Data & Society, 7*(2), 2053951720948087.

Möller, D. (2020). *Cybersecurity in digital transformation: Scope and applications*. Springer.

Moor, J. (2006). The Dartmouth College Artificial Intelligence Conference: The next fifty years. *AI Magazine, 27*(4), 87.

Mugge, P., Abbu, H., Michaelis, T. L., Kwiatkowski, A., & Gudergan, G. (2020). Patterns of digitization: A practical guide to digital transformation. *Research-Technology Management, 63*(2), 27–35.

Mukhopadhyay, S., & Bouwman, H. (2019). Orchestration and governance in digital platform ecosystems: A literature review and trends. *Digital Policy, Regulation and Governance, 21*(4), 329–351.

Murdoch, W. J., Singh, C., Kumbier, K., Abbasi-Asl, R., & Yu, B. (2019). Interpretable machine learning: Definitions, methods, and applications. arXiv preprint arXiv:1901.04592.

Muscatella, D. L. (2020). Data protection officer: Tasks and responsibilities of a key role for the innovation of the relationship between data and data subjects' rights. *Journal of Data Protection & Privacy, 3*(4) , 403–417.

Navath, S. (2021). Predictive analytics: Extracting value from big data. *Journal of Business Intelligence and Data Analytics, 1*(1), 1–2.

Nazerian, F., Motameni, H., & Nematzadeh, H. (2019). Emergency role-based access control (E-RBAC) and analysis of model specifications with alloy. *Journal of Information Security and Applications, 45,* 131–142.

Nemes, N., Scanlan, S. J., Smith, P., Smith, T., Aronczyk, M., Hill, S., ... Stabinsky, D. (2022). An integrated framework to assess greenwashing. *Sustainability, 14*(8), 4431.

Newman, J. (2020). Joined-up government: The politics of partnership. In: Leslie Budd, Julie Charlesworth and Rob Paton (eds.), *Making policy happen* (pp. 194–200). Routledge.

Noy, N., Gao, Y., Jain, A., Narayanan, A., Patterson, A., & Taylor, J. (2019). Industry-scale knowledge graphs: Lessons and challenges: Five diverse technology companies show how it's done. *Queue, 17*(2), 48–75.

Ofner, M. H., Otto, B., & Österle, H. (2012). Integrating a data quality perspective into business process management. *Business Process Management Journal, 18*(6), 1036–1067.

Oliveira, M.I.S., Oliveira, L.E.R.A., Ribeiro Batista, M.G., and Farias Lóscio, B. (2018). Towards a meta-model for data ecosystems. In: Anneke Zuiderwijk and Charles C. Hinnant (Eds.), Proceedings of the 19th Annual International Conference on Digital Government Research, May 30–June 1, 2018, Delft, Netherlands. ACM, New York, NY, USA, 10 pages. https://doi.org/10.1145/3209281.3209333

Orji, C. I. (2019). Digital business transformation: Towards an integrated capability framework for digitization and business value generation. *Journal of Global Business and Technology, 15*(1), 47–57.

Panigrahi, R., & Borah, S. (2018). A detailed analysis of CICIDS2017 dataset for designing Intrusion Detection Systems. *International Journal of Engineering & Technology, 7*(3.24), 479–482.

Panitz, J. C., Wiener, M., & Amberg, M. (2010). A balanced scorecard for compliance-requirements of a comprehensive compliance-reporting. AMCIS 2010 Proceedings. Paper 160. http://aisel.aisnet.org/amcis2010/160

Pappas, I. O., Mikalef, P., Giannakos, M. N., Krogstie, J., & Lekakos, G. (2018). Big data and business analytics ecosystems: Paving the way towards digital transformation and sustainable societies. *Information Systems and e-Business Management, 16,* 479–491.

Parker, G., Petropoulos, G., & Van Alstyne, M. W. (2020). Digital platforms and antitrust. Bruegel Working Paper, No. 06/2020, Bruegel, Brussels. http://hdl.handle.net/10419/237620

Parsons, C. (2015). Beyond privacy: Articulating the broader harms of pervasive mass surveillance. *Media and Communication, 3*(3), 1–11.

Pasquale, F. (2012). Privacy, antitrust, and power. *George Mason Law Review, 20,* 1009.

Patel, J. (2019). Bridging data silos using big data integration. *International Journal of Database Management Systems, 11*(3), 1–6.

Patel, J. (2020, August). The democratization of machine learning features. In *2020 IEEE 21st International Conference on Information Reuse and Integration for Data Science (IRI)* (pp. 136–141). IEEE.

Paulheim, H. (2017). Knowledge graph refinement: A survey of approaches and evaluation methods. *Semantic Web, 8*(3), 489–508.

Perkin, N., & Abraham, P. (2021). Building the agile business through digital transformation. *Journal of Business Research, 124*, 610–619.

Peukert, C., Bechtold, S., Batikas, M., & Kretschmer, T. (2022). Regulatory spillovers and data governance: Evidence from the GDPR. *Marketing Science, 41*(4), 746–768.

Plotkin, D. (2020). *Data stewardship: An actionable guide to effective data management and data governance.* Academic Press.

Politou, E., Michota, A., Alepis, E., Pocs, M., & Patsakis, C. (2018). Backups and the right to be forgotten in the GDPR: An uneasy relationship. *Computer Law & Security Review, 34*(6), 1247–1257.

Popovič, A., Hackney, R., Tassabehji, R., & Castelli, M. (2018). The impact of big data analytics on firms' high value business performance. *Information Systems Frontiers, 20*(2), 209–222.

Power, D. J. (2015). Creating a data-driven global society. In Iyer, L. S., & Power, D. J. (Eds.), *Reshaping society through analytics, collaboration, and decision support. Annals of Information Systems* (Vol. 18), 13–28. Springer.

Praveena, M., Sinhku, S., Mythri, V., & Moida, R. (2018). Analytical study on quantum computing and its initial role on big data. *Journal of Advanced Research in Dynamical and Control Systems, 10*(2), 66–72.

Provost, F., & Fawcett, T. (2013). Data science and its relationship to big data and data-driven decision making. *Big Data, 1*(1), 51–59.

Quach, S., Thaichon, P., Martin, K. D., Weaven, S., & Palmatier, R. W. (2022). Digital technologies: Tensions in privacy and data. *Journal of the Academy of Marketing Science, 50*(6), 1299–1323.

Rajabi, Z., & Abade, M. N. (2012). Data-centric enterprise architecture. *International Journal of Information Engineering and Electronic Business, 4*(4), 53.

Randstad. (2017). Annual report. https://www.randstad.com/s3fs-media/rscom/public/2020-02/randstad-annual-report-2017.pdf. Accessed 21 May 2021.

Ranjan, J., & Foropon, C. (2021). Big data analytics in building the competitive intelligence of organizations. *International Journal of Information Management, 56*, 102231.

Ranjan, J., Foropon, C., Sarkar, J. G., & Sarkar, A. (2022). Corrigendum to "Big data analytics in building the competitive intelligence of organizations" [*International Journal of Information Management* 56 (2021) 102231].

Richter, P. C., & Bruehl, R. (2020). Ahead of the game: Antecedents for the success of shared service centers. *European Management Journal, 38*(3), 477–488.

Ridsdale, C., Rothwell, J., Smit, M., Ali-Hassan, H., Bliemel, M., Irvine, D., ... Wuetherick, B. (2015). Strategies and best practices for data literacy education: Knowledge synthesis report. https://dalspace.library.dal.ca/bitstream/handle/10222/64578/Strategies%20and%20Best%20Practices%20for%20Data%20Literacy%20Education.pdf

Ridzuan, F., & Zainon, W. M. N. W. (2019). A review on data cleansing methods for big data. *Procedia Computer Science, 161*, 731–738.

Rios, N., de Mendonça Neto, M. G., & Spínola, R. O. (2018). A tertiary study on technical debt: Types, management strategies, research trends, and base information for practitioners. *Information and Software Technology, 102*, 117–145.

Rivera, R., Pazmiño, L., Becerra, F., & Barriga, J. (2022). An analysis of cyber espionage process. In: Rocha, Á., Fajardo-Toro, C.H., Rodríguez, J.M.R. (eds) *Developments and advances in defense and security* (pp. 3–14), vol. 255. Springer.

Robol, M., Breaux, T. D., Paja, E., & Giorgini, P. (2022). Consent verification monitoring. *ACM Transactions on Software Engineering and Methodology, 32*(1), 1–33.

Romanosky, S., Ablon, L., Kuehn, A., & Jones, T. (2019). Content analysis of cyber insurance policies: How do carriers price cyber risk? *Journal of Cybersecurity, 5*(1), tyz002.

Russell, S. J., & Norvig, P. (2016). *Artificial intelligence: A modern approach*. Pearson Education Limited.

Salas, J., & Domingo-Ferrer, J. (2018). Some basics on privacy techniques, anonymization and their big data challenges. *Mathematics in Computer Science, 12*(3), 263–274.

Sakpal, M. (2021). How to improve your data quality – Gartner, 14 July. https://www.gartner.com/smarterwithgartner/how-to-improve-your-data-quality

SAS. (n.d.). White paper Artificial Intelligence and ethics. https://www.sas.com/content/dam/SAS/documents/marketing-whitepapers-ebooks/ebooks/en/artificial-intelligence-and-ethics-111452.pdf. Accessed 13 May 2022.

Sayler, K. M., & Harris, L. A. (2020). *Deep fakes and national security*. Congressional Research SVC Washington United States.

Schlatt, V., Sedlmeir, J., Feulner, S., & Urbach, N. (2022). Designing a framework for digital KYC processes built on blockchain-based self-sovereign identity. *Information & Management, 59*(7), 103553.

Schmidhuber, J. (2015). Deep learning in neural networks: An overview. *Neural Networks, 61*, 85–117.

Schmitz, M., Dietze, C., & Czarnecki, C. (2019). Enabling digital transformation through robotic process automation at Deutsche Telekom. In: Nils Urbach and Maximilian Röglinger (eds.), *Digitalization cases* (pp. 15–33). Springer.

Schneier, B. (2015). NSA plans for a post-quantum world. https://www.schneier.com/blog/archives/2015/08/nsa_plans_for_a.html. Accessed 25 July 2021.

Scriney, M., McCarthy, S., McCarren, A., Cappellari, P., & Roantree, M. (2019). Automating data mart construction from semi-structured data sources. *The Computer Journal, 62*(3), 394–413.

Scupola, A., & Mergel, I. (2022). Co-production in digital transformation of public administration and public value creation: The case of Denmark. *Government Information Quarterly, 39*(1), 101650.

Semenov, N. A., & Poltavtsev, A. A. (2020). Cloud-based data architecture security. *Automatic Control and Computer Sciences, 53*(8), 1056–1064.

Serrano, W. (2022). Verification and Validation for data marketplaces via a blockchain and smart contracts. *Blockchain: Research and Applications, 3*(4), 100100.

Shor, P. W. (1994). Algorithms for quantum computation: Discrete logarithms and factoring. In *Proceedings the 35th Annual Symposium on Foundations of Computer Science*, Santa Fe, NM, 20th–22nd November.

Shor, P. W. (1998). Quantum computing. *Documenta Mathematica, 1*(1000), 467–486.

Siderska, J. (2020). Robotic process automation—A driver of digital transformation? *Engineering Management in Production and Services, 12*(2), 21–31.

Silverston, L. (2011). *The data model resource book, Volume 1: A library of universal data models for all enterprises*. John Wiley & Sons.

Sion, L., Dewitte, P., Van Landuyt, D., Wuyts, K., Emanuilov, I., Valcke, P., & Joosen, W. (2019, March). An architectural view for data protection by design. In *2019 IEEE International Conference on Software Architecture (ICSA)* (pp. 11–20). IEEE.

Singh, A., & Hess, T. (2020). How chief digital officers promote the digital transformation of their companies. In: Robert D. Galliers, Dorothy E. Leidner and Boyka Simeonova (eds.), *Strategic information management* (pp. 202–220). Routledge.

Singh, A., Klarner, P., & Hess, T. (2020). How do chief digital officers pursue digital transformation activities? The role of organization design parameters. *Long Range Planning, 53*(3), 101890.

Singhal, A. (2012). Introducing the Knowledge Graph: Things, not strings. 16 May. https://blog.google/products/search/introducing-knowledge-graph-things-not/. Accessed 25 July 2021.

Spiekermann, M. (2019). Data marketplaces: Trends and monetisation of data goods. *Intereconomics, 54*(4), 208–216.

Squicciarini, M., & Nachtigall, H. (2021). Demand for AI skills in jobs: Evidence from online job postings. *OECD Science, Technology and Industry Working Papers*, No. 2021/03, OECD Publishing, Paris.

Statista. (2018). Big data market size revenue forecast worldwide from 2011 to 2027. March 2018. https://www.statista.com/statistics/254266/global-big-data-market-forecast/. Accessed 17 July 2021.

Steane, A. (1998). Quantum computing. *Reports on Progress in Physics, 61*(2), 117.

Stöger, K., Schneeberger, D., Kieseberg, P., & Holzinger, A. (2021). Legal aspects of data cleansing in medical AI. *Computer Law & Security Review, 42*, 105587.

Studer, R., Benjamins, V. R., & Fensel, D. (1998). Knowledge engineering: Principles and methods. *Data & Knowledge Engineering, 25*(1–2), 161–197.

Suliman, A., Husain, Z., Abououf, M., Alblooshi, M., & Salah, K. (2019). Monetization of IoT data using smart contracts. *IET Networks, 8*(1), 32–37.

Sustainalytics. (2020). Utilising ESG in the Covid-19 Recovery. https://connect.sustainalytics.com/esg-in-the-covid-19-recovery. Accessed 28 August 2021.

Svahn, F., Mathiassen, L., Lindgren, R., & Kane, G. C. (2017). Mastering the digital innovation challenge. *MIT Sloan Management Review, 58*(3), 14.

Tayi, G. K., & Ballou, D. P. (1998). Examining data quality. *Communications of the ACM, 41*(2), 54–57.

Teece, D. J. (2007). Explicating dynamic capabilities: The nature and microfoundations of (sustainable) enterprise performance. *Strategic Management Journal, 28*(13), 1319–1350.

Tian, X., He, J. S., & Han, M. (2021). Data-driven approaches in FinTech: A survey. *Information Discovery and Delivery, 49*(2), 123–135.

Treder, M. (ed.) (2020). Typical challenges of a CDO. In *The chief data officer management handbook: Set up and run an organization's data supply chain* (pp. 193–212), Apress.

Trieu, V. H., Burton-Jones, A., Green, P., & Cockcroft, S. (2022). Applying and extending the theory of effective use in a business intelligence context. *MIS Quarterly, 46*(1), 645–678.

Tsai, C. W., Lai, C. F., Chao, H. C., & Vasilakos, A. V. (2016). Big data analytics. In: Borko Furht and Flavio Villanustre (eds.), *Big data technologies and applications* (pp. 13–52). Springer.

Tsegaye, T., & Flowerday, S. (2020). A Clark-Wilson and ANSI role-based access control model. *Information & Computer Security, 28*(3), 373–395.

Tumbas, S., Berente, N., & Brocke, J. V. (2018). Digital innovation and institutional entrepreneurship: Chief Digital Officer perspectives of their emerging role. *Journal of Information Technology, 33*(3), 188–202.

Turing, A. M. (1950). Mind. *Mind, 59*(236), 433–460.

United Nations. (n.d.a). Sustainable development goals. https://sdgs.un.org/goals. Accessed 13 May 2022.

United Nations. (n.d.b). Will robots and AI cause mass unemployment? Not necessarily, but they do bring other threats. https://www.un.org/en/desa/will-robots-and-ai-cause-mass-unemployment-not-necessarily-they-do-bring-other. Accessed 13 May 2022.

Vaia, G., Arkhipova, D., & DeLone, W. (2022). Digital governance mechanisms and principles that enable agile responses in dynamic competitive environments. *European Journal of Information Systems, 31*(6), 662–680.

Valdez-de-Leon, O. (2016). A digital maturity model for telecommunications service providers. *Technology Innovation Management Review, 6*(8), 19–32.

Vermeulen, A. F. (2018). *Practical data science: A guide to building the technology stack for turning data lakes into business assets.* Apress.

Vial, G. (2023). Data governance and digital innovation: A translational account of practitioner issues for IS research. *Information and Organization, 33*(1), 100450.

Visnjic, I., Neely, A., & Jovanovic, M. (2018). The path to outcome delivery: Interplay of service market strategy and open business models. *Technovation, 72*, 46–59.

Wand, Y., & Wang, R. Y. (1996). Anchoring data quality dimensions in ontological foundations. *Communications of the ACM, 39*(11), 86–95.

Wang, R. Y., & Strong, D. M. (1996). Beyond accuracy: What data quality means to data consumers. *Journal of Management Information Systems, 12*(4), 5–33.

Wang, Z., Zhang, J., Feng, J., & Chen, Z. (2014, June). Knowledge graph embedding by translating on hyperplanes. In *Proceedings of the AAAI Conference on Artificial Intelligence* (Vol. 28, No. 1), AAAI Press.

Warner, K. S., & Wäger, M. (2019). Building dynamic capabilities for digital transformation: An ongoing process of strategic renewal. *Long Range Planning, 52*(3), 326–349.

Waters Technology. (2020a). Covid-19 is raising the ESG stakes. https://www.waterstechnology.com/data-management/7521151/covid-19-is-raising-the-esg-stakes. Accessed 20 November 2021.

Waters Technology. (2020b). Fuzzy data stalls ESG alpha hunt. https://www.waterstechnology.com/data-management/4844651/fuzzy-data-stalls-esg-alpha-hunt. Accessed 20 November 2021.

Waters Technology. (2020c). Four asset managers explain how they incorporate ESG data. https://www.waterstechnology.com/data-management/7535166/four-asset-managers-explain-how-they-incorporate-esg-data. Accessed 20 November 2021.

Watson, G. J., Desouza, K. C., Ribiere, V. M., & Lindič, J. (2021). Will AI ever sit at the C-suite table? The future of senior leadership. *Business Horizons, 64*(4), 465–474.

Watt, E. (2017). The right to privacy and the future of mass surveillance. *The International Journal of Human Rights, 21*(7), 773–799.

Weill, P., Apel, T., Woerner, S. L., & Banner, J. S. (2019). It pays to have a digitally savvy board. *MIT Sloan Management Review*, 60(3), 41–45.

Westerman, G., Calméjane, C., Bonnet, D., Ferraris, P., & McAfee, A. (2011). Digital Transformation: A roadmap for billion-dollar organizations. *MIT Center for Digital Business and Capgemini Consulting, 1*, 1–68.

Wiedemann, A., Forsgren, N., Wiesche, M., Gewald, H., & Krcmar, H. (2019). Research for practice: The DevOps phenomenon. *Communications of the ACM, 62*(8), 44–49.

Wixom, B. H., Piccoli, G., & Rodriguez, J. (2021). Fast-track data monetization with strategic data assets. MIT Sloan Management Review, 62(4), 1–4.

Wixom, B. H., & Ross, J. W. (2017). How to monetize your data. *MIT Sloan Management Review, 58*(3), 10–13.

Wixom, B. H., & Todd, P. A. (2005). A theoretical integration of user satisfaction and technology acceptance. *Information Systems Research, 16*(1), 85–102.

Wolff, A., Gooch, D., Montaner, J. J. C., Rashid, U., & Kortuem, G. (2016). Creating an understanding of data literacy for a data-driven society. *The Journal of Community Informatics, 12*(3), 9–26.

Wolf, M. (2017). Emerging technologies. In Wolf, M. (Ed.), *The physics of computing* (pp. 221–228). Morgan Kaufmann.

XBRL. (2020). Green reporting headed digital? https://www.xbrl.org/news/green-reporting-headed-digital/. Accessed 12 December 2022.

Xiaofeng, M., & Xiang, C. (2013). Big data management: Concepts, techniques and challenges. *Journal of Computer Research and Development, 50*(1), 146.

Xu, Y., & Koivumäki, T. (2019). Digital business model effectuation: An agile approach. *Computers in Human Behavior, 95*, 307–314.

Yablonsky, S. (2019). Multidimensional data-driven artificial intelligence innovation. *Technology Innovation Management Review, 9*(12), 16–28.

Zetlin, M., & Olavsrud, T. (2020). What is a chief data officer? A leader who creates business value from data. 28 September. https://www.cio.com/article/3234884/what-is-a-chief-data-officer.html. Accessed 19 July 2021.

INDEX

Note: **Bold** page numbers refer to tables and *italic* page numbers refer to figures.

Printed in the United States
by Baker & Taylor Publisher Services